PLAYING
THE TAKEOVER
MARKET

PLAYING THE TAKEOVER MARKET

How to Profit from Corporate Mergers, Spinoffs, Tender Offers, and Liquidations

Judith H. McQuown

SEAVIEW BOOKS/NEW YORK

The author and publisher gratefully acknowledge permission to reprint from:
W. T. Grimm & Co. Lehman Brothers Kuhn Loeb. Securities Research Co.,
A division of United Business Service Co., 208 Newbury Street, Boston, MA
02116. *Trendline,* A division of Standard & Poor's Corp. Conoco, Inc. Disclosure, Inc. Council of Economic Advisers. *Barron's Weekly. Forbes Magazine.*

Seaview Books/A Division of PEI Books, Inc.

Library of Congress Cataloging in Publication Data
McQuown, Judith H.
        Playing the takeover market.

        Bibliography: p.
        1. Consolidation and merger of corporations.
2. Corporate reorganizations. I. Title.
HD2746.5.M35   658.1'6   81-50323
ISBN 0-87223-707-9   AACR2

For Robert Willens, for the idea
and
For Risa Weinreb, for the help

Contents

Acknowledgments

This book owes much to the help of many experts, for whose time, patience, and enthusiasm I am indebted.

Special thanks go to Stanley Sanders, Haas Securities Corporation; E. Michael Metz, Oppenheimer & Co.; Robert J. Farrell, Merrill Lynch, Pierce, Fenner & Smith; and to the many arbitrageurs and corporate executives who requested anonymity; to professors Michael Keenan and Lawrence J. White of the New York University Graduate School of Business Administration; and to Nancy Dunnan.

At Seaview Books I am grateful for the help of Anne Harrison, my editor, whose support and enthusiasm for the book never flagged.

Finally, as always, my deepest thanks go to Alfred Bester for his constant love and patience.

PLAYING THE TAKEOVER MARKET

1

Special Situations

Every time someone makes money in the market, somebody else loses an equal and opposite amount—in actual dollars or lost profits by selling too early. It's the Newton-McQuown law of investing. The purpose of this book is to help *you* get on the winning side of this equation by showing you how to invest—and how not to invest—in special situations.

"Special situations" is the name that professional investors give to certain types of investments whose potential profits are not expected to come about through increased earnings performance (the most common reason for stock price rises), but rather through something "special" in the nature of the company itself.

As their name implies, special situations are unique in the sense that they combine the potential for high profits with the relative freedom from the significant risks normally associated with a potentially lucrative investment. These investment opportunities are special in another sense, too: They require methods that differ from the traditional tools and mental approach normally used by an investor to analyze a stock. In fact, characteristics that would typically lead an investor to reject a particular stock are often the very factors that make a company especially ripe for a takeover or more likely to effect a spinoff or liquidation.

The special situations discussed in this book involve the following forms of corporate upheavals:

1. the *merger:* a process in which one company acquires the assets of another in exchange for stock of the acquiring company;

2. the *tender offer:* a process similar to redemption (see below), but with another company offering to purchase the shareholders' stock. (Tender offers are often opening gambits to corporate takeovers and mergers.)

3. the *spinoff:* a process of corporate splitting in which a company forms a new company and distributes the new company's stock to its stockholders;

4. the *liquidation:* the termination of corporate life, in which a company converts its assets to cash and distributes the money to its shareholders in exchange for their stock;

5. the *redemption:* a process by which a corporation repurchases stock from its shareholders.

Although these transactions share many common characteristics (the most important being their uniformly beneficial effect on the investor lucky enough to hold their shares), there are significant differences that must be understood. One of the most important distinctions is the potential tax treatment associated with special situations. The investor's tax treatment may run the gamut from highly taxed dividend income (as high as 50% in federal taxes alone, in some cases) to a complete deferral of the taxes normally payable when the stock is disposed of. Accordingly, this chapter will describe the actual mechanics of each special situation, with particular emphasis on its potential tax treatment.

MERGERS

Normally, an investor purchases securities based on his assessment of the company's prospects. Sale decisions are made on the same basis. In a merger, an investor sells his stock not to another investor but to another corporation—again, at a profit.

The term "merger" is one of the most abused words in the financial writer's lexicon. While most sophisticated investors understand that a merger normally involves what might be termed a "corporate marriage," the tax professional is concerned with the question of whether a merger constitutes a "tax-free reorganization" according to the Internal Revenue Code. If a merger can be classified this way, the owners of the acquired (or target) corporation will not have to pay taxes when they exchange their stock for the stock of the acquiring company.

Legally, a merger is a transaction in which one corporation acquires the assets and liabilities of another corporation, and the acquired corporation's legal existence is terminated. If this absorption is carried out in accordance with the corporation laws of the parties' states of incorporation, it will constitute a merger. Similarly, a merger may involve the acquisition of one corporation's stock by another. In this case, the target's legal existence is not terminated; instead, it remains in existence as a subsidiary of the buyer.

In either case, however, the investor's prime concern is whether the merger is a tax-free reorganization. Under the Internal Revenue Code, this determination is based primarily on the type of payment (also called "consideration") received by the target's shareholders in exchange for their stock. If more than 50% of the total payment consists of the buyer's stock, the deal will be termed a reorganization and will not be taxable immediately. For many investors, the deferred taxes are one of the major advantages of playing the merger game.

Conversely, if the payment consists primarily of "nonstock" —including cash, notes, or even long-term debentures (a form of bond)—the transaction will be considered a taxable sale, and the investor's gain will be taxable immediately at capital-gains rates.

(Note: Even in a reorganization, the investor will be taxed on the cash received. Thus, even though a transaction is properly termed a "tax-free reorganization," investors will still have to pay tax on the property—other than stock—that they receive.)

Example: ABC Corporation acquires XYZ Corporation in a transaction qualifying as a merger under Delaware law. (Most publicly held corporations are registered in Delaware because the state's corporate laws are extremely liberal.) ABC pays the shareholders of XYZ a total of $10 million: 60% in stock and 40% in cash. Thus the transaction is a reorganization, since over 50% of the payment is stock. Mr. Nitgedeiget owns 100 shares of XYZ, which cost him $1,000, and receives ABC stock worth $1,800 and $1,200 cash in exchange. Mr. Nitgedeiget's gain is $2,000 ($1,800 + $1,200 less $1,000), but only $1,200 of his gain is currently taxable; the balance of the gain ($800) is deferred until he sells his ABC stock.

TENDER OFFERS

Tender offers are another area of potential profits for the shrewd investor.

Tender offers are often a prelude to a merger. In many cases, a prospective suitor will make open-market purchases of a significant percentage (usually slightly less than 5%, to avoid SEC reporting requirements) of the target's stock and then seek representation on the target's board of directors. This action is often followed by a formal merger proposal.

In recent months, the tender offer has been the most widely publicized of the special-situation scenarios. This trend has its roots in the efforts of companies such as Esmark, Inc., to dispose of highly profitable divisions (in Esmark's case, its Vickers Petroleum subsidiary) and to use the sales proceeds to repurchase a substantial portion of its outstanding stock.

This type of tender offer is called a "partial liquidation." It differs from the more traditional tender offer because it guarantees capital-gains tax treatment even though the funds may be distributed pro-rata (according to the number of shares held) among the shareholders. The distinction between a partial liquidation and a redemption is a function of the events that prompt the distribution. In a partial liquidation, the distribution results from a "genuine contraction" of the entity's productive capacity; as such, the Internal Revenue Code provides for capital-gains treatment. A redemption, on the other hand, may be the result of a decision by a corporation to distribute its excess liquid assets, whose disposal does not cause a reduction in its business activity.

Owing to the natural aversion of an entrenched management to reducing the productive assets under its direct control, the partial liquidation has rarely taken place in the past. Thus, the potential universe of companies for which this technique may be advantageous is virtually limitless. As in the more traditional tender offer, the benefits to the investor are extremely attractive: undervalued corporate assets are converted into cash, and the investor realizes the "real-life" market value of the company's underlying assets at long-term capital-gains tax rates. In Esmark's case, this phenomenon was demonstrated graphically: Before the announcement of the Vickers sale, the stock was traded in the high 20s; within a period of three months, the stock was hovering around 60. This was a better than 100% gain for the smart-money investor.

SPINOFFS

The spinoff transaction has also made headlines in the past several months. For reasons rather like those prompting the trend toward partial liquidations, corporations have been testing the theory that the sum of the parts is indeed more valuable than the whole. For example, in mid-1980, IU International distributed stock of its wholly owned shipping subsidiary, Gotaas-Larsen, Inc. The result: With no other change or improvement in the companies' prospects, the stocks of the newly separated entities were recently trading at a 46% premium over the price of IU International alone prior to the transaction.

In a spinoff, investors do not sell their stock to another company; instead, they retain their stock and receive stock in other, subsidiary corporations as well. In a sense, it's like changing your dollar bill for four quarters—but with the hope that at least one of the quarters may be pre-1965 silver, and thus be worth more than the original dollar.

Spinoff transactions may be viewed as the exact opposite of

mergers: They are manifestly a process of corporate divorce. In a spinoff, a company distributes the stock of one or more of its subsidiaries to its shareholders. Here, the tax aspects are extremely important. If the distribution constitutes a spinoff within the meaning of the Internal Revenue Code, the shareholders pay no tax when they receive their new stock. *But* if the detailed requirements of the Code are not satisfied, the distribution is currently taxable as a dividend at rates as high as 50% in federal taxes alone.

These exacting requirements—plus the fact that the spinoff is unattractive to an entrenched management because it reduces the amount of corporate assets under their control—have made the spinoff the rarest type of special situation. Nevertheless, the prolonged stock-market slump of 1979–80 revived this form of special situation on the theory that a leaner, sleeker, more easily understandable corporate structure would increase the market value of the distributing corporation by an amount that would exceed the reduction in its assets caused by the spinoff.

As mentioned earlier, a "tax" spinoff is completely tax-free to the recipients. Where before the transaction they owned the stock of one corporation whose assets consisted of subsidiaries, they now directly own the stock of two or more corporations whose combined value often exceeds the predistribution value of their stock in the distributing corporation.

One of the best-documented spinoffs of the past several years involves M-G-M's separation of its hotel and gaming business from its film business. Here, the announced reason for the separation was that it would allay the fears of scriptwriters and other film talents who felt that they were dealing with a corporation whose primary interest was hotels and gambling, not films. To satisfy their demands, the old M-G-M now consists of two independent companies, each conducting one aspect of the former consolidated business.

Again, a trend may be in the offing. The desire to simplify operations and to make a corporation's business more clearly understood, and hence more attractive to suppliers and investors, indicates that the spinoff may be coming into its own. If this hypothesis is valid, the conglomerates and multi-industry companies constructed in the 1960s provide a dazzling array of companies that may potentially employ this device.

LIQUIDATIONS

To continue our marriage-divorce analogy, a liquidation may be looked at as corporate death. Here the ordinary meaning of the word parallels its meaning for tax purposes. Liquidation is the process in which corporate assets are converted into cash and the cash is distributed to the shareholders in exchange for and in retirement of their stock. Once the final liquidating distribution is made, the corporation ceases to exist.

Since the conversion of stock into cash is a fully taxable transaction, investors will realize capital gains equal to the difference between the original cost of the stock they surrender and the value of the liquidating distribution they receive. If they have held their stock for at least 12 months prior to their surrender, their capital gains will be long-term and will be taxed at favorable rates—no more than 20%.

The corporation's tax treatment with regard to the conversion of *its* assets to cash depends primarily on the alacrity with which the process is effected. If the corporation completes the distribution to its shareholders within a 12-month period, it will not have to pay any tax on gains it realizes from the sales of its properties. This benefit is substantial, and many companies therefore try to complete their liquidation in time to benefit from this favorable provision. Thus, when a corporation sells off a major asset at a substantial gain, it is a good bet that the company plans complete liquidation in order to avoid paying taxes on this gain. *This action alone can be a valuable clue for investors who play the special-situations market.*

The benefits of liquidation are easily recognized when we consider the large number of companies that are selling at prices demonstrably below book value. When the stock market fails to recognize the underlying value of a company's assets, management may decide that the shareholders' returns may be maximized by converting these undervalued assets into cash in amounts that are often double the preliquidating market evaluation of the company's corporate worth.

REDEMPTIONS

A tender offer or redemption (often referred to as a "repurchase") may be viewed as a partial liquidation. In this type of transaction, the corporation repurchases only a portion of its stock and remains in existence as a smaller version of its former self. Again, investors typically (but not always) realize capital gains in this transaction. However, where the repurchase is undertaken on a proportionate (pro-rata) basis, so that the corporation buys back the same *percentage* of stock from each shareholder, the distribution will be taxed as a dividend. Conversely, as is often the case, a non-pro-rata redemption will offer shareholders tax-favored capital gains.

The primary reasons for redemption are varied; however, in many cases, management wishes to shrink the number of outstanding shares and thereby increase earnings per share. (This concept will be discussed more fully in chapter 3.) If nonproductive assets can be disposed of and the proceeds used to retire a portion of the stock, the enhanced return on the remaining assets divided by a smaller base of outstanding shares will often yield dramatic improvements in earnings per share. This increase alone is often the cause of sharp price rises in the stock.

Again, from a tax viewpoint, the redemption transaction is treated primarily according to the manner in which the funds are distributed. If the funds are distributed pro rata, the transaction will usually be treated as a dividend: High-bracket investors are hereby warned. However, if management decides to "take out" only the small, public shareholders (which simultaneously increases the relative influence of the insiders), capital-gains treatment will be assured. (For example, a 5% pro-rata, across-the-board redemption would be treated generally as a dividend, but a "to-whom-it-may-concern" offer for 5% of the stock, which is usually accepted by small stockholders, would be given capital-gains treatment.)

WHAT ABOUT RISK?

Many times in the past months, we've heard or read this sort of financial news: "The market was down, except for merger-and-acquisition stocks," or "Yesterday's market rally was fueled by merger-and-acquisition stocks." And, in fact, special situations seem relatively immune to the four classic types of economic risk:

1. *Interest-rate risk*—the risk that interest rates will rise and that the price of fixed-income investments (corporate, government, and municipal bonds and preferred stocks) will decline until they yield the new, higher rate. Thus, if interest rates rise from 10% to 12%—an increase of 20%—a bond or preferred stock selling at 100 and yielding 10% may decline to 83, so that it yields 12% and matches the current yields of 12% on new issues.

2. *Inflation risk*—the risk that future purchasing power will be eroded by inflation. Among financial instruments that are especially vulnerable to inflation are long-term bonds, savings certificates, insurance policies, and straight annuities—in fact, anything that pays off in "straight dollars," unadjusted for inflation.

3. *Business risk*—the risk that a particular business or industry outlook will sour. One well-known example was the downturn in Americans' purchase of large cars, which created havoc in the auto industry and was the fundamental cause of Chrysler's near-collapse.

4. *Investment risk*—the risk that an investment will be unprofitable. This risk is linked closely to interest-rate risk, inflation risk, and business risk, because an investment can lose value for all of these reasons.

Special situations are usually not affected by interest-rate risk, because, in most cases, the acquiring company's stock or surplus cash is exchanged for stock of the target company. Unless borrowing is unusually heavy and galloping interest rates jeopardize the deal, ordinary interest-rate fluctuations pose no great risk to special situations.

Special situations are also not vulnerable to inflation risk, because their time frame is much shorter. These stocks are generally held for a year or less, as opposed to five, ten, or twenty years for many bonds and insurance vehicles. Only hyperinflation would substantially erode purchasing power within a year or so.

Special situations are, almost by definition, not vulnerable to business risk. Their very existence as special situations indicates that they are desirable. Other companies recognize their value either as going concerns or as liquidation candidates.

Special situations possess only one major investment risk: If the deal is not consummated, investors who buy shares in a target company at overpriced levels will lose part of their investment if the stock retreats because the deal fell through. Later sections of *Playing the Takeover Market* will show you how to judge whether a deal may fall through and will teach you several strategies to protect your profits.

For now, though, let's look at some of the big special-situation winners of 1980. Out of the 100 best performers of 1980, the companies listed in table 1 were actual or rumored special situations. All of the stocks more than doubled from December 31, 1979 to December 31, 1980.

TABLE 1
Best Stock Performers of 1980

		PRICE			
				CHANGE	
RANK	COMPANY	12/31/79	12/31/80	%	OUTCOME
2	Shearson Loeb Rhoades	$10.50	$37.50	+257.1	Deal
12	E. F. Hutton	11.25	33.00	+193.3	Rumor
18	Dean Witter Reynolds	8.81	23.88	+170.9	Rumor
25	Franklin Mint	9.63	25.00	+159.7	Deal
28	Zapata	28.50	72.75	+155.3	Rumor
30	Morrison-Knudsen	17.88	45.38	+153.8	Rumor
32	Florida Steel	17.13	43.00	+151.1	Deal
34	Paine Webber	9.13	22.63	+147.9	Rumor
36	Lennar	9.06	22.13	+144.1	Rumor
38	Natomas	15.13	36.75	+143.0	Rumor
39	U.S. Home	12.38	30.00	+142.4	Deal
40	Geosource, Inc.	25.31	61.25	+142.0	Rumor
58	Bache Group	9.78	21.75	+122.4	Deal

| | | PRICE | | CHANGE | |
RANK	COMPANY	12/31/79	12/31/80	%	OUTCOME
63	Union Pacific	36.13	78.75	+118.0	Deal
66	Mesa Petroleum	29.56	63.50	+114.8	Rumor
70	Rowan Companies	21.06	45.00	+113.6	Rumor
71	Hardee's Food Systems	12.75	27.13	+112.7	Deal
72	Wabash, Inc.	14.25	30.25	+112.3	Deal
73	New England Nuclear	23.25	49.25	+111.8	Deal
87	Iowa Beef Processors	23.50	48.00	+104.3	Deal
88	Crouse-Hinds	18.88	38.50	+104.0	Deal
89	Alexander's	6.38	13.00	+103.9	Rumor
92	Chris-Craft	16.50	33.50	+103.0	Rumor

While these results were achieved in 1980, and similar profits were certainly made by knowledgeable investors in 1981, there can be no guarantee about future profits. However, it is certainly reasonable to assume that the long-term factors responsible for the popularity of special situations will be with us for some years to come. Shrewd investors will profit from identifying these situations.

2

Identifying the Candidates

In June 1981 there were 1,532 common stocks listed on the New York Stock Exchange and 904 common stocks listed on the American Stock Exchange.

How should an investor know which ones hold "special situation" potential? Here are some of the clues that top-ranking professionals look for to narrow down the field.

SOME LIKE IT HOT

Just like restaurants and summer resorts, industries, too, can be "fashionable"—from a special-situation point of view. In the first half of 1981, for example, mining companies were the hot takeover targets. Kennecott was gobbled up by Standard Oil of Ohio, and St. Joe Minerals was acquired by Fluor.

Before the mining companies, the insurance and finance companies enjoyed superstardom. ITT bought up Hartford Insurance, and RCA acquired CIT Financial.

A review of an industry's recent performance in merger, tender-offer, spinoff, and liquidation activity offers a good indication of likely behavior in the future. Looking just at mergers, for example, we see that certain industries have dominated selling activity over the past five years. In table 2,

TABLE 2
Top Ten Industry Classifications

INDUSTRY CLASSIFICATION OF SELLER	1976	1977	1978	1979	1980
Finance, Banks & Insurance	313 (1)	291 (1)	253 (1)	326 (1)	301 (1)
General Services	221 (2)	266 (2)	240 (2)	222 (2)	215 (2)
Wholesale & Retail	202 (3)	190 (3)	192 (3)	213 (3)	190 (3)
Machinery, Equipment & Farm Equipment	112 (5)	116 (5)	95 (5)	91 (5)	80 (4)
Food Processing & Agriculture	106 (6)	134 (4)	112 (4)	126 (4)	70 (5)
Drugs, Cosmetics & Medical Equipment	62 (11)	60 (9)	60 (10)	62 (9)	69 (6)
Electronics	60 (12)	65 (8)	66 (8)	82 (6)	68 (7)
Public Utilities	72 (9)	84 (6)	68 (7)	67 (8)	60 (8)
Printing & Publishing	58 (13)	57 (10)	65 (9)	57 (12)	57 (9)
Petroleum	96 (7)	55 (12)	47 (14)	52 (13)	56 (10)

SOURCE: W. T. Grimm & Co.

the number in parentheses next to each year's total indicates that industry's ranking as a merger target the preceding year. As you can see, industry rankings have remained fairly stable, an indication that these trends will probably persist for the near future.

Patterns of popularity indicate more than a simple follow-the-leader mentality; they reflect underlying economic realities—and point out a consensus of savvy business people about where profitable opportunities lie. For example, in table 2, the strong showing of the Finance, Banks & Insurance category owes much to the recent high interest rates and a generally sluggish economy, which have greatly enhanced the attractiveness of insurance companies as takeover targets. Insurance companies provide stable earnings growth, generate lots of cash, and are largely immune to business cycles.

Similarly, the increase in ranking of the Drugs, Cosmetics & Medical Equipment and Electronics sectors reflects the belief that they will be high-growth areas in the 1980s.

In addition to examining industries with the greatest absolute numbers of special situations, investors may also want to look at those industries with the greatest percentage increase in activity. Once again taking mergers as an example, table 3 shows which industries have demonstrated the greatest growth.

To profit most, however, investors should watch for emerging trends that can help boost activity in new areas. As Eric Gleacher of Lehman Brothers Kuhn Loeb, investment bankers, points out, "A few years ago, copper and silver companies sold at very low prices; now there is a three- to fourfold rise in their stock. A few years ago, you couldn't sell cement companies; now there's a shortage of cement capability in North America and people are buying them."

In other words, investors should follow the economic picture as a whole to try to predict which industries will benefit in the future.

STOCK PURCHASES OF ONE COMPANY BY ANOTHER

Whenever a company buys 5% or more of the stock of another—a move that often signals a possible takeover strat-

TABLE 3
Increased Merger Activity

SELLER INDUSTRY CLASSIFICATION	1979	1980	% INCREASE
Conglomerate	7	13	+86%
Transportation	26	36	+38%
Valves, Pumps & Hydraulics	22	30	+36%
Health Services	20	27	+35%
Textiles	15	19	+27%
Machine Tools	19	24	+26%
Miscellaneous	36	44	+22%
Drugs, Cosmetics & Medical Equipment	62	69	+11%
Electrical Equipment	34	37	+ 9%
Machined Metal Products	13	14	+ 8%
Petroleum	52	56	+ 8%
Packaging & Containers	16	17	+ 6%

SOURCE: *W. T. Grimm & Co.*

egy—it must report the purchase to the SEC within ten days in a 13D filing. The SEC publishes the data daily in the *SEC News Digest* and in a comprehensive monthly publication, *Official Summary of Security Transactions and Holdings.* Both publications can be bought from the SEC or consulted at SEC regional offices and many libraries.

Under new SEC regulations, companies seeking control of other companies must make their offers within five days of their 13D filing. Most companies are understandably reluctant to tip their hands so quickly. Therefore, to keep their options open and still stay legal, many companies filing 13D's list "investment" as the sole reason for their purchases. Companies with such "toeholds" can later go on to

1. make takeover offers;
2. buy additional stock to increase holdings above the 20% level and allow for equity accounting to reflect that interest in the target's earnings;
3. stage a proxy fight for control;
4. sell the stock back to the company—usually at a tidy profit.

INSIDE MOVES: OVER THE COUNTER

SEC regulations define an insider as an officer or director of a company, or the principal holder of more than 10% of any class of equity securities—preferred as well as common stock. Insider trading in a stock is permissible—as long as it's reported to the SEC on the appropriate forms.

Each week the SEC compiles a publicly available report of stock purchases, sales, and exercises of options by corporate insiders; this information also appears in the *Official Summary of Security Transactions and Holdings,* mentioned earlier. According to many securities analysts, this insider movement may indicate that a special situation is brewing—particularly when insider activity abruptly increases or decreases.

According to Larry Unterbrink, a partner in the "consensus of insiders" newsletter, insider buys of a company's stock provide a better guide to its future than insider sales, because people sometimes sell stock for reasons other than the souring of a company's prospects (buying a new house or paying off the IRS or Junior's orthodontist, for example). "But there's only one reason to buy," Mr. Unterbrink says. "To make money."

Fortunately, SEC regulations do protect the public and minority shareholders by preventing insiders from cashing in on advance information—and/or manipulating stock prices. SEC rule 16B states that insiders must return to the company any profits they make on the stock in short-term trading (in this case, stock held less than six months). Similarly, although the SEC does not treat 5% shareholders as insiders, the agency requires them to file form 13D within 30 days if they acquire an additional 5% of a company's stock.

Penalties for violations of SEC rules are stiff; they range from censure and dismissal to criminal charges.

INSIDE MOVES: UNDER THE TABLE

It's illegal, it's immoral, and—who knows?—it may even be fattening; but nevertheless, insiders sometimes do start taking advantage of their privy knowledge. A tip to a tennis partner or a brother-in-law, a friendly securities analyst, and soon word begins to whisper . . . echo . . . roar down Wall Street's granite canyons. One investment banker recounts how an industrial company's top-ranking executives based in different cities discussed how much to bid for another company on a conference-call hookup: "Within thirty minutes after we hung up, the information was on the floor of the New York Stock Exchange, and trades were being executed on that basis [of the secret information]."

Of course, some insider trading in advance of a merger announcement is entirely proper: The acquiring company itself may be buying up shares in the open market to gain a firmer toehold.

Fortunately for the smart-money investor, there's no need to remain out in the cold about hot inside information—legal or illegal. Trading patterns published every day in the financial press provide good clues about pending special situations. Here are some indicators to watch out for:

Sudden price changes.   Stock of General Portland, a major cement producer, had been holding relatively steady. Suddenly, "mysteriously," the stock shot up from 24¼ on a Tuesday to 33⅝ on Friday. The reason was disclosed only a week later: Canada Cement was making a $45-per-share cash merger offer.

New highs.   Price changes can turn into new highs for a stock as more and more investors latch on to a special-situation candidate's rising star.

A study by Lehman Brothers Kuhn Loeb (see table 4) shows a clear pattern of preannouncement trading in stocks of takeover targets. Lehman analysts who studied 24 unopposed cash takeovers in the first three quarters of 1980 found that the average premium of the transaction price over the stock's market price shrank to 60% the day before the announcement from 82% a month before.

Sudden volume changes.   When rumors of an American Cyanamid takeover surfaced in February 1980, its usual volume quintupled. Similarly, in the late spring and early summer of 1981, as Wall Street buzzed with speculation of a Cities

TABLE 4
Market Action in Takeover Situations

BUYER/TARGET	TARGET'S STOCK PRICE A MONTH BEFORE ANNOUNCEMENT	TARGET'S STOCK PRICE A DAY BEFORE ANNOUNCEMENT	TRANSACTION PRICE
Blue Bell/Jantzen	$16.00	$20.50	$30.00
British General Electric/Scriptomatic	$7.50	$10.75	$16.25
Dana/Tyrone Hydraulics	$11.50	$15.50	$24.28
Federal-Mogul/Huck Manufacturing	$20.00	$25.75	$41.00
SmithKline/Allergan Pharmaceuticals	$29.50	$39.88	$54.40
Tenneco/Southwestern Life	$22.88	$27.25	$42.45

SOURCE: *Lehman Brothers Kuhn Loeb*

Service takeover, volume ebbed and flowed with each new development.

May 18. Volume less than 100,000 shares.

May 21. Nu-West Group Ltd., a Canadian oil and real-estate company, announces purchase of 6.3% of Cities Service. Cities Service volume spurts to nearly 500,000 shares.

May 21–June 24. Volume in Cities Service fluctuates violently from around 70,000 shares a day to over 550,000 shares a day, depending on the temporary popularity of merger/no-merger rumors.

June 24–25. Trading is halted in both Cities Service and Conoco as the companies hold merger talks. The talks themselves halt on June 25 when Seagram's bids for Conoco.

June 28–July 3. Volume averages around 450,000 shares.

July 6. Texaco is said to be interested in acquiring Cities Service. Volume zooms to over 750,000 shares.

July 7. No news good news? Volume up again to just under 1 million shares.

July 8. Cities Service denies that it is holding merger talks with any company—including Texaco. Volume plummets to 550,000 shares.

August 7. A month later, with no new specific takeover rumors, volume is once again a "normal" 320,000 shares.

WHO'S GOT THE BACON?

For stalking mergers, another useful approach involves zeroing in on which companies are the most likely acquirers—and then psyching out what kinds of companies they are likely to buy.

Today, who *are* the most likely acquirers?

Many experts believe that the acquirers have some important characteristics in common. "Whenever you have a giant company making a determination that it wishes to grow by merger, it is a suggestion that their own business doesn't fully require, or warrant, the reinvestment of their cash flow," says Sigmund Wahrsager, general partner at Bear, Stearns.

Using this criterion, many observers as early as 1979 singled out the oil industry as a likely acquirer because of its exhaustible petroleum supply and huge cash flows. "Oil companies have a tremendous amount of cash which they can't put in their business," said Oppenheimer vice-president Norman Weinger in the *Wall Street Journal* of February 9, 1979. "They are therefore looking around for what they feel could be potential future business."

According to analysts, the new business was likely to include natural-resource companies because oil-company executives were already familiar with that field and could easily transfer their oil expertise to the acquired mineral companies.

Recent events, of course, have proved the accuracy of these forecasts. Shortly before this book went to press, Mobil made an unsuccessful $8.8-billion offer for Conoco, the nation's ninth-largest oil company and second-largest coal producer. Texaco and Gulf were also reportedly readying acquisition bids.

By this point you must be saying to yourself, "Wait a minute! The author's saying that oil companies are *acquirers.* From what I've been reading, I thought that the oil companies have been *takeover targets!*" Indeed, an August 7, 1981, *New York Times* article listed 12 major oil companies as takeover candidates.

The confusion is simple to clear up. Just as big fish eat little fish, big companies acquire smaller companies.

Many of the characteristics that make companies likely acquirers—large cash flows and hefty lines of credit—also make them vulnerable targets. For example, the second-tier oil companies such as Cities Service, Getty, and Marathon Oil, previously included in our list of potential acquirers, also became widely rumored merger bait during the summer of 1981. Big as they were, these companies ranked as mere nibbles to such leviathans as Mobil, Texaco, and Gulf Oil.

Other mature industries—such as food processing and railroads—are also likely acquirers. Investment analysts also expect merger activity from industries plagued by cyclical downturns, such as businesses related to automobiles and agriculture. Still other potential acquirers include companies enjoying a temporary earnings spurt. "These companies recognize that over the longer term, the boom isn't sustainable, so rather than reemploy the cash in their own business, they look elsewhere," says Donald Trott, director of research at A. G. Becker.

Divestitures also point out potential purchasers. Increasingly, companies are selling off marginal or "poor fit" divisions. According to Morgan Stanley & Company, the first quarter of 1981 saw the announcement of 26 divestitures valued at a total of $3.5 billion—compared to 13 divestitures worth $1.4 billion in the first quarter of 1980.

Having rid itself of unsuitable divisions, the seller frequently uses the profits to make new—and hopefully more lucrative—acquisitions. Bendix, for example, sold off its forest-products division and stock in a mineral company in 1980 because, to accomplish its strategic objectives, the company wanted to concentrate on high-technology areas. By selling off these unwanted assets, Bendix estimated that it had added $575 million in cash to its balance sheet—quite a healthy bankroll with which to shop for the desired high-tech companies.

Similarly, Joseph E. Seagram & Sons, often described as the world's largest liquor company, sold off the domestic holdings of its Texas Pacific subsidiary for $2.3 billion, and used these funds less than a year later to make its historic, unsuccessful offer for Conoco.

Once you've pinpointed companies as likely buyers, your next task involves figuring out who might be on their shopping list.

While acquirers tend to congregate in certain industries, targets run the full gamut. As Goldman, Sachs partner Stephen Friedman says, "It's almost like saying what kinds of girls do people marry."

There will be much more detail about the reasons one company buys another in later chapters. Some key factors include:

Strategic fit.   As more and more *Fortune* 500 companies set up corporate-planning departments, the concept of strategic fit becomes increasingly important. Today, says Joseph G. Fogg, codirector of mergers and acquisitions for Morgan Stanley, "the vast majority of transactions have clear and obvious strategic planning purposes. This was not the case in the 1960s, when many acquisitions had strictly an accounting rationale."

The recent takeovers of natural-resource companies by the huge oil companies furnish excellent examples of strategic fit. The purchases allowed the oil companies both to spend the piles of cash they had on hand and add years to the expected life-span of their resource reserves.

Technological breakthroughs. For companies looking to develop new products in high-technology areas, it's often cheaper to purchase an ongoing high-technology concern than to start from scratch on their own. Although generally optimistic expectations about these companies has driven up their stock prices for both prospective corporate acquirers and private investors, John C. Ball, an analyst with A. G. Becker, reports that "the big guys are aggressively looking for telecommunications and advanced semiconductor technology. The prices today are not cheap, but some of these companies are growing at hellacious rates."

Earnings growth. According to a special report prepared by Argus Research Corporation for Thomson McKinnon Securities in the summer of 1980, earnings growth stands as the most crucial factor in takeovers. Surveying the financial statistics for the 35 largest takeover targets from October 1979 through March 1980, the Argus study found that the five-year average compound growth rate in earnings for these companies was 17%—compared with 12% for the typical industrial company in the same five-year period. That's a difference of 42%—perhaps well worth paying a premium for!

SQUARE PEGS IN ROUND HOLES

The opposite of strategic fits is, of course, strategic misfits —square-peg-in-round-hole subsidiaries that have no place in their parent's future. Often the misfits are otherwise healthy companies that just don't belong in the parent's strategic long-term plan.

Esmark, seeing its future in consumer goods and specialty chemicals, sold off its highly profitable Vickers Energy Corporation for $1 billion. Then Esmark used the proceeds to buy back half of its 22 million shares outstanding—and thus boost earnings per share. Esmark stock, which had been trading at $25, zoomed to $60.

Square pegs have good potential for either acquisitions, spin-offs, or outright sale as an independent entity. To correctly diagnose them, scan the business press for interviews with chief executives, who often talk about what business their company wants to be in.

It often indicates what business they want to be out of!

THE CASE OF THE JILTED BRIDES

At the end of 1980, the final score for acquisitions of publicly held companies stood at 1,889 completed or pending and 178 canceled—roughly 9% of the total. Whether the announced deals fell through because of warts, wars, or wrongdoing, yesterday's takeover candidates—often called "jilted brides"—have one thing in common: They're candidates for *future* takeovers.

Look at Blue Bell, the manufacturer of Wrangler jeans, which defended its honor against a takeover bid by Allegheny Ludlum—only to succumb to a similar challenge less than six months later from Bass Brothers Enterprises.

As merger consultant William E. Chatlos of Georgeson & Company, specialists in investor relations, says: "The kill rate for targeted companies has been running between ninety and ninety-five percent. In other words, if somebody makes an offer, somewhere down the road the independent company will cease to exist."

The same financial charms that attracted the original suitors to these jilted brides should draw other corporate swains in the future. Consequently, your review of companies recently left at the altar will turn up many takeover candidates.

FANCY FOOTWORK

If computers give you a terminal case, skip this section. However, for the binomially inclined, the new calculators and home computers allow investors to run programs that can speed the special-situation-identification process.

Both Texas Instruments and Hewlett-Packard offer self-programmable calculators, as well as ready-made programs for securities analysis. Texas Instruments also sells a securities-analysis-application program for its home computer.

All of these techniques allow investors to narrow down the field of special-situation contenders. However, as *Wall Street Journal* columnist Tim Metz points out, where there's smoke, there's not always fire: "There's nothing like Wall Street take-over rumors to heat up a stock price these days. Or is it that there's nothing like a stock price spurt to kindle a blaze of takeover rumors?"

The following chapters will help investors differentiate between fool's gold and the genuine article.

3

Analyzing the Annual Report

Okay, now you've winnowed out the potential candidates and have obtained some 20 or 30 shiny annual reports, staring you down from your coffee table. What next?

Conquering their fears of the unfamiliar terrain known as the annual report, investors, armed only with pocket calculators, can evaluate an investment by using the same key ratios used by Wall Street securities analysts to identify a company's hidden strengths and weaknesses.

In fact, investors even have a valuable competitive edge over securities analysts that compensates, in part, for their lack of professional training and experience. When a securities analyst finds a special situation, her report must go through corporate channels and be approved at various levels of her brokerage house. And this process takes time. If her report is turned down, she can then buy the stock for herself or her family. But if her report is approved and the stock is recommended by the brokerage house, she cannot buy that stock until her report has been in the firm's customers' hands for a certain period of time.

On the other hand, if an investor finds a promising special situation, she simply calls her broker and places a buy order. She can buy the stock in less than 24 hours, rather than having to wait at least two weeks before acting on her discovery. And in special situations, where timing is probably the most important factor, since news at any time can drastically affect stock prices, this two-week lead is crucial.

For investors trying to diagnose special-situation potential, a company's annual report provides the vital information. Annual reports contain two basic sections.

First comes the window dressing: a narrative, decked out in pretty pictures, that describes (glowingly) the firm's operating results during the past year and discusses any new developments that might affect future operations.

Second, there's the nitty-gritty: four basic financial statements, including the balance sheet, income statement, statement of retained earnings, and statement of changes in financial position.

When viewed in combination, these statements reveal a firm's operations and financial position. The annual report provides detailed information for the two most recent years, along with summaries of key operating statistics for the past ten years. Companies also file an even more detailed statement with the SEC—the 10-K—which gives financial breakdowns for each major division or subsidiary. Far more austere than the glossy annual report, the 10-K narrative furnishes more detail, more straightforwardly, than the annual report. Consequently, it's generally a good idea to request the 10-K from the company at the same time as the annual report.

Once investors familiarize themselves with the financial statements at the *backs* of the annual reports—far away from the pretty pictures—analyzing a company to identify its potential as a special situation should take only about an hour or so. The company's multimillion-dollar assets, liabilities, profits, and losses are translated into key ratios—figures that are more easily understood and compared. Only basic arithmetic is necessary—but don't forget those decimal points! They may look almost the same, but 2.5:1 is *ten times the size* of .25:1!

The following sections aim to teach you how to perform basic ratio calculations and analysis—not to turn you into certified financial analysts. Any exceptions or subtleties to the rules are noted to provide you with an overview of appropriate factors for consideration, not to send you running off to buy finance textbooks.

BALANCE-SHEET RATIOS

A balance sheet shows a company's assets and liabilities on a specific date. It is like a photograph: one particular instant frozen in time. Assets are listed first, and are broken down into current assets and fixed (essentially long-term) assets.

Current assets are assets such as cash, securities, receivables, and inventory—any assets that can be converted into cash within a year.

Current liabilities are liabilities such as accounts payable, bank notes and loans, employees' salaries, taxes, and the current portion of any long-term debt—any liabilities that must be paid within a year.

The *current ratio* is obtained by dividing current assets by current liabilities:

$$\text{Current Ratio} = \frac{\text{Current Assets}}{\text{Current Liabilities}}$$

The *quick ratio* is similar to the current ratio, but more finely calibrated; it excludes inventories from its calculation:

$$\text{Quick Ratio} = \frac{\text{Current Assets} - \text{Inventory}}{\text{Current Liabilities}}$$

Thus the quick ratio measures pure liquidity, since it disregards inventory, which might have to be sold off at a substantial discount.

In most cases, a current ratio greater than 2:1 and a quick ratio greater than 1.5:1 are considered high.

Let's look at several examples and their significance to a securities analyst.

Example 1: A company's current assets are $5 million and its liabilities are $4.5 million.

$$\text{Current Ratio} = \frac{\$5,000,000}{\$4,500,000} = 1.11\!:\!1$$

This current ratio is much too low; it barely covers current liabilities and leaves no "breathing space" for the company— or its shareholders. If inventories had to be sold off for less than their balance-sheet valuation, or if the investment portfolio declined, the company might not be able to pay off its current liabilities without going deeper into debt.

A current ratio of 1.5:1 to 2:1 would be far healthier.

Example 2: A company's current assets are $8 million and its current liabilities are $3 million.

$$\text{Current Ratio} = \frac{\$8,000,000}{\$3,000,000} = 2.67{:}1$$

For industrial and manufacturing companies, a current ratio greater than 2:1 is considered high. A high current ratio may indicate management's failure to utilize its current assets profitably, to deploy potentially productive assets in its business operations—in other words, to convert them into fixed long-term assets like plant and equipment. A high current ratio can identify a company as "fat," cash-rich—just the kind that the lean and hungry hunter companies are looking for.

If an investor finds a company with an extremely high current ratio, he may have spotted a potential merger candidate. Companies with significant amounts of cash and other quick assets are very attractive to aggressive companies whose management feels that they can make better use of those assets and can earn a greater rate of return on those assets by investing them in their business. Historically, many companies with high current ratios and quick ratios have been singled out as merger candidates.

For financial companies (banks, insurance companies, brokerage houses, et al.), high current ratios and quick ratios are not as significant as they are for industrial companies. In periods of rising interest rates, very high current or quick ratios might well indicate highly sophisticated money managers who chose to load their investment portfolios with short-term government securities and commercial paper to maximize their rate of return.

But all this must now be taken with a pinch of salt—a grain just isn't enough. Ideally (read: "before the 1979–80 interest-rate cycle"), a well-run company should have on hand current assets just sufficient to discharge its current liabilities through an operating cycle (generally a year). The balance will be invested in its business. A company that has a current ratio greater than 2:1 is either not paying attention to money management, or, alternatively, is earning a higher rate of return on its investments than on its own business operations. Such a ratio may indicate that the company is not earning the rate of return it should be.

But—the wildly fluctuating 1979–81 interest cycle can justify high current and quick ratios. There's our pinch of salt. After all, if a company could earn 20% by investing its excess cash in short-term commercial paper, as it could have in the summer of 1981, it *would* seem foolish for it to have reinvested those funds in its own business and to have worked hard to try to achieve an equivalent rate of return.

However, with the resumption of more-normal interest rates, an unusually high current or quick ratio indicates that the company isn't earning what it should be and that the company is converting itself—unwittingly, perhaps—into an investment company. These ratios alert a potential acquirer— and the investor who uncovers these ratios—that this company might perform much better under different, more aggressive management.

The *ratio of accumulated depreciation to the book value of property, plant, and equipment,* which is usually expressed as a percentage, is another important number to look at. *Depreciation* refers to the loss in *book value* (stated value, usually its cost) of an asset over time, even though the asset may not actually lose market value. *Accumulated depreciation,* which is listed that way on the balance sheet, is the *total amount depreciated to date* on all the property, plant, and equipment.

To an investment analyst, this ratio indicates the age and possible obsolescence of the target company's plant and equipment, because the ratio increases with the length of time an asset has been depreciated. Generally, any number over 50% is regarded as high; the higher the number, the less attractive the target is on this basis.

Let's look at two examples.

Example 1: Hazleton Laboratories, a small high-technology company, showed accumulated depreciation of $8,174,000 and book value of $22,875,000 on its June 30, 1979, balance sheet.

$$\frac{\text{Accumulated Depreciation}}{\text{Book Value}} = \frac{\$8,174,000}{\$22,875,000} = 35.73\%$$

This ratio indicates that most of Hazleton's equipment is fairly new, especially if Hazleton is using accelerated—rather than straight-line—depreciation.*

Example 2: Singer Company's 1979 annual report showed accumulated depreciation of $492.3 million and property, plant, and equipment of $781.4 million.

$$\frac{\text{Accumulated Depreciation}}{\text{Book Value}} = \frac{\$492.3}{\$781.4} = 63.00\%$$

This ratio shows that Singer's plant and equipment are much older—an important negative factor because it indicates that a potential acquirer may have to invest heavily in new plant and equipment for the target in the near future. Such expenditures will absorb resources that might be more productively allocated elsewhere.

On this basis, Hazleton would be considered a good takeover candidate because its low ratio of 35.73% tells a potential acquirer that it will not have to make significant new investments in equipment in the near future and that its funds will thus be available for other, more profitable uses. Singer's high ratio of 63.00% suggests that much of its plant and equipment may be obsolete and may require expensive replacement in the near future.

Note also that the use of ratios makes it easy to compare companies whose numbers are vastly different; in this case, Singer's book value is 34 times larger than Hazleton's, and its accumulated depreciation is 60 times larger. When their

*Under the straight-line method of depreciation, the same amount of depreciation is taken—or written off—every year over the asset's useful life. Under accelerated depreciation, higher write-offs are taken during the early years of the asset's life, and correspondingly lower write-offs are taken during the later years of the asset's life. In inflationary periods, accelerated depreciation is more advantageous because it is much more desirable to take large write-offs early and smaller ones sometime in the future than to take a flat write-off each year. The Reagan tax act of 1981 recognized the need for accelerated depreciation and accordingly liberalized depreciation rules.

balance-sheet figures are converted into ratios, their significant differences show up strikingly.

Some balance-sheet figures refer to *intangible assets.* Unlike
plant and equipment, intangible assets are, in a sense, an accounting fiction: They are set up for accounting purposes.
Goodwill is the best example of an intangible asset. If a company has a figure for goodwill on its balance sheet, it probably
made an acquisition in the past in connection with which it
paid a certain amount in excess of the acquisition's fair market
value. Thus goodwill is considered a *phantom asset.* This over-
payment doesn't necessarily mean that the acquisition was a
bad deal, just that accountants and investment analysts may
feel that the hunter paid for the "going-concern value" of the
target company—e.g., its customer list or reputation—rather
than for just its assets. But since the hunter can't dispose of
goodwill or use it for any productive purpose, as it could with
other assets, goodwill should be subtracted in making balance-
sheet calculations.

The *debt/equity ratio* is another useful measure of a company's strength and is easily determined from the balance
sheet. To derive this ratio, divide long-term liabilities by the
sum of the common and preferred shareholders' equity, which
are labeled clearly:

$$\text{Debt/Equity Ratio} = \frac{\text{Long-term Liabilities}}{\text{Common + Preferred Stockholders' Equity}}$$

Let's look again at Singer's 1979 balance sheet, with long-
term liabilities of $427 million, preferred shareholders' equity
of $25 million, and common shareholders' equity of $71 million (total $396 million):

$$\text{Debt/Equity Ratio} = \frac{\$427}{\$396} = 1.08{:}1$$

Analysts generally regard a ratio greater than 1:1 as a yellow
flag and a ratio greater than 2:1—which means twice as much
borrowing as shareholders' stake in the corporation—as a very
red flag. High debt/equity ratios are unfavorable because they

signify that a company is probably at the outer limit of its borrowing capacity, and thus cannot leverage and increase its growth and profits through further borrowing.

Debt/equity ratios are so important that a company with a low debt/equity ratio might well become the target of a high-debt/equity-ratio company; the latter, by acquiring the former, would pick up substantial borrowing capacity—much like acquiring an unused line of credit. By making such an acquisition, a company can shore up its own depleted borrowing capacity.

Not surprisingly, the IRS has looked at debt/equity ratios, too. In conjunction with regulations that the IRS issued in mid-1980 on whether an interest in a company (potential acquisition) will be viewed by the IRS as debt or equity, the IRS has indicated that 60% of the companies filing tax returns have a debt/equity ratio of less than 1:1 (less debt than equity). Thus there is reasonable evidence that a debt/equity ratio of 1:1 is really the break point for both tax and investment purposes.

This IRS finding creates a valuable yardstick for investors examining merger candidates: The farther away a target moves from a debt/equity ratio of 1:1, the less attractive it will be as an acquisition candidate.

Let's take debt/equity ratios one step further. By refining them slightly, we can make them a more useful, more sophisticated tool. The more venturesome investor can make a small adjustment in the debt/equity ratio to allow for favorable treatment of any low-interest long-term loans. Obviously, a 30-year loan at 5% that still has 15 years to run should be treated differently from recent borrowings at 15%. Thus, if a company has a $1-million loan at 5%, it certainly makes sense to convert that liability to present interest rates—say, $417,000 at 12%—

$$\$1,000,000 \times 5\% = \$50,000 \text{ annual interest payment}$$
$$\$ \quad ? \quad \times 12\% = \$50,000$$
$$\$ \quad 417,000 \times 12\% = \$50,000$$

—by using a simple equation, and to use that equivalent liability ($417,000) in computing a more reasonable and realistic debt/equity ratio.

Clearly, cheap long-term debt is similar to a cheap mortgage. And, like a cheap mortgage, cheap long-term debt is a kind of hidden asset: It signifies more borrowing capacity than is immediately apparent. Potential hunters are aware of this factor and focus very heavily on the cost (interest rates) of the target's borrowings in determining whether the target would make an attractive acquisition.

Interest rates for corporate borrowings are shown clearly in balance-sheet footnotes. Without spending a great deal of time on precise calculations, investors can note whether the interest rates for most of the company's borrowings are well below the current rate of 12%–15%. If they are, the debt can be reduced proportionately for the debt/equity ratio calculation.

Book value per share is the last—and to many analysts the most important—of the balance-sheet ratios. Book value represents the net worth of the corporation if it were liquidated: what would remain after all the assets were sold and all the liabilities were paid. Book value per share is simply this figure divided by the number of shares outstanding, and indicates what a stockholder might expect to receive per share of stock if the corporation were liquidated.

To illustrate, let's look at a company with $50 million in total assets, $10 million in total liabilities, and 2 million shares outstanding.

Book Value = Total Assets − Total Liabilities
Book Value = $50,000,000 − $10,000,000 = $40,000,000

$$\text{Book Value per Share} = \frac{\$40,000,000}{2,000,000} = \$20$$

Analysts regard book value per share as the crucial ratio because it quickly and easily indicates exactly how the market values a company's stock (selling price) vis-à-vis its real assets (book value per share). If investors accept the proposition—and many do—that a company's book value per share indicates the value of its assets, the book value per share becomes a kind of shorthand that tells investors how the market evaluates that company. Because of its significance, *book value per share is*

*important in examining every single type of special situation: mergers,
tender offers, spinoffs, and liquidations.* If the book value is at least
one-third higher than the stock's present market price, there's
a good chance that at some point there will be a move made
to tender for, merge, spin off, or liquidate the company. The
"trigger" is the same; only the means to a profitable end differ.

The investor's Holy Grail is the company that is trading at
a substantial discount from book value. Seasoned investors
will recognize this strategy as the Benjamin Graham approach.* Many money managers and investment analysts actually design computer programs to identify stocks selling at
some minimum specified discount from book value—generally
at least one-third. Some investment managers base their investment decisions on these criteria, using the stocks identified by the programs as their universe of potential buys.

Lest this book-value approach be labeled as overly naïve or
simplistic, investors should be aware that there is usually a
difference between book value and asset value; they rarely
correlate 100%.

Even if book value and market value coincide, the price tags
might not reflect the company's true worth. Buried beneath
the black-and-white of financial statements or stock quotations
can be a mother lode of gold in the form of "hidden assets."

Known in financial circles as "off-balance-sheet assets," hidden assets are not assets that are concealed fraudulently.
Rather, the term describes those assets a company possesses
but does not have to specifically report or clearly label in
financial statements. Since most merger deals today involve a
substantial premium over indicated book value, how much of
that premium is justified often depends on these hidden assets. They can include:

Real estate. Real estate is generally carried on the books at
cost, and that cost becomes part of the book-value calculations. But the land and its buildings could have been bought
50 years ago, and the original price may be only 5% of its
current worth.

Leases. Property doesn't have to be owned by a company;

---

*Benjamin Graham, David L. Dodd, et. al., *Security Analysis: Principles and
Technique*, 4th ed. (New York: McGraw-Hill, 1962).

even leases can be valuable hidden assets. Many investors and securities analysts know that Chock Full o' Nuts' most valuable assets include some very long-term leases, many of which still have 20 to 30 years to run. The leases govern prime-location store rentals for as little as $100 per month—with these fixed costs locked in, regardless of inflation, for the next quarter of a century.

Long-term energy-related contracts. These agreements do not provide for price increases in keeping with current market trends. Prices are often fixed at what now are clearly unusually low levels.

Assets carried at historical purchase price. One leading oil company's reserves, for example, are carried on a 1930 cost basis —a tremendous understatement of present value.

LIFO vs. FIFO. LIFO and FIFO are accounting acronyms for two methods of valuing inventory: Last In, First Out; and First In, First Out. Under FIFO the goods sold are matched against the first goods bought to calculate profit. Under LIFO, they're matched against the most recent goods bought.

During periods of rising costs—especially when prices may trail costs or may not permit the full passing along of the increased costs—LIFO accounting (sales price minus high cost) artificially depresses earnings, while FIFO accounting (sales price minus low cost) artificially inflates earnings. Investors should know which method is used in order to judge the "real value" of a company's earnings: artificially low (LIFO) or artificially high (FIFO). An easy mnemonic: *Low earnings = LIFO.*

Companies must state whether they use LIFO or FIFO accounting in their annual reports. This information usually appears as a note to "inventory" on the balance sheet.

Miscellaneous. This catchall includes practically everything. International Banknote—the venerable printer of foreign currencies, stamps, traveler's checks, and stock certificates—has vast archives of printing proofs and plates dating back two centuries. Insured for $20 million, the archives are carried on the books for exactly $1! Furthermore, as has been borne out by the sale figures at recent major numismatic auctions, some analysts believe that these old engraving plates and samples are worth substantially more than their $20-million insured value.

Hidden assets can also include the prosaic. As Lee Hackett, president of the American Appraisal Company of Milwaukee, points out, even engineering drawings can become crucial. "[The drawings] may be buried somewhere because the production people know the product is completed and don't need them. But in case of a strike, there may be no way to keep going if these drawings are unavailable."

Other assets may be worth *less* than their book value. Think of all the 1980 inventory that couldn't be sold: U.S. Olympic souvenirs, Rely tampons, American gas-guzzling cars.

Such skeletons in the closet come in myriad varieties. In broadcasting, for example, the three TV networks generally write off around 75% of the cost of a show or film the first time it airs and the remaining 25% when they rebroadcast the program. But what if the show really bombs and there is no rerun? Although auditing requires that shows axed from the prime-time schedule be duly exorcised from the balance sheet, some industry observers suggest that the networks have been deferring write-offs of turkeys. (Such practices were common in the movie industry, too, until 1973, when official scrutiny intensified.)

Meanwhile insurance companies—popular acquisition candidates because of the hefty cash premiums they collect each year—can have warts all their own. If a company acquires an insurance company whose investment portfolio includes large unrealized capital losses, the buyer must assume the portfolio's losses as well as its profits. Taking these losses would leave the acquiring company with a reduced surplus and might even require a transfusion of cash from the hunter to the target to maintain certain "solvency ratios" demanded by state insurance examiners. Not exactly a desirable outcome when the original goal was to *take* cash from the target!

So beware of overvalued assets when you size up a company's potential as a takeover target. Sometimes the "skeletons" are "phantom assets," which appear on the balance sheet for accounting purposes only. As mentioned before, goodwill is the best example of an intangible asset. If a company shows a figure for goodwill on its balance sheet, it probably acquired a company in the past for which it paid a certain amount in excess of the fair market value. While this premium doesn't necessarily mean that the acquisition was a bad deal, it indicates that both accountants and investment analysts may feel that the purchaser paid for the "going concern" value of the target, rather than only its assets.

Since the purchaser can't dispose of goodwill or use it for any productive purpose, investors should subtract goodwill from total assets when making balance-sheet calculations.

OTHER FACTORS AFFECTING BOOK VALUE

Of the major factors affecting book value, perhaps the two most important are *net operating loss* and *replacement cost.*

Net operating loss is defined literally as the excess of a company's allowable deductions over its gross income. This excess may be carried back to the three preceding years to recover actual tax dollars previously paid, or forward to the succeeding seven years to reduce the amount of taxes subsequently due: thus the terms *loss carry-back* and *loss carry-forward.* Accordingly, a net operating loss is a valuable asset; in effect, a corporate tax shelter that serves to reduce a corporation's effective tax rate.

Of course, a net operating loss is worthless unless the corporation can generate taxable income against which to offset those losses. If this future income is not likely, the company may then become the target of acquisition efforts by a profitable suitor seeking to shelter its *own* earnings. Hence, a net operating loss is actually a hidden asset that can provide the impetus for a takeover.

However, the Internal Revenue Code will prohibit the availability of a target's net operating losses to a suitor if it appears that the transaction was undertaken principally to secure the loss. Since this test is a subjective one (note the word "principally"), there is always the possibility that the IRS will rule against the suitor. That possibility of failure explains why net operating losses do not always command premium prices. Indeed, net operating losses may not even command a "fair" price—roughly, 46 cents on the dollar. In practice, the risk of IRS disallowance translates into a price of roughly 25 cents for each dollar of loss.

In any event, a net operating loss is a "hidden" asset, an intangible. As such, any company possessing a net operating loss will reflect an artificially low book value.

Replacement cost of an asset is, quite simply, the price, at current costs, of purchasing an asset in the current market. Typically, this amount is used by analysts to compute a company's "true" earnings, which include depreciation calculated on the basis of replacement amounts, as opposed to historical costs.

Although the use of replacement value—"inflation accounting"—is not required for the presentation of financial statements, companies with over $1 billion of assets are required to present replacement-cost data as footnotes. These footnotes have indicated the degree of overstatement in many corporations' reported earnings, particularly those with older plant and equipment, whose depreciation deductions are based on historical costs and are therefore abnormally low by today's standards.

These differences from book value become more significant in some situations, less so in others. Once again, our purpose here is not to transform investors into securities analysts, but merely to alert investors to look carefully at assets and to modify book-value calculations when necessary, rather than regarding them as immutable gospel. Fortunately, in most cases, book value should be adjusted up, rather than down; thus the investor who simply calculates book value will generally wind up understating assets rather than overstating them and will therefore tend to be less aggressive in making investment decisions involving those stocks.

Finally, investors should note a tantalizing sidelight to the evaluation of book value. Some companies are so extremely undervalued on the stock market that there's no need to find capital to buy them. How and why?

Because the acquirer can raise the money by using the borrowing power of the target itself—perhaps the ultimate form of leveraged buyout. (In a leveraged buyout, the purchaser

antes up very little of his or her own money; most of the
purchase price is borrowed.)

Using a computer screen, Oppenheimer & Company analysts Norman Weinger and E. Michael Metz identified "those
companies that, on the basis of their balance-sheet entries,
would be particularly attractive to an acquirer since their assets
could theoretically provide sufficient collateral values to permit borrowing the entire purchase price. In essence, a buyer
could possibly use the borrowing power of the acquired company to completely finance the purchase of it."

Limited to those companies whose stock-market values were
greater than $10 million, the screen turned up over 80 compa-
nies, some of them household words. Among the candidates:
Boeing, Gulf Oil, E. F. MacDonald, U.S. Steel, and Ford Motors.

PROFITABILITY RATIOS

As their name indicates, these ratios measure a company's
profitability. They are derived from the profit-and-loss statement, which follows the balance sheet.

Profitability ratios are not as important for our purposes as
balance-sheet ratios. Profitability ratios reflect the capability of
the company as a going concern, rather than as a special situation. Nevertheless, an acquiring company will also pay attention to certain profitability ratios in its decision-making
process.

The *gross profit ratio*—also called the *gross profit margin*—is
simply

$$\text{Gross Profit Margin} = \frac{\text{Net Sales} - \text{Cost of Goods Sold}}{\text{Net Sales}}$$

Similarly, the *net profit margin* examines profitability after
general administration and operating costs and income taxes
have been subtracted.

$$\text{Net Profit Margin} = \frac{\text{Net Income}}{\text{Net Sales}}$$

All of these numbers appear clearly in the profit-and-loss statement.

To securities analysts, the gross profit margin indicates how well—or badly—a company is doing in its primary business (as opposed to its investments). Gross profit margins are very different (and much higher) than net profit margins. Net profit margins measure how successfully the company operates its business.

Because net profit margins vary widely from industry to industry, with supermarket net profit margins historically low (1%–2%) and high-technology profit margins high (sometimes over 30%), investors should examine net profit margins in the context of the company's particular industry. Both Standard & Poor's and Moody's company reports, which can be found in large-city business libraries or can be obtained from investors' stockbrokers, rank companies' gross and net profit margins within their industries. Thus, a company might be ranked fifth in its 20-company group on gross profit margin and eighth on net profit margin. These figures signify that while the company ranks high in its group on both gross and net profit margins, it fares better on pricing and selling its goods than on keeping its general, administrative, and other costs down.

Net earnings and *net earnings per share*—sometimes shown as *net income* and *net income per share.* Both net earnings and net earnings per share are shown on the income statement; they do not have to be calculated.

Net earnings and net earnings per share are traditional measures of profitability: the return on investment after all expenses have been subtracted.

Earnings per share is a significant investment concept for traditional investing because it is used in calculating the familiar price/earnings ratio: current market price divided by last year's known earnings or this year's estimated earnings per share. The price/earnings ratio is so commonly used that it is part of the daily stock-market pages in the *Wall Street Journal* and *The New York Times* and is abbreviated and spoken of as P/E. Even more important to traditional investing is the trend of earnings, shown by several years' earnings per share, with earnings per share projected several years into the future.

Special-situation investors, however, are not interested in earnings trends or their projections. They are *very* interested in stocks with low price/earnings ratios, because low P/E's are a quick and easy way of identifying cheap stocks. In fact, many investors use P/E's as a screening device before they even begin to calculate book value and its relation to market price. It's a lot faster.

EARNED YIELD

Another measure of stock value has emerged: the concept of earned yield. To calculate the earned yield, the after-tax earnings per share are divided by the stock price:

$$\text{Earned Yield} = \frac{\text{After-tax Earnings per Share}}{\text{Stock Price}}$$

Only now coming into prominence in the United States, the earned-yield technique has long enjoyed popularity in England and abroad. Earned yield offers an advantage over the classic price/earnings ratio because of its applicability to both stocks and bonds, which enables investors to compare the two types of securities directly.

Despite the importance of the price/earnings ratio and earned yields for traditional investing, the emphasis differs for stalking special-situation targets. Here securities analysts concern themselves much more with book value than with earnings per share.

Most securities analysts use profitability ratios to fine-tune their original evaluation of a company obtained from calculating the balance-sheet ratios. High profitability ratios tell the potential acquirer that the target company's management is competent and successful; the hunter may then decide to retain the management and to continue operating the target as a going concern. In fact, very often the target company's management is the primary asset involved in the acquisition.

In contrast, low profitability ratios often show that management of the target company is not utilizing balance-sheet assets to maximize profitability. The potential acquirer might then decide (1) to install new management to run the target and substantially increase profitability—this is the classic "turnaround situation"; or (2) to strip the target and sell off its assets.

Cash flow per share, which is derived from earnings per share, is the final ratio to examine. It can be calculated from the financial statement called "Changes in Financial Position." This financial statement analyzes the company's expenses, which are shown on the profit-and-loss statement, and subtracts those that do not require the actual outlay of money. Depreciation is the primary example. Depletion and amortization can count heavily, too, and are often lumped together with depreciation.

For our purposes, we need only add depreciation per share (found in the income statement) to earnings per share. This will give us a rough but workable estimate of cash flow per share. Thus, if depreciation per share were $.50 and earnings per share were $2.50, cash flow per share would be $3.00.

Investment analysts regard cash flow as a more accurate indicator of "true" earnings and liquidity because it more accurately reflects a company's ability to earn money by putting differing accounting systems on a comparable basis. Huge depreciation substantially decreases a company's earnings per share—perhaps unfairly, since it usually reflects investments in efficient new equipment that can generate high profits. Accelerated depreciation, which most companies use to offset the diminishing value of money during inflation, accentuates this difference. Using cash flow per share in conjunction with earnings per share puts the company's earning power in perspective.

Finally, it is important to remember that no ratio is "good" or "bad" in itself; it's only relative. Investors should compare a company's ratios with those of other companies in the same industry.

Various sources make comparative ratios available. *Dun & Bradstreet* compiles one set of useful data that lists 14 ratios for a large number of industries. Another good resource is the *Annual Statement Studies* published by Robert Morris Associates, the national association of bank loan officers. The Federal Trade Commission's *Quarterly Financial Report* gives ratios for manufacturing firms by industry group and size of company. Trade associations and credit departments of individual companies also compile useful industry averages.

Now, as a final check, let's analyze the 1980 annual report for Conoco, selected because of the lusty pursuit of this company as a merger "bride." Conoco's balance sheet and income statement are reprinted on the following pages. The ratios— and the interpretation an investment analyst might make of them—appear at the end of this chapter. Then, in chapter 6, we'll see what these ratios meant to the companies that bid for Conoco in the largest merger in financial history.
The information you need to find is:

1. Current ratio
2. Quick ratio
3. Ratio of accumulated depreciation, depletion and amortization to book value
4. Debt/equity ratio
5. Book value
6. Book value per share
7. Gross profit margin
8. Net profit margin
9. Cash flow per share

First we'll calculate and comment on the six balance-sheet ratios, then the three profitability ratios.

1. Current ratio
   The current ratio is:

$$\frac{\text{Current Assets}}{\text{Current Liabilities}} = \frac{\$4.004 \text{ billion}}{\$2.992 \text{ billion}} = 1.34 \text{ to } 1$$

2. Quick ratio
   The quick ratio is:

$$\frac{\text{Current Assets} - \text{Inventories}}{\text{Current Liabilities}}$$

$$= \frac{\$4.004 \text{ billion} - \$859.7 \text{ million}}{\$2.992 \text{ billion}}$$

$$= 1.05 \text{ to } 1$$

3. *Ratio of accumulated depreciation, depletion and amortization to book value of property, plant, and equipment*
   Is:

$$\frac{\text{Accumulated Depreciation, Depletion and Amortization}}{\text{Book Value of Property, Plant, and Equipment}}$$

$$= \frac{\$3.761 \text{ billion*}}{\$9.975 \text{ billion}} = 37.7\%$$

4. *Debt/equity ratio*
   Is:

$$\frac{\text{Long-term Debt}}{\text{Common and Preferred Stock}}$$

$$= \frac{\$1.378 \text{ billion}}{\$4.585 \text{ billion}} = .30 \text{ to } 1$$

5. *Book value*
   Book value is:

   Total assets — total liabilities
   = $11.036 billion — $6.451 billion
   = $4.585 billion

6. *Book value per share*
   Book value per share is:

$$\frac{\text{Book Value}}{\text{Number of Common Shares}}$$

$$= \frac{\$4.585 \text{ billion}}{107,780,000}$$

$$= \$42.54$$

*From Note 3 of balance sheet

Consolidated Balance Sheet

	December 31	
	1980	1979
	($000)	
Assets		
Current assets:		
Cash, including time deposits.	$ **605,874**	$ 520,296
Marketable securities at cost, which approximates market	**140,173**	548,553
Accounts and notes receivable	**2,161,207**	1,595,014
Inventories (Note 1)	**859,676**	719,109
Other current assets	**236,698**	41,260
Total current assets	**4,003,628**	3,424,232
Investments and advances (Note 2)	**234,790**	217,327
Long-term receivables	**90,607**	121,213
Property, plant, and equipment, at cost (including oil and gas properties accounted for by the successful efforts method of accounting), less accumulated depreciation, depletion, and amortization (Note 3):		
Owned	**6,214,845**	5,120,313
Leased under capital leases	**210,661**	227,907
	6,425,506	5,348,220
Prepaid and deferred charges	**281,744**	200,179
	$11,036,275	$9,311,171

Liabilities and Stockholders' Equity

Current liabilities:

Notes payable (Note 4)	$ 60,718	$ 79,225
Accounts payable	1,699,773	1,359,748
Accrued taxes, including income taxes	782,298	656,768
Other accrued liabilities	410,250	330,800
Long-term debt due within one year (Note 4)	22,930	49,250
Capital lease obligations due within one year (Note 6)	16,132	15,526
Total current liabilities	2,992,101	2,491,317
Long-term debt (Note 4)	1,378,448	1,367,392
Capital lease obligations (Note 6)	238,054	254,253
Minority interest in subsidiaries	323,286	284,797

Deferred credits and other liabilities:

Income taxes	999,099	716,597
Employee benefits (Note 8)	312,413	260,418
Other	208,345	153,286
	1,519,857	1,130,301

Stockholders' equity (Note 5):

Preferred Stock	399	502
Common Stock (shares outstanding 1980—107,831,164; 1979—107,673,296)	567,268	566,469
Capital surplus	536,630	532,310
Retained earnings	3,512,221	2,715,296
	4,616,518	3,814,577
Less Common Stock in treasury	31,989	31,466
Total stockholders' equity	4,584,529	3,783,111

Contingent liabilities (Note 9)

	$11,036,275	$9,311,171

Notes to Consolidated Financial Statements

Note 1 — Inventories

	1980	1979
	($000)	
Crude oil and refined products	$486,696	$444,858
Chemicals	66,017	44,499
Coal	32,059	27,488
Other	44,921	43,340
	629,693	560,185
Materials and supplies	229,983	158,924
	$859,676	$719,109

The excess of replacement or current cost over stated value of inventories for which cost has been determined under the LIFO method approximated $1,400,000,000 and $1,185,000,000 at December 31, 1980 and 1979, respectively. Net income in 1980 includes a $92,000,000 benefit from a reduction of crude oil and refined products inventory quantities valued under the LIFO method.

Note 2 — Investments and advances

At December 31, 1980, Conoco's investments in and advances to companies accounted for under the equity method aggregated $218,896,000, which approximates the Company's equity in their net assets. Conoco's equity in net income of these companies is included in other income for 1980, 1979, and 1978 in the amounts of $52,606,000, $53,042,000, and $37,992,000, respectively. Dividends received from these companies were $21,501,000,

In the fourth quarter of 1980, Conoco adopted a policy of capitalizing interest cost as required by Statement No. 34 of the Financial Accounting Standards Board. Accordingly, $45,000,000 was capitalized as part of the historical cost of certain qualifying assets, which increased 1980 net income by $23,700,000.

Note 4 — Notes payable and long-term debt

Notes payable represent borrowings under various bank financing arrangements, primarily foreign, having an average interest rate at December 31, 1980 and 1979 of approximately 16% and 15%, respectively. The maximum and average amounts outstanding were $115,838,000 and $86,632,000, respectively, in 1980 and $95,200,000 and $51,400,000, respectively, in 1979. The weighted-average annual interest rate approximated 14% in 1980 and 12% in 1979.

Long-term debt at December 31, 1980 is summarized in the table at the top of page 37. Annual maturities on long-term debt during the next five years are: 1981 — $22,930,000; 1982 — $34,593,000; 1983 — $85,228,000; 1984 — $64,868,000; and 1985 — $68,217,000. Subsequent to December 31, 1980, Conoco issued $300,000,000 of 30-year 13¼% debentures and Hudson's Bay Oil and Gas Company Limited issued $100,000,000 of 25-year 14¾% debentures. Mandatory annual sinking fund payments commence in 1992.

Note 5 — Stockholders' equity

There are 2,100,000 authorized shares of $2 cumulative convertible Preferred Stock, without par value, of which 109,360 shares were outstanding at December 31, 1980 and 137,453 shares were outstanding at December 31, 1979. Each share of Preferred Stock is entitled to one vote and is convertible into 2.68 shares of

$33,597,000, and $15,714,000 in 1980, 1979, and 1978, respectively.

Conoco is obligated to certain affiliates and corporate joint ventures, in which it has substantial stock investments, to provide specified minimum revenues from crude oil and refined products shipments or purchases. No significant loss is anticipated by reason of such agreements.

Note 3 — Property, plant, and equipment

	1980		1979	
	Owned	Leased under capital leases	Owned	Leased under capital leases
	($000)			
Petroleum production	$5,583,720	$ —	$4,585,264	$ —
Refineries and natural gas processing facilities	1,169,689	4,000	1,036,924	4,000
Petroleum marketing	277,008	23,684	281,611	29,001
Petroleum supply and transportation	388,574	197,274	343,105	196,492
Chemicals	617,299	26,224	515,435	26,224
Coal and related activities	1,750,866	31,931	1,583,767	32,189
Minerals	52,535	—	45,846	—
Other	136,191	47,183	76,318	45,963
	9,975,882	330,296	8,468,270	333,869
Less accumulated depreciation, depletion, and amortization	3,761,037	119,635	3,347,957	105,962
	$6,214,845	$210,661	$5,120,313	$227,907

Common Stock. The Preferred Stock is callable at and has a liquidation value of $60 per share plus accrued dividends.

There are 120,000,000 authorized shares of Common Stock, $5 par value, of which 113,453,633 shares were issued at December 31, 1980 and 113,293,884 shares were issued at December 31, 1979. At the same dates, there were 5,622,469 and 5,620,588 shares, respectively, of Common Stock in the treasury, shown at par for shares held at December 31, 1969, and at cost for subsequent acquisitions, including 4,255,318 shares received in exchange for a portion of the Company's investment in a consolidated subsidiary recorded at the Company's carrying value of the investment plus expenses related to the exchange. At December 31, 1980, 1,526,607 shares of Common Stock were reserved for issuance, including 1,125,700 shares in connection with stock options; 293,084 shares for conversion of Preferred Stock; and 107,823 shares for other purposes. During 1980, 75,222 shares of Common Stock were issued upon conversion of 28,093 shares of Preferred Stock.

At December 31, 1980, options were outstanding to purchase 733,400 shares of the Company's Common Stock under a 1971 nonqualified stock option plan for officers and other key employees. Under the plan, options for a maximum term of 10 years may be granted at prices not less than the market price of the Company's Common Stock on the date of grant. Options do not become exercisable until at least one year after date of grant. As an alternative to exercise, optionees may surrender options granted under the plan, subject to acceptance by the Company's Compensation Committee, for payment to the optionees of an amount equal to the difference between the option price and the fair market value of the shares. Such payments may be made in shares, cash, or both, at the discretion of the Compensation Committee. The cost thereof is accrued over the vesting period of the options and is adjusted for subsequent changes in the fair

Ten-Year Review 1971–1980 (millions of dollars, except per-share amounts)

	1980	1979	1978	1977	1976	1975	1974	1973	1972	1971
Revenues by Product										
Refined petroleum	9,092.6	7,138.0	5,116.9	4,470.7	4,030.4	3,766.8	3,479.3	2,355.9	1,911.1	1,593.6
Crude oil	6,014.2	2,663.4	2,208.0	2,190.3	1,979.1	1,889.7	2,218.7	1,020.5	838.0	744.9
Natural gas	683.3	549.0	448.0	392.7	336.6	221.3	158.8	132.2	105.5	94.8
Coal	1,334.5	1,322.9	961.6	1,105.5	1,152.3	1,026.3	747.0	473.7	421.0	320.9
Chemicals	874.7	792.0	601.9	441.9	385.1	293.3	376.8	221.0	200.0	200.3
Other sales and services	489.1	386.1	351.1	339.2	319.9	302.2	298.3	267.6	173.3	146.4
Other operating revenues	24.0	31.0	80.5	32.2	41.3	57.8	19.6	8.7	12.7	17.3
Nonoperating revenues	253.9	200.5	103.8	79.3	107.6	108.7	45.2	11.4	34.0	3.5
Total from continuing operations	**18,766.3**	**13,082.9**	**9,871.8**	**9,051.8**	**8,352.3**	**7,666.1**	**7,343.7**	**4,491.0**	**3,695.6**	**3,121.7**
Costs, Expenses, and Taxes										
Purchases of crude oil	6,381.4	3,419.0	2,763.5	2,826.4	2,630.2	2,441.6	2,751.0	1,291.8	868.3	726.9
Other costs and operating expenses	5,529.8	4,416.8	3,310.7	2,775.5	2,470.3	2,343.5	2,091.2	1,166.6	1,129.7	985.2
Selling, general, and administrative expenses	756.4	624.8	486.9	466.4	430.4	374.1	324.2	278.5	227.3	219.2
Exploration expenses(1)	354.1	237.8	233.9	213.4	180.6	174.8	145.4	103.0	81.3	89.0
Depreciation, depletion, and amortization	466.9	398.3	343.3	340.3	318.8	297.9	243.1	238.9	181.1	161.4
Loss on long-term natural gas sales contract	—	—	—	—	—	29.6	—	—	—	—
Interest and debt expense	143.3	167.0	147.1	117.9	120.5	119.3	104.6	82.1	68.3	67.4
U.S. federal income taxes	319.4	244.2	146.9	174.7	194.3	137.5	86.2	40.6	33.8	3.4
U.S. state income taxes	10.0	8.1	4.9	6.4	7.0	4.4	4.2	3.4	2.2	1.0
Foreign income taxes	2,121.7	1,407.8	794.4	742.2	623.7	517.9	493.6	250.3	205.5	175.1
U.S. excise taxes	187.0	203.4	232.3	239.9	246.4	246.5	238.2	256.3	234.6	211.1
Other taxes	1,413.3	1,089.4	915.0	723.5	635.3	618.5	530.1	539.2	472.8	359.7
Minority interest in subsidiaries' net income	56.8	50.9	41.6	44.6	38.6	34.1	29.6	20.2	14.9	11.7
Total from continuing operations	**17,740.1**	**12,267.5**	**9,420.5**	**8,671.2**	**7,896.1**	**7,339.7**	**7,041.4**	**4,270.9**	**3,519.8**	**3,011.1**

Income										
Income from continuing operations	1,026.2	815.4	451.3	380.6	456.2	326.4	302.3	220.1	175.8	110.6
Income from discontinued plant foods and related operations	—	—	—	—	—	—	—	—	—	4.4
Income before extraordinary items	**1,026.2**	**815.4**	**451.3**	**380.6**	**456.2**	**326.4**	**302.3**	**220.1**	**175.8**	**115.0**
Extraordinary items	—	—	—	—	—	—	—	—	—	(19.4)
Net Income	**1,026.2**	**815.4**	**451.3**	**380.6**	**456.2**	**326.4**	**302.3**	**220.1**	**175.8**	**95.6**
After-Tax Foreign Currency Adjustments(2)										
Long-term debt	(5.9)	(6.8)	(14.2)	(9.0)	(1.5)	12.5	(15.1)	(16.0)	6.7	(13.6)
Other	13.0	2.7	(17.5)	(13.1)	5.0	3.4	(12.5)	(4.0)	3.6	(8.8)
Total	**7.1**	**(4.1)**	**(31.7)**	**(22.1)**	**3.5**	**15.9**	**(27.6)**	**(20.0)**	**10.3**	**(22.4)**
Per Common Share Data(3)										
Income before extraordinary items(4)	**9.52**	**7.58**	**4.20**	**3.55**	**4.34**	**3.20**	**2.98**	**2.18**	**1.75**	**1.14**
Net income(4)	9.52	7.58	4.20	3.55	4.34	3.20	2.98	2.18	1.75	.94
Dividends	2.13	1.70	1.43	1.35	1.15	1.00	.85	.76	.75	.75
Book value(5)	42.45	35.06	29.20	26.43	24.22	20.52	18.31	16.17	14.72	13.61
Market price — high	73.00	49.25	32.13	38.00	40.88	37.50	29.25	27.63	20.13	19.88
— low	41.00	28.00	24.50	27.50	29.75	20.25	14.50	13.38	12.50	12.25
— at year-end	65.38	47.25	28.13	30.00	37.50	30.44	22.31	27.31	20.00	14.44

(1) Comprises cash exploration expenses, dry hole costs, and impairment of unproved properties; differs from exploration expenses shown on page 54 by including 100% of exploration expenses for Hudson's Bay Oil and Gas Company.

(2) Comprises balance sheet translation adjustments, including those of affiliates accounted for under the equity method, and gains and losses on forward exchange contracts.

(3) Amounts give retroactive effect to the share-for-share stock distribution declared in May 1976.

(4) Based on weighted-average number of Common shares outstanding and after deducting dividends paid on Preferred Stock.

(5) At December 31.

Ten-Year Review 1971–1980 (millions of dollars, except as indicated)

	1980	1979	1978	1977	1976	1975	1974	1973	1972	1971
Rates of Return (%)[1]										
Return on stockholders' average equity	**24.5**	**23.5**	**15.1**	**13.9**	**19.3**	**16.3**	**17.1**	**13.9**	**12.0**	**8.2**
Return on average borrowed and invested capital	18.6	17.9	12.0	11.1	14.0	12.0	12.3	10.4	8.9	6.7
Balance Sheet Data[2]										
Net working capital:										
Cash and marketable securities	746.0	1,068.8	695.4	748.5	1,054.7	530.6	547.9	287.4	196.0	143.6
Other	265.5	(135.9)	210.1	171.9	(74.8)	37.9	73.2	181.2	127.4	263.1
Investments and advances	234.8	217.3	179.4	160.6	128.2	114.8	106.1	103.7	103.0	97.1
Net property, plant, and equipment:										
Owned	6,214.8	5,120.3	4,090.2	3,488.6	3,064.7	2,796.9	2,433.4	2,117.2	2,079.1	1,879.5
Leased	210.7	227.9	233.2	262.4	357.9	322.6	303.9	323.7	227.1	202.9
Total assets	**11,036.3**	**9,311.2**	**7,445.2**	**6,625.2**	**6,409.4**	**5,519.8**	**4,949.4**	**4,009.5**	**3,491.4**	**3,255.0**
Long-term debt	1,378.4	1,367.4	1,219.6	1,066.1	1,041.4	904.1	892.5	700.2	702.0	711.0
Long-term capital lease obligations	238.1	254.3	268.9	283.0	377.9	342.9	319.0	337.6	246.1	219.1
Minority interest in subsidiaries	323.3	284.8	250.7	222.5	191.0	165.9	143.8	123.8	112.2	114.2
Deferred credits and other liabilities	1,519.9	1,130.3	811.7	626.2	531.7	466.6	368.4	311.9	263.1	234.2
Stockholders' equity	4,584.5	3,783.1	3,147.8	2,849.6	2,609.3	2,112.5	1,880.2	1,659.6	1,513.8	1,404.3
Changes in Financial Position										
Funds available:										
Funds from operations	1,832.0	1,520.9	1,013.5	890.1	872.4	745.1	654.6	567.6	408.9	356.6
Sales of fixed assets and investments	136.8	98.1	152.8	95.4	137.6	126.0	83.2	56.8	67.2	132.7
Addition to long-term debt	52.4	233.3	310.0	88.1	214.1	105.8	230.4	51.7	65.6	76.2
Addition to capital lease obligations	.2	1.0	—	2.5	59.3	47.5	9.6	107.1	43.6	35.5

Issuance of equity securities	138.8	67.3	—	—	148.7	—	—	—	—	—
Other sources (net)	—	—	—	48.3	13.1	—	38.4	11.4	8.2	11.8
Total	**2,160.2**	**1,920.6**	**1,476.3**	**1,124.4**	**1,445.2**	**1,024.4**	**1,016.2**	**794.6**	**593.5**	**612.8**
Funds applied:										
Capital expenditures	1,762.2	1,561.6	1,107.2	834.6	775.3	796.4	667.6	372.7	457.8	387.4
Investments and advances	4.7	21.9	5.4	15.5	2.9	3.5	3.2	4.8	11.5	20.0
Addition to assets under capital leases ...	1.2	2.1	.2	2.6	19.0	44.5	9.7	99.7	40.0	23.4
Reduction of long-term debt	49.7	92.4	171.4	74.8	77.9	82.1	58.6	71.1	67.1	53.3
Reduction of capital lease obligations	16.4	15.7	14.0	97.4	24.3	23.6	28.2	15.6	16.6	13.6
Dividends on Common Stock	229.0	182.9	153.0	144.7	120.3	101.6	85.9	76.5	74.9	74.8
Dividends on Preferred Stock	.2	.3	.4	.5	.6	.8	.9	1.2	1.5	1.5
Dividends to minority interests	18.2	16.3	13.6	13.8	13.5	12.0	9.6	7.8	7.4	6.5
Other applications (net)	—	—	25.9	—	—	12.6	—	—	—	—
Total	**2,081.6**	**1,893.2**	**1,491.1**	**1,183.9**	**1,033.8**	**1,077.1**	**863.7**	**649.4**	**676.8**	**580.5**
Increase (decrease) in working capital	78.6	27.4	(14.8)	(59.5)	411.4	(52.7)	152.5	145.2	(83.3)	32.3

Stockholder and Employee Data

Shares outstanding (thousands):										
Common[3]—weighted-average for year ..	107,780	107,580	107,396	107,183	104,920	101,608	101,011	100,333	99,906	99,774
—at year-end	107,831	107,673	107,423	107,354	107,021	101,838	101,244	100,810	100,045	99,878
Preferred—at year-end	109	137	191	211	278	370	442	483	681	723
Number of stockholders at year-end:										
Common	73,394	71,532	70,588	70,125	66,681	64,813	69,192	71,361	79,329	84,712
Preferred	1,231	1,547	2,056	2,274	2,815	3,274	3,650	3,919	4,481	4,727
Number of employees at year-end	41,503	40,502	42,780	43,141	43,899	44,028	41,174	39,796	38,092	40,509

(1) See Definition of Terms, page 60.
(2) At December 31.
(3) Amounts give retroactive effect to the share-for-share stock distribution declared in May 1976. Common shares outstanding on February 18, 1981, the date of this report, were 107,843,000.

How should we interpret this information? Nancy Dunnan, financial analyst and writer, has provided the following analysis of Conoco, based on the company's 1980 annual report.

Conoco's current ratio is 1.34 to 1. In our earlier discussions, we indicated that the current ratio should be approximately between 1.5 to 1 and 2.0 to 1. According to *Dun & Bradstreet's Key Business Ratios,* the industry average for crude-petroleum and natural-gas companies is 1.40 to 1. Therefore, Conoco's ratio is a bit low, but not significantly.

Next, let's examine the quick ratio. Conoco's quick ratio of 1.05 to 1 falls well within our guideline for this ratio.

Therefore, neither of Conoco's liquidity ratios suggests that Conoco is either a cash cow or has lazy management. Instead, a current ratio of 1.34 to 1 and a quick ratio of 1.4 to 1 fall near or within the mainstream of American business. These ratios don't touch off a "buy" signal.

The ratio of accumulated depreciation to book value of fixed assets indicates the age of the corporation's equipment: The higher the value, the older the equipment. Since many mergers stem from the belief that it's cheaper to buy than to build, a comparatively young stock of fixed assets can attract acquirers. Conoco's ratio of 37.7% is quite good. Generally, investors should look for a ratio that is less that 40%, indicating that the fixed assets have a substantial useful life remaining.

However, when using this ratio, remember to check whether the corporation uses accelerated or straight-line depreciation. Accelerated depreciation will artificially *raise* this ratio, making assets seem older.

The debt/equity ratio measures borrowing power by indicating the relative percentage of outside versus inside (shareholder) financing composing the corporate capital structure. A low debt/equity ratio suggests expansion potential: The company could support additional debt to expand either its own activities or those of an acquirer. Since banks use this ratio as a primary indicator of creditworthiness, a low debt/equity ratio indicates that a firm can raise more capital if desired. Conoco's debt/equity ratio is .30 to 1—extremely favorable. In fact, according to *Standard & Poor's* May 1981 industry survey, Conoco had the seventh-lowest debt/equity ratio among the domestic integrated oil companies. The company's light leverage would enhance its attractiveness to acquirers.

So far, however, the results of our Conoco analysis would only mildly interest a special-situation investor. Although the company shares some characteristics with special-situation candidates, none of the numbers we've come up with so far would clinch a "buy" decision.

The last figures to analyze are book value and book value per share. Book value roughly measures a corporation's liquidation value. Consequently, if book value per share is less than market price per share, a company may be a takeover candidate; the company is a bargain—a raider can purchase it for an amount that is less than the underlying assets. On the other hand, an undervalued firm may defend itself against unwanted takeover by reacquiring some of its shares, spinning off a subsidiary, or liquidating—all special situations that can mean profits for smart-money investors.

Of course, book value is an accounting concept that does not purport to measure the actual fair market value of the assets. Although land may be valued on the books at $1, it may in reality be worth several million dollars. Investors must adjust these undervalued assets to arrive at a company's true value.

Conoco's book value is about $42.50 per share. From a look at Conoco's "Ten Year Review," we see that, instead of being a bargain, the stock has sold *above* book value: In 1980, its high was $73 while its low was $41.

But is Conoco's book value realistic—or are undervalued assets artificially depressing Conoco's worth?

At last we strike pay dirt. Conoco's annual report and 10-K fully describe the company's proven worldwide reserves of oil, gas, and coal. By looking at various independent analysts' reports—or doing some homework on calculating the value of natural-resource reserves—an investor would discover that Conoco might be worth between $147 and $160 per share—roughly triple Conoco's 1981 low.

To give you a further idea of how Conoco's balance sheet understates asset value, let's look at its oil reserves. Conoco's

1980 balance sheet carried its oil reserves at $2.50 to $4.00 per barrel (the original oil exploration cost). Meanwhile, on the spot market, oil was selling for $30 to $40 per barrel. Analysts call this phenomenon the "Inflationary Psychology Factor"— inflation, combined with a bear market, has made it cheaper these days to buy assets than to invest in new production.

By carefully examining other information in Conoco's annual report and 10-K, an investor discovers other tidbits that enhance the company's attractiveness.

Conoco had extensive in-ground reserves in the United States. Because of the precariousness of world politics, domestic reserves have become increasingly important for American companies. In April 1981, when Conoco sold for around $53 a share, the company's in-ground reserves totaled some $256.50 per share according to estimates by *Value Line*. Of that amount, $85.50 was in the United States. Among the other so-called second-tier oil companies, only Marathon Oil had a higher figure: $262-per-share value of in-ground reserves, of which $118 was domestic.

Also, during 1980, Conoco had added to its oil and gas reserves, at a time when many U.S. companies did not, because of the oil glut and high interest rates.

Finally, an investor should perform a two-part analysis, studying the broader economic, industrial, and political trends as well as the balance-sheet details. From such an investigation, potential investors in Conoco would find that

—Conoco's stock price, along with that of the rest of the industry, was depressed because of the oil glut. During 1979–80, for six consecutive quarters, the oil industry posted spectacular gains. Then came the oil glut. Earnings went flat and the price of oil shares began to decline. In particular, the integrated oil companies, such as Conoco, pressed by unprofitable operations in some divisions, were soon greatly undervalued in relation to their assets. As a result, Conoco, which had traded as high as $73 in 1980, drooped to a 1981 low of $47.50.

This drop in prices made oil companies in general—and Conoco in particular—a good buy.

—Although Conoco had substantial American reserves, the company also has extensive assets in Libya. With U.S.-Libyan relations rapidly deteriorating over recent years, Wall Street became increasingly nervous about the security of Conoco's Libyan supplies.

—The United Mine Workers were on strike in Conoco's coalfields.

Combined, these external factors made many large institutional investors place Conoco high on their "dump" lists, further depressing the company's stock price and making it even more of a bargain.

Finally, let's turn to the income-statement ratios, which are concerned with profitability.

7. *Gross profit margin*
   The gross profit margin is:

$$\frac{\text{Net Sales} - \text{Cost of Goods Sold}}{\text{Net Sales}}$$

Net sales are a company's gross operating receipts from its principal business activity, less allowances, rebates, and returns. Therefore, Conoco's gross profit margin is:

$$\frac{(\$18,766.3 \text{ million} - \$253.9 \text{ million}) - (\$6,381.4 \text{ million} + \$5,529.8 \text{ million})}{(\$18,766.3 \text{ million} - \$253.9 \text{ million})}$$

$$= \frac{\$18,512.4 - \$11,911.2}{\$18,512.4}$$

$$= \frac{\$6,601.2}{\$18,512.4}$$

$$= 35.7\%$$

8. *Net profit margin*
   The net profit margin is:

$$\frac{\text{Net Income}}{\text{Net Sales}}$$

$$= \frac{\$1,026.2 \text{ million}}{\$18,512.4 \text{ million}}$$

$$= 5.5\%$$

9. *Cash flow per share*
   The cash flow per share is:
   Net Income per Share $+ \dfrac{\text{Total Depreciation}}{\begin{array}{c}\text{Average Number of}\\ \text{Shares Outstanding}\end{array}}$

$$= \$9.52 + \frac{\$466,900,000}{107,780,000}$$

$$= \$9.52 + \$4.33$$
$$= \$13.85$$

The gross profit margin measures the corporation's productive efficiency: how much of each sales dollar is consumed by the direct costs of producing the product. Therefore, the percentage of gross profit on net sales indicates whether the average markup on goods will normally cover expenses and result in a profit.

Although the gross profit margin will vary greatly among firms within the same industry, according to volume, location, and scale of operations, it tends to remain fairly constant within a firm. If a company's gross profit margin has dropped over the years, it indicates a possible problem in its bottom line.

By calculating gross profit margins for the past five years the same way as was worked out in number 7 above, we can see that Conoco's gross profit margins, which fluctuated between 37.6% and 38.1% during 1976–78, rose sharply to 39.2% in 1979 and fell even more sharply to 35.7% in 1980, as shown in table 5.

These figures should raise a question in the investor's mind, but we should certainly not a jump to a hasty and perhaps erroneous conclusion. Rather than extrapolate on the basis of only five numbers, we should keep the drop in the 1980 gross profit margin in mind and examine the net profit margin to see whether it bears out the declining profitability suggested in table 4.

The net profit margin concerns itself with all the corpora-

TABLE 5
Gross Profit Margin

1980	35.7%
1979	39.2
1978	37.8
1977	37.6
1976	38.1

tion's expenses—direct and indirect—to earn a dollar of sales. A firm's net profit margin becomes meaningful when compared to averages in specific industries. Compared to the averages for crude-petroleum and natural-gas producers in Dun & Bradstreet's 1980 *Key Business Ratios,* we see that Conoco's performance is indeed inferior: Conoco's net profit margin is about 5.5%, compared to an industry average of about 12%.

Finally, we can use cash flow per share as an alternative measure of liquidity—an adjunct to the current and quick ratios. Conoco's cash flow per share is $13.85. In comparison, Sun Oil, a similar domestic integrated oil company in the same price range as Conoco, had a cash flow per share of $10.99: $5.92 in earnings per share (versus Conoco's $9.52) and $5.07 in depreciation per share (versus Conoco's $4.33). Conoco's 1980 earnings were much better than Sun's; its depreciation per share slightly worse (because it was lower). In fact, compared not only to Sun but to other domestic integrated oils, Conoco's cash flow per share ranked high.

In sum, although several of Conoco's ratios indicated that the company might be a takeover candidate, the main clue was its adjusted book value.

Conoco illustrates perfectly the importance of book value and undervalued assets for spotting a special-situation candidate. Although investors might discover the key to a special situation in a detailed study of the balance sheet, a diligent search for the hidden or undervalued assets lurking behind the figures frequently has equal or greater importance.

In chapter 6 we'll take an in-depth look at how Conoco's hidden assets finally paid off for investors, many of whom doubled their money in less than three months.

4

Technical Analysis

Technical analysis is the study and interpretation of stock prices and volume trends. The theory behind it is that stock price and volume patterns can indicate future stock performance—and thereby future profits.

While the best-known use of technical analysis, the famous Dow theory, is generally applied to the long-term market as a whole (Dow believed that his major movement—the "primary trend"—covered at least four years), some of its techniques can be applied to special-situation stocks. Let's look at the clues and trading patterns that tell special-situation investors that something interesting and unusual is happening to a company's stock.

SPEAKING VOLUMES

According to Dow theory, volume figures as importantly as price in forecasting the direction of stock-market (or individual stock) trends. As the Wall Street adage says, "It takes volume to really move a stock"—either up or down.

Trading volume measures the intensity of investor emotions —how widespread demand is. When a stock moves up accompanied by heavy volume, it indicates a bullish trend: a strong, broad-based desire by investors to buy a stock because they believe the price will rise and they will make a profit. Conversely, a stock's decline on heavy volume signals bearishness: investor sentiment that it's time to bail out before the stock declines even further. Sometimes, however, a price reversal on *light trading* may occur during general bullishness, as a small group of investors embarks on profit taking.

CHARTING THE ACTION

Bar charts provide one of the simplest and best ways to track price and volume patterns for individual stocks. For each trading day, the investor plots the stock's high and low prices on graph paper and draws a vertical line connecting the two points. Then the investor draws a small horizontal line at the stock's closing price, and a vertical line at the bottom of the chart to indicate the stock's trading volume.

Weekly charts are prepared the same way, and are often used in conjunction with daily charts for another view of what's happening, since weekly charts smooth out small fluctuations and highlight larger ones. Monthly charts are sometimes used as well.

What exactly should investors watch out for?

Any unusual behavior—suggesting that something may be happening.

- Unusual trading volume.
- Gaps in the price action (when the stock *opens* a point or more higher or lower than it *closed* the previous day).
- Volatility changes. This is when a stock moves up or down in wider than usual swings (for example, when a stock that generally closes up or down ¼ to ½ point now closes up or down 1 to 2 points). This kind of movement can indicate that insiders or institutional investors know something that you don't know—yet. Meanwhile, their buying and selling are apparent to technical analysts.

Let's take a look at several bar charts and see how they can be interpreted.

Figure 1 shows our old friend Conoco in graphic form. This daily chart from *Trendline*'s August 7, 1981, issue shows that

FIGURE 1
Daily Bar Chart

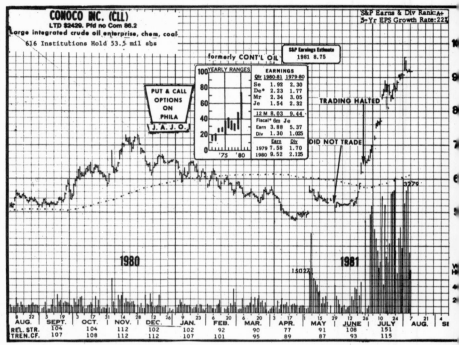

SOURCE: *Trendline (Standard & Poor's)*

volume, which often averaged 100,000 shares a day in late April and early May 1981, shot the stock up more than 13% in one day: from 49⅞ to 56½.

The white space between the 49⅞ close on May 5 and the trading range of 56–58 on May 6 is called an "upside gap" and is considered extremely bullish—a buy signal. Note that there are similar upside gaps, created by unprecedented volume on June 25 (the Seagram offer) and July 6 (the du Pont offer). Even buying at the last of these gaps, with Conoco selling at $77, investors could have made 20% in a month by tendering to Seagram for $92 cash, or 27% in about two months, by tendering to du Pont for $98—assuming that they received cash, rather than stock.

Moral: Upside gaps are a buy sign, in most cases. The probability increases with the number of gaps when it means that there are multiple bidders for your stock.

Figure 2 is a weekly chart from Securities Research Com-

FIGURE 2
Weekly Bar Chart

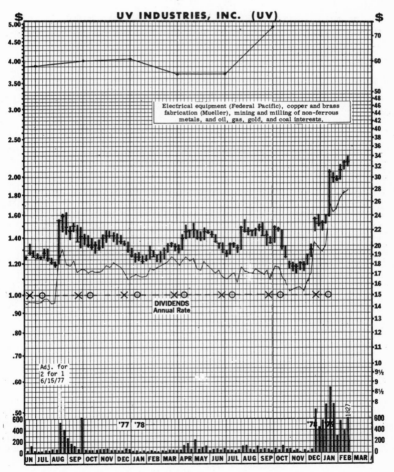

UV INDUSTRIES, INC. (UV)

Electrical equipment (Federal Pacific), copper and brass fabrication (Mueller), mining and milling of non-ferrous metals, and oil, gas, gold, and coal interests.

DIVIDENDS
Annual Rate

Adj. for
2 for 1
6/15/77

source: 3-Trend Security Charts (United Business Service)

pany's 3-Trend Security Charts, March 1979 issue. In this chart, UV Industries, a liquidation candidate that is discussed in chapter 9, shows a similar upside gap on unprecedented volume in mid-December 1978. The stock, which had been trading between 17 and 18½ in late October and early November on weekly volume averaging 5,000 shares, started climbing to 20 in early December.

The upside gap between 20¼ and 21⅞ clued investors that something interesting was happening at UV. Investors who bought then at 22 could have sold out at 34—a 50% profit— only three months later.

Figure 3, a monthly chart from Securities Research Company's 3-Trend Security Charts, June 1981 issue, illustrates

FIGURE 3
Monthly Bar Chart

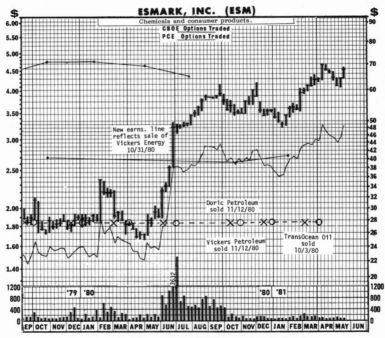

SOURCE: 3-Trend Security Charts (United Business Service)

how Esmark's announced sale of Vickers Energy, TransOcean Oil, and Doric Petroleum in late 1980 sent the stock spurting from 23 to 40 in just one month—on high volume, of course.

Esmark's repurchase of its own stock with the profits from these sales boosted the stock even higher—to 58—by the end of June 1981.

Esmark benefited from these moves as much as the investors who took their profits. By boosting the stock price from 23 to 58, Esmark guaranteed that it would not become a takeover candidate; this was a substantial risk when Esmark, with a book value of $36, had sold in the mid-20s—a discount of one-third from book value.

As we discussed in chapter 2, "Identifying the Candidates," new price highs can signal stocks with special-situation potential. However, as Robert J. Farrell, chief market analyst at Merrill Lynch, Pierce, Fenner & Smith, remarks, a stock's trading suddenly, significantly, and "inexplicably" above its usual price and volume levels suggests that you weren't the first kid on the block to unearth that company's hidden assets, accounting wizardy, or tax loopholes. Other informed investors may also have started bidding up the stock price. Their presence can be either good or bad:

Good, because their participation indicates that a deal may be taking place very soon; hence this investment may be profitable for you over the *very* short term—even a week or two!

Bad, because they may already have boosted the stock price near the level of the special-situation deal price. Not only can this price rise cut into your potential profit, it can also increase the danger that the stock price will tumble below what you paid for it if the deal blows up.

Then how do you know whether the stock's worth buying?

Once again, it's a question of book value. If the stock has a book value of $47 and it's already trading at $45, there's only a $2-per-share (or 4.4%) profit likely. The stock isn't worth chasing—especially if its trading range over the last two years was $20–$27. If the deal doesn't go through, the stock will generally plummet back to its old trading range as disappointed speculators dump their stock, and speculators who were suckered in at $45 will see an almost instant loss of 40% —back to $27 per share.

However, if the stock has a book value of $47 and is trading at $30, there's about a 50% profit potential. Even if the deal sours and it drops back to the $25 level, an investor would be risking only about 16% of his investment. For some investors, a 50% potential profit versus a 16% potential loss is an acceptable risk parameter.

Technical analysis has suffered from an overuse of buzz words, Computerese, and Greek-alphabet equations in recent years. Bob Farrell, for one, wants to take the entrail-reading voodoo out of it. "There's a lot of mumbo jumbo about technical analysis, unfortunately a lot of it promulgated by technical analysts themselves," says Farrell, who thinks that too much high-tech overkill has intimidated investors from adapting the practical methods of technical analysis to their advantage.

Farrell should know. As chief market analyst for Merrill Lynch, Pierce, Fenner & Smith, he writes a weekly market commentary distributed to the company's 400 offices worldwide. An annual poll taken by *Institutional Investor* magazine has placed him at the top of his category for the past five years.

Farrell offers some simple advice on how technical analysis can help special-situation investors:

1. Watch out for the unusual. Sudden changes in the price, volume, or volatility of a stock can indicate that something's cooking. To help spot unusual activity, check four recaps that appear in the daily financial press:

Stocks with new highs/new lows

The most active list

Stocks up the most (as percentage)

Stocks down the most (as percentage)

2. Start charting the stocks you're interested in. It's not complicated—a pencil and some graph paper for bar charts are all you need. For past performance data, either subscribe to a charting service—such as Standard & Poor's, United Business Service, or Horsey's—or use your local business library. Just concern yourself with direction: Is the stock price moving up or down? If it's moving up, it means that other investors may also have recognized its special-situation potential. If it's moving down, see point 3.

3. The crowd is generally wrong. By definition, a special-situation stock is an out-of-favor stock—one currently under-valued by the market. The average investor doesn't even start getting interested in a stock until its price has already peaked. Don't be scared away if no one else believes that one of your prospects is the hottest merger belle to grace Wall Street since Conoco. Remember, instead, that on May 1, 1981, a scant two months before the Conoco bidding war erupted, Conoco sold at $49.875—not very far above its 1980 low of $41. Du Pont eventually made a successful $98-per-share offer to Conoco owners, some of whom doubled their money in less than four months.

An Oppenheimer partner likes to examine possible special-situation candidates relative to the market as a whole. Here are his criteria:

Is this stock unduly sensitive to the market? Is it more or less volatile than the market? (In portfolio-manager jargon, is its *beta* greater than 1.0 or less than 1.0?) A stock doesn't have to have a small trading volume or capitalization to be market-sensitive. Two giants—IBM and General Motors—are very market-sensitive; they will not resist a declining market, but instead often lead it downward. *He avoids market-sensitive stocks* because they're too likely to decline in weak markets.

What is the stock really worth? And how much cheaper than its worth is the stock selling? You guessed it—it's book value again.

Is there anything that indicates that the stock is too cheap? The best indicator: *Other investors are buying the stock, too.* After all, very few investors have the financial resources to push up the price of a stock all by themselves. Declining markets may actually be a blessing in disguise, says the Oppenheimer partner. "When a stock suddenly stops declining in a down market and flattens out or moves up on some volume, it's an indication that the stock is not going to remain unusually cheap. Other

investors have spotted the stock and are buying it. Their buying is halting the decline or fueling the rise against the declining market. Strong performance relative to the market as a
whole tips me off."

THE CASE AGAINST TECHNICAL ANALYSIS

Although technical analysis has gained popularity in recent
years, many observers question its validity. It does have some
useful applications for the special-situation investor, but you
should know and consider the arguments against it. According to its detractors, technical analysis is fundamentally opposed to the efficient-capital-markets theory, which holds
that

—a large number of independent investors are always
analyzing and evaluating securities, seeking to maximize their
own profits;

—new information concerning securities arrives in the market in a random fashion; that, in general, releases of new
information are independent from each other;

—security prices should change nearly instantaneously to
reflect the new information.

As Frank K. Reilly summarizes in his text, *Investment Analysis
and Portfolio Management:* "The combined effect of (1) information coming in at random, and (2) numerous investors who
adjust stock prices rapidly to reflect this new information is
that *price changes are independent and random. . . .* The security
prices that prevail at any point in time should be an unbiased
reflection of all currently available information."

Thus, for Reilly, it's impossible for the average investor
to know what the stock market as a whole doesn't already
know.

"That's fine in theory," says Farrell. "But academic theories
that markets operate efficiently and immediately ignore the
real-world vagaries of time lags and information leaks. Con-
trary to what academics say, the marketplace presents many
inefficiencies. Technical analysis can enable investors to detect

unusual, nonrandom events which suggest that something is going on."

On the basis of actual trading patterns and the success of some investors, Farrell seems to be correct more often than not.

5

Mergers

Looking for a Horatio Alger rags-to-riches story? Check out the Wall Street merger market.

March 11, 1981. Kennecott closes at 27.

March 12, 1981. Standard Oil of Ohio agrees to purchase Kennecott for $62 per share. That's right—a 120% profit *overnight*.

July 20, 1981. Colt Industries closes at 63⅛.

July 23, 1981. Colt surges 21⅛ points to 84¼, following the announcement that Penn Central has offered to acquire the company for $100 per share in cash or stock.

Mergers don't even need final consummation to send stock prices soaring. Early in June 1981, General Portland, the nation's second-largest cement producer, sold in the mid-20s—just as it had for the past few months. Within three days, the stock zinged to 33⅝ on speculation that the company was targeted for takeover. That's a better than 30% rise. (Eventually, General Portland accepted a $47-per-share offer from Canada Cement—a 50% premium over its premerger price.)

In the past year, the urge to merge has hit epidemic proportions. According to W. T. Grimm & Co., although merger and acquisition announcements in 1980 fell 11% from 1979, the total dollar volume of all transactions increased about 2% to a record $44.3 billion.

The sizzling pace increased in 1981. In the first quarter alone, American businesses spent $17.5 billion to buy other business, up from $7.2 billion the year before. Mergers are getting bigger, too. In 1975, only 14 deals surpassed the $100-million mark; in 1980, there were 94 agreements of that size. In the first quarter of 1981, companies announced 25 $100-million-plus mergers, headed by two proposed multi*billion*-dollar takeovers in the mining industry: Standard Oil of California's proposed $3.9-billion purchase of Amax, Inc. (which was rejected), and Standard Oil of Ohio's successful $2-billion bid for Kennecott.

As this book went to press, Tomislava Simic, Grimm's research director, acknowledged: "There's every possibility that the full year 1980 record total of $44.3 billion will be surpassed by the end of the third quarter [of 1981]." That prediction was virtually assured by the July announcement of the largest merger in corporate history: the $7.6-billion acquisition of Conoco by du Pont.

What exactly is a merger? Broadly, a merger is any legal combination that forms one economic unit from two or more previous ones—a corporate marriage, so to speak.

Why do some companies acquire other companies? Surveys have turned up a mixed bag of merger motives, ranging from lofty financial aspirations to megalomania.

Increased Shareholder Value

Mergers can enhance returns for company shareholders through:

1. *Synergy.* The whole is greater than the sum of its parts. One partner's skills and knowledge are applicable to problems and opportunities facing the other.

2. *Economies of scale.* By investing in markets closely related to current operations, a company can reduce its long-run costs through economies of scale of production, capital, distribution, promotion, research and development, and other expensive areas.

3. *Milking cash cows.* Divisions with a cash surplus—nicknamed "cash cows"—can furnish money to other units that are long on potential but short on funds. The company thus does not have to borrow funds externally at high interest rates.

4. *Risk-pooling.* Because of its diversification gained through

mergers and acquisitions, a company can reduce its cost of debt and leverage itself more than its nondiversified competitors.

5. *Reducing the likelihood of bankruptcy.* Findings of a January 1981 conference on mergers and acquisitions, held by the Salomon Brothers Center for the Study of Financial Institutions at New York University's Graduate School of Business Administration, indicate that the desire to decrease the risk of bankruptcy (through improving the quality of the debt or the debt/equity ratio) also helps explain merger activity.

It's Cheaper than Growing Your Own

Three separate factors have made it less expensive to buy a going concern than to build up an operation from scratch:

1. *Inflation.* Because inflation raises asset values, it's cheaper for a company to purchase another owning a plant, equipment, natural resources, or land than to acquire these assets on its own.

2. *Undervaluation of stock.* Despite the 1980–81 recovery of the stock market, many solid companies remain extremely undervalued, based on their assets and expected cash flow. Writing in the *Wall Street Journal* on June 2, 1980, James H. Lorie, Professor of Business Administration at the University of Chicago, said: "When stock market historians look back upon the 1970s, they are likely to refer to what happened during that decade as the Great Crash. . . . Between the end of 1969 and the end of 1979, the value of common stocks on the New York Stock Exchange declined by about 42%." A company whose stock is undervalued is an attractive acquisition prospect.

3. *High cost of money.* With the prime rate hitting 20% + with deading frequency over the past 18 months, companies have become leery of launching new products, new technologies, or new lines of business themselves because of the high failure rate. To reduce risk, companies prefer to buy going concerns with known brand names, established distribution systems, and successful track records.

Increased Use of Corporate Strategic Planning

Strategic planning has become the key buzzword in American industry. According to Lazard Frères general partner Louis Perlmutter, "Nearly every *Fortune* 500 company is deeply involved in a strategic study, trying to learn how it should be structured and what businesses it should be in to maximize growth in the 1980s. These deliberations are going to produce a steady flow of merger-and-acquisition transactions regardless of the short-term economic climate."

Tax Benefits

As explained in chapter 3, corporate tax losses in one year can be carried forward and used to offset future income (loss carry-forward) or be applied retroactively to taxes already paid (loss carry-back).

However, a firm with large losses and bleak future prospects may find itself unable to utilize this potential tax break. Acquiring a profitable corporation—or being acquired by one—allows the company to cash in on its tax loss.

Spare Change

Many U.S. corporations have huge cash holdings and are finding it hard to resist going on a shopping spree with undervalued assets all around them. The oil companies figure prominently among the leading shoppers. Texaco, for example, ended the first quarter of 1981 with $3.6 billion cash on its books.

The Corporate Jungle: Eat or Be Eaten

A July/August 1978 *Harvard Business Review* article, entitled "What Today's Directors Worry About," reported that a fairly large number of corporate directors had takeover fears on their minds.

To help keep the acquisition wolves from their doors, many companies have themselves embarked upon active takeover programs. Acquisitions not only consume the cash surpluses that make a company an attractive takeover prospect, but also make the candidate too big, and therefore too expensive to buy out.

Political Climate

During 1979 and 1980, observers attributed the rapid merger pace to pending legislative prohibitions on business combinations. Acquirers scurried to close their deals before the Justice Department banned them.

But political winds shift as rapidly as meteorological ones. Following the conservative landslide in the 1980 election, one Justice Department trustbuster sighed, "It looks like it's all over."

During its first few months in office, the Reagan administration has created a probusiness atmosphere. In a move ripe with symbolic import, Federal Trade Commission prosecutors advised the commission to drop its seven-year-old antitrust suit against the nation's eight largest oil companies. Similarly, the commission called off its five-year-old antitrust investigation into the automobile industry. Meanwhile, William Baxter, the new chief of the Justice Department's antitrust division, went on record as saying that big businesses are "very valuable things" because they tend to be the most efficient operations. Mr. Baxter stated that antitrust law should aim for only one goal: efficiency—maximum production at the lowest price. This is surely a promerger position.

Do It for the Gipper

According to at least one expert, the Big Acquisition has become a way for chief executives nearing retirement to leave their imprint on the corporation. Acquisitions can also enhance an executive's self-image as an aggressive manager who knows a good thing when he or she sees it.

Having seen some of the motives acquirers have in common, let's take a look at the characteristics of the merger targets.

There are a number of tip-offs that a company may belong on someone's shopping list. For the investor who has identified a list of potential candidates, these signs will help to spot impending action.

13D Filings

Since companies and individuals must file a 13D report with the SEC after buying 5% or more of another company's stock, 13D reports should be on every special-situation investor's reading list. Such toehold stakes frequently act as preludes to merger moves.

According to Robert Willens, a partner at Peat, Marwick, Mitchell, if a company acquires a 10% or greater stake in another company, the probability is fairly high that a merger attempt will follow. If the acquiring company is known as a takeover company, that probability is heightened. For example, if Gulf & Western, whose track record for acquiring companies goes back to the go-go era of the 1960s, typically starts with 10%–20% of a target company's stock, a merger offer within the year is highly probable.

How can investors find out? Acquiring companies must file a 13D form with the SEC within ten days, stating that they have acquired a fairly sizable block (5% or more) of another company's stock. In at least half the cases, a merger attempt will follow within a matter of months. Many of these announcements also appear in the *Wall Street Journal, The New York Times,* and the business sections of other major newspapers.

In addition, the SEC publishes the data daily in the *SEC News Digest* and monthly in a comprehensive publication entitled *Official Summary of Security Transactions and Holdings.* Investors can buy both publications from the SEC or consult them at SEC regional offices (see Appendix) and many libraries.

Undervalued Shares

As you'll see in succeeding chapters, *undervalued shares are probably the single most important factor that causes any company to become a special-situation candidate.*

"Undervalued shares" means that a company's adjusted book value is greater than its current market value. Once again, note the word "adjusted." As you saw in chapter 3 and the financial analysis of Conoco, many companies have hidden assets on their balance sheets, such as LIFO reserves, real estate, patents, and trademarks. And why are they hidden? For camouflage—few companies want to disclose how vulnerable they are to takeovers.

The 1970s were not kind to Wall Street. The value of common stocks on the New York Stock Exchange declined about 42% from 1969 to 1979. During the 1970s, once again citing Professor James H. Lorie's article in the *Wall Street Journal,* "The average annual rate of return in constant dollars for a tax-exempt investor who invested in all stocks in the New York Stock Exchange in proportion to their initial value and reinvested the dividends was about minus 1.5%."

Because of both the undervalued stock market and high inflation, many companies, as noted earlier, find that it's cheaper to buy than to build—i.e., that it costs less to acquire a going concern and its assets than to start a new one.

The Council of Economic Advisers calculates a statistic known as Tobin's q, which measures a firm's market value as a percentage of the current replacement costs of its net assets. During the 1960s, the ratio stayed at approximately 1.000. Since 1972, however, it has dropped by half. (See table 6.)

TABLE 6
Market Value as % of Replacement Cost

1960	0.956
1965	1.250
1970	0.863
1972	1.012
1974	0.663
1976	0.740
1978	0.602
1980	0.526

SOURCE: *Council of Economic Advisers, based on data for nonfinancial corporations.*

In 1981, companies have continued trading at an enormous discount from their replacement value—the average is 50%. To help determine whether a particular company is bargain-basement-priced, investors should look at its 10-K, which lists inflation-adjusted values for plant, equipment, and other fixed assets. However, the 10-K will *not* include replacement-value figures for certain natural resources (such as timberland), which balance sheets frequently undervalue.

Cash Cows and Companies with Low Debt/Equity Ratios

A potential acquirer may want to buy only the target company's assets or its investment portfolio. Sometimes a company may make an acquisition just to obtain the target company's cash and securities to pay off its own debt, or use the target's low debt/equity ratio to increase its own borrowing capacity. The acquiring company would plan to buy the target's assets cheaply and use the money, in turn, to pay off its own debt or to invest in its own business, to generate a higher rate of return than the target company has achieved.

Not surprisingly, management of the target company regards this strategy as looting or stripping their company of its assets. And there is some justification for their crying corporate rape. Many companies are so asset-rich they can be acquired by what tax experts call a "bootstrap" acquisition: The acquiring company uses the *target's own assets* or debt capacity to acquire the company.

Trendiness

Michael Metz, vice-president of Oppenheimer & Company, says: "At the risk of sounding cynical, there are fads in mergers. If there's a major acquisition in an industry—whether it's toilet paper or oil companies—it can be the beginning of a trend."

Du Pont's takeover of Conoco, for example, set off huge repercussions in the oil industry. Following the du Pont deal, Eugene Nowak, an analyst with Dean Witter Reynolds, said:

"[The offer] presages other oil and chemical mergers of this kind."

"Presages" was the wrong word—"detonated" describes it better. Within 24 hours of the du Pont victory, medium-size oil companies led off the heavy trading as analysts speculated on which would be the next acquisition target. One oil-industry executive joked: "Don't leave anything sitting around on a table or we'll buy it."

All the candidates moved up sharply, including Pennzoil, up $4.875; Mesa Petroleum, up $1.875; and Superior Oil, up $2.75.

Broken Deals

Metz offers another interesting trading proposition: Always look at "broken deals"—mergers that fall through. As you'll see in more detail later on, the target's price generally drops precipitously in the day or two after a merger falls through, as traders scurry to unload their positions.

"But where there's smoke, there's fire," says Metz. The same factors that made a company an attractive target in the first place may lure other acquirers in the future. By moving in on a stock immediately after a deal "blows," you may be able to buy a promising special-situation stock at bargain prices.

Desirable Industry

Sure, many steel companies and apparel manufacturers may be selling at only one-quarter of their book value, but who wants to get involved in those depressed, stagnant industries? Most merger targets are in healthy or growing areas of the economy.

Death of a Major Stockholder

Despite overtones of ghoulishness, "death watches" hold a legitimate place on Wall Street. If a major stockholder dies, very frequently his or her shares soon come on the market in order to raise cash to settle the estate. An acquirer may be waiting in the wings, ready to snap up the block of shares and obtain control of the company.

Worth of the Target

Before investing in any merger candidate, perhaps the most important question investors should answer is, How much is the target worth? Unfortunately, there's no simple solution. But there *are* yardsticks. Acquirers today use three major valuation methods to determine how much a company is worth.

1. *Historical price/earnings multiples.* The simplest technique, this approach relies upon the prices, as multiples of most-recent annual earnings, paid for other companies in the same industry as the target. If a company sold for six times its most recent annual earnings of $1 million, or a total of $6 million, then a close competitor with $1.5 million in earnings should be worth $9 million.

Although this method offers simplicity, it lacks validity when applied to the real world. In 1981, for example, three major mining-company deals produced three different multiples: Standard Oil of California offered 10.5 times target Amax's 1980 earnings (maybe that's why the offer was rejected); Fluor paid 23 times earnings for St. Joe Minerals; and Standard Oil of Ohio shelled out 19.1 times Kennecott's 1980 earnings (excluding an extraordinary gain).

2. *Liquidation value.* This method asks, "How much money would a company fetch if it sold off each of its divisions at auction?" As an investment banker explains it, "The seller can tote up the price, including assumed premiums for each piece. Studies show that the total can be expected to exceed the price that would be paid for the company as a single unit." In other words, it's synergy: the sum of the parts is greater than the whole. A company's liquidation value generally is close to its adjusted book value, which we discussed in chapter 3.

3. *Discounted cash flow.* Today, according to a recent article in *Business Week,* over half of the major acquisition companies use the discounted-cash-flow (DCF) technique to analyze take-

overs. DCF explicitly takes into account the time value of money: the fact that $1 received today can be invested and can earn interest, and therefore it is worth more than $1 received a year from today. (Inflation is confusingly similar in that it, too, recognizes the time value of money—but from the standpoint that the $1 received today will *buy more* than the $1 received a year from today. Thus inflation has a multiplier effect on the time value of money.)

HOW TO APPLY THE DCF TECHNIQUE

According to Professor Michael Keenan of the New York University Graduate School of Business Administration, the DCF technique puts a price tag on a company in a three-step procedure.

Step one is to *determine the cash flow of the company.* How much cash is the company expected to "throw off" in future years? In establishing a time horizon, how far in the future do you feel comfortable predicting corporate performance? In most cases, the forecasts will range from five to ten years.

Step two is to *establish an appropriate discount rate.* As explained above, DCF recognizes the time value of money. By discounting the *future* cash flows of a company by a certain percentage, DCF considers such factors as:

• Inflation—which erodes value through decreasing purchasing power.

• Cost of capital: If the hunter has to borrow money to buy the target, the hunter must pay interest on those funds. This interest must be deducted from any profits the target will generate.

• Forgone interest or investments: If a company buys a target through the use of its own internally generated funds, the acquirer may not have to pay interest. However, it is *losing* the interest or profits it could have received by investing in either government securities or alternate projects.

Step three is to *determine the residual value of the company.* At the end of the time horizon, how much money might an acquirer pay? This is a useful gauge for investors: If the figure is only 10% more than what the stock of the company is worth, then they are not going to get a good return; if it's 40% to 50% over the worth of the stock, then it should be a good deal.

In-depth explanations of calculating the net present value of a company by using DCF techniques go far beyond the general, popular-consumption nature of this book. Interested readers should consult one of the excellent financial texts on the subject.

Despite the detailed scenarios, sophisticated graphs, and sensitivity analyses generated by DCF, experts admit that the projections are only as good as the assumptions that go into them. "I don't want to be identified with saying this," admitted one corporate-finance specialist, "but do you realize that the very best any investment banker can hope to do in a price-fairness opinion is come up with a figure that is within ten to fifteen percent above or below the true value?"

As the *Wall Street Journal* headlined in a March 1981 article, "Deciding how much a company is worth often depends on whose side you're on."

How much, then, are estimates of a company's worth *worth*?

The head of a Wall Street investment banker's mergers-and-acquisitions department summed it all up: "You can have a two-foot-high stack of data backing a specific price range, but the client's top management may determine not to be bound by it. Often in the heat of battle, it gets to be a matter of guts and ego in the chairman's office."

Thus, investors trying to determine a target's worth should understand that there's no definitive answer. Their best strategy would be to develop a multipronged approach.

• On your own, analyze the company's annual report and calculate its adjusted book value.
• Check various investment-service and brokerage-house reports.
• Ask your broker and his or her research department.

By using information from many sources, investors can obtain a *range* of values in which a final price tag will probably fall.

TYPES OF MERGERS

True love, corporate style, frequently runs more smoothly than its human counterpart. After identifying a target, the potential acquirer analyzes how willing the candidate might be to accept a merger offer. Is the target's stock selling far below its book value? Is there a single aging major owner with multiple heirs who might want to facilitate settling of an estate? Is the target a recently founded high-technology company that's long on know-how but short on capital? Has a key member of the target's management dropped a hint at the golf course, a testimonial dinner, or in the sanctity of the commuter train?

If the acquirer believes that the target will be receptive to its overtures, it generally approaches the target's management directly with a deal. If the two companies work out mutually acceptable terms, the two management groups will recommend that their shareholders approve the merger. After stockholder approval, the acquiring firm will buy the target company's shares from its stockholders, paying either with cash, its own shares, or some combination of the two.

In July 1981, for example, shareholders of Standard Brands and Nabisco overwhelmingly approved the merger of the two food-industry giants in a tax-free swap valued at $1.9 billion.

An alternative scenario: The acquirer makes a "friendly" tender offer for the shares of the target. We'll discuss tender offers in depth later in this chapter.

Sometimes companies, like sweethearts, fan a suitor's passions by playing hard-to-get.

In June 1981, Société Nationale Elf Aquitaine (Elf Aquitaine), France's state-controlled oil company, offered $50 per share for Texasgulf's common stock and $159.375 per share for Texasgulf's preferred stock. (Texasgulf's common stock had traded as low as $28 in 1980; the preferred had traded as low as $47 that year.)

Despite several long meetings with the French, Texasgulf's management maintained a discreet, suspenseful silence on the offer. Two weeks after its original proposal, Elf Aquitaine sweetened the pot, upping its bid to $56 per share for the common and $178.47 for the preferred.

Texasgulf immediately said "I do" to this new proposal. Chairman Richard D. Mollison stated: "In light of the increased offer, the Texasgulf board decided to facilitate our shareholders' making their investment decisions with respect to the acceptance of the Elf Aquitaine offer and will not oppose the offer."

Tenders in the Night: The Hostile Takeover

Not all romances have such blissful endings. Sometimes the target company's management resists the offer—either because they think the price is too low or because they want to maintain their company's independence (read: They're afraid of losing their jobs).

In such cases, the target firm's directors are said to be hostile. The hunter can then attempt to gain control either by making large open-market stock purchases, which are followed by a proxy fight—a time- and money-consuming procedure— or by appealing directly to the target firm's shareholders with a tender offer.

In a tender offer, a company offers to buy stock from shareholders at a specified price, generally at a substantial premium over the current market price. If successful, the hunter ends up with a majority of the outstanding shares—sufficient to force a merger.

Tender offers are subject to the 1968 Williams Act, which requires a company to make all such offers to all stockholders at the same price. The SEC considers a tender offer to begin with any detailed public announcement of the essential terms of the deal: i.e., the specific price and the number of target-company shares sought at that price.

To give the target company's shareholders adequate time and information to evaluate the tender offer, the potential acquirer must file detailed information (in a 14D-1 filing) within five business days of the announcement. Similarly, SEC regulations require that the target company's board respond within ten days (in a 14D-9 filing) to any publicly disclosed offer, including a justification of its point of view.

Two other terms become important for shareholders hit by tender offers:

Proration date. When a company makes a tender offer for some—not all—of a target's outstanding stock, more shares may be tendered than were sought. Similarly, if an acquirer offers both cash and stock in payment, the cash portion may be oversubscribed. In such cases, the SEC requires proration —proportional stock purchases from all eligible tenderers based on the total number of shares sought and tendered. For example, if a company makes a tender offer for 5 million shares and 10 million are tendered, the company could accept 50% of each tenderer's stock. If the offer were $100 per share and the stock later dropped down to $50, shareholders would have received $100 per share for half their stock and $50 per share for the remainder—if they wanted to sell it and close out their position—or an average value of $75 per share.

According to SEC rules, everyone who tenders stock by the proration date must receive the same treatment. If the tender price is increased, the acquirer must set a new proration date.

The law contains two important twists. First, shareholders who tender their stock under the original offer must receive any increases in the offer price. Furthermore, shareholders who tendered before a price increase—and before an offer was "oversubscribed"—are *not* subject to proration. Consequently, they are guaranteed the *highest price* offered for *all* their shares. Acquiring companies frequently use this leverage to encourage early tenders.

The proration date, then, allows shareholders to "get in line" to sell their stock.

Withdrawal date. According to SEC rules, stockholders who "get in line" to tender their shares can also "get out of line" until an offer's withdrawal date, several business days after the proration date. After the withdrawal date, stockholders cannot take back their stock. If the tender is successful, the bidder will pay out the cash or stock within a week or two. If the tender fails, people get their stock back.

Consequently, in hotly contested takeovers in which more than one company makes a tender offer, a shareholder can tender his or her stock to one bidder and still move the stock to another potential acquirer before the withdrawal date. However, it's rather like check-out lines in the supermarket:

If you attempt to jump out of one line and into another (because of a better deal), you lose your place in the first line—and may find no room in the second line. Therefore, it pays for investors to decide where to line up before the proration deadlines. We'll discuss how investors should select their queues later on.

BEFORE THE MERGER ANNOUNCEMENT

"To buy or not to buy . . ." That is the question facing investors. In making a decision, investors should ask themselves two very important questions:

- What is my potential risk?
- What is my potential reward?

Potential Risk

For merger candidates, an investor's risk equals the difference between what he or she paid for a stock and what price the stock would trade at if the merger failed to materialize—"what the animal is worth if the deal blows apart," as one arbitrageur put it. Investors can estimate that price using simple, conventional securities analysis discussed in chapter 3: price/earnings ratio; yield; book value versus market value.

In many cases, if investors buy a merger candidate before it's even a gleam in an acquirer's eye, they will not pay a substantial premium over this base value. Therefore, since there's little probability that its price will slip below what they paid for it, the investment has minimal risk.

Potential Reward

In mergers, there's no telling how much the potential reward—the final merger price—might be. One anonymous risk arbitrageur said, "You never really know what someone will pay for a stock. You can't manage your profit; you can manage only your risk."

As previously mentioned, the best methods for estimating a company's worth include:

- using adjusted book value
- using discounted cash-flow value
- checking various investment-service and brokerage-house reports.

As a general rule, investors should stay away from "possible-merger" stocks that are trading at or near book value. If your analysis of a stock shows that its book value (therefore, probable merger value) is $45, but it's now trading at $42, the meagerness of the potential reward does not justify the risk. You can do a lot better—at less risk—by plunking your dollars into a money-market fund. Get out your calculator and a new stack of annual reports, and try to find a juicier merger candidate.

EVALUATING THE DEAL

Once a merger is officially announced, what action should the stockholder take? Tender his or her shares? Oppose the deal during the ensuing proxy fight? Wait until the deal is consummated and sell the stock received in the merger?

According to Wall Street professionals, the most important consideration for investors after a merger proposal is, What are the chances that the companies will consummate the deal? A merger's probable success or failure will help investors determine strategy, discussed later on.

In addition to considering whether a deal will succeed, investors should concern themselves with how long the deal will take for completion.

As the earlier description of the discounted-cash-flow method pointed out vividly, time is money. During the time an investor has money tied up in a given stock, he or she can't use those funds for other investments—which might pay off bigger and faster. Not only stock investments—investors could have earned 18% in August 1981 with virtually no risk, simply by investing in a money-market fund.

Both shareholders in the target and other investors will probably first learn of merger proposals in the financial papers, which generally feature articles about proposed mergers. For tender offers, the papers may also carry large "tombstone" advertisements detailing the terms of the offer. Subsequently, copies of the offer to purchase will be sent to the target's shareholders.

As soon as the announcement has been made, investors should carefully read the offer and accompanying newspaper articles for the following key information, which will help to predict whether or not the deal will go through:

1. What kind of deal is it, friendly or hostile?

According to ongoing studies by Dr. Douglas V. Austin, who has been researching tender offers for 24 years, 96% of all uncontested tender offers between 1972 and 1979 were fully or partially successful. In contrast, in 1978 and 1979, only about 75% of all hostile tender offers were completed. This is an enormous increase of 50% over 1976–77, when only 50% of all contested offers succeeded.

Besides signaling the probability of a deal's success, the friendly-versus-hostile question indicates the likely price at which the merger will be consummated. Generally, friendly deals go through at the announced price. Hostile deals can smoke out other suitors and spark bidding wars that move the takeover price way up from the initially proposed level. That's the advantage of a hostile deal, as you'll see more clearly in the next chapter. But there are disadvantages, too. Hostile deals frequently take more time to complete—and they can crumble entirely.

2. What are the terms and form?

How much money (or cash equivalent—i.e., stocks or bonds) is the acquirer offering? How does that offer compare with the "real" value of the target, using both book value and analysts' reports? Even in friendly deals, other bidders may try to elbow their way in if they think that the offer price is too low.

3. Is the deal for cash or for securities? If it's for securities, what kind? Common stock? Preferred stock? Straight or convertible debentures? In hostile tenders that utilize stock, the

target's management frequently disparages the quality of the offeror's securities. Since no one can belittle the integrity of cash, cash offers enhance the chances of success of hostile tenders.

However, investors should remember the important tax advantages of mergers for stock. If more than 50% of the total merger payment consists of the acquirer's stock, shareholders can defer tax payments on the stock portion until they sell their shares. Because of this deferment, many large institutional investors (e.g., banks, mutual funds, pension funds) prefer receiving stock, rather than immediately taxable cash.

In 1970 only 28% of all mergers were cash-financed. Following the stock-market debacle of the 1970s, that figure soared to 54% by 1977. The reasons for this "dash to cash" were twofold:

A sweetener. Shareholders of targets were reluctant to receive volatile stock. During the go-go conglomerate years of the 1960s, stock swaps and exchanges of other securities comprised the favorite payment medium. When the conglomerate bubble burst, however, many stockholders were left holding the bag. The price of Litton Industries, for example, nosedived from 86⅜ in the early 1960s to 11 in 1968.

Avoidance of dilution. At the same time, because the market seriously undervalued most stock prices, a hunter had to issue too many new shares in order to effect a purchase. Issuing all this new stock diluted earnings disproportionately.

But now, along with the resurgence of the stock market in the 1980s, has come a renewed popularity of stock in takeovers. One major factor: Stock is particularly advantageous for hunters when the prime rate hovers around 20%.

According to W. T. Grimm, the Chicago-based financial consultants, 31% of all reported 1980 merger payments involved stock, in contrast to 26% the year before. Cash deals declined to 47% of transactions, compared to 53% in 1979.

Figure 4, compiled by W. T. Grimm, retraces the payment trends since 1974, the year in which cash first began dominating acquisition deals.

4. Is the offer conditional?

Whether friendly or hostile, most tenders are conditional on the bidder's receiving a minimum number of shares. Particu-

FIGURE 4
Payment Trends
1974-1980

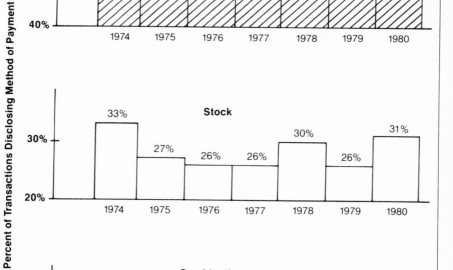

Percent of Transactions Disclosing Method of Payment

Cash

50% — 48% 48% 52% 54% 46% 53% 47%

40% —

1974 1975 1976 1977 1978 1979 1980

Stock

33% 27% 26% 26% 30% 26% 31%

30% —

20% —

1974 1975 1976 1977 1978 1979 1980

Combination

16% 23% 20% 18% 23% 20% 21%

20% —

10% —

1974 1975 1976 1977 1978 1979 1980

Source: W.T. Grimm & Co.

larly in hostile bids, the raider may specify that the offer is conditional upon its receiving a minimum of 50.01% of the target's outstanding shares—sufficient to force a subsequent merger.

Yes, Virginia, this means that there may be no Santa Claus. A company could make a tender offer, you could turn in your shares, and boom!—the prospective acquirer backs out. Although you get tendered shares back, the stock, which had been trading at a substantial premium over market value, falls back to its old level unless a new bidder emerges.

Therefore, with a conditional offer, if you think there's a good chance that the raider will drop out, sell your shares on the open market, rather than tendering them.

5. Is the target in a regulated industry?

Hostile deals rarely occur in regulated industries, since regulatory commissions tend to favor the target's position. Within days of receiving an unfriendly takeover offer from American Express, for example, McGraw-Hill elicited concern about the move from the SEC, FTC, FCC, the Federal Reserve Board, the U.S. controller of the currency, a House banking subcommittee, the New York State attorney general, and the New York State Banking Department. Even if hostile offers eventually succeed, they can take a year or more to consummate (for example, it took Texas International Airlines a year and a half to complete its hostile takeover of Continental Airlines)—time during which your stock (a money equivalent) is tied up and cannot earn interest.

Even with friendly offers deals in regulated industries creep along far more slowly than deals in unregulated industries. Although Westinghouse and Teleprompter agreed to merge in October 1980, the FCC didn't approve the deal until July 1981. Other agencies can move even more slowly. The ICC, which controls such industries as railroads and trucking, has a statutory 30-month waiting period.

6. Is the acquirer foreign?

A foreign company will seldom attempt—and even less often complete—a hostile takeover. Foreign companies are very nervous that a messy takeover battle might cause a backlash, in which the United States might severely curtail foreign investment in this country.

However, the involvement of a foreign purchaser can slow the pace of even friendly offers by six months to a year. And when the foreign buyer is involved in a regulated industry, investors can count on waiting a year and a half to two years before consummation of a deal. Thus, when Hong Kong & Shanghai Banks purchased a portion of Marine Midland Bank, and when National Westminster Bank purchased part of Crocker National, the California bank holding company, investors had to wait nearly two years to see the deals completed.

Following a tender offer or merger announcement, investors should also investigate the following factors, which can also strongly influence a deal's success or failure.

Current Ownership

Look for this information in a company's most recent proxy statement, which accompanies the notice of the annual meeting.

1. Is the company closely held—with at least 50% of the stock owned by a few people, often the founding family? Such a pattern of ownership virtually assures success of a friendly offer—and makes hostile offers virtually impossible.

2. Is a substantial amount of the stock owned by people over the age of 60? Such shareholders are generally interested in mergers as a way to avoid future estate problems—especially if the market for the stock is thin, with fewer than 1,000 shares traded per day. A thin market would make it difficult for heirs to sell their stock without depressing the price of their remaining shares.

To obtain this trading information, look at the volume column of the stock-market pages over the past week or two, or divide the last month's sales in the *Standard & Poor's Stock Guide* by 22—the approximate number of trading days in a month.

3. What percentage of shares is owned by corporate management and company directors? If the percentage is substantial, this pattern enhances the probable success of a friendly offer —and presages the failure of a hostile offer.

Frequently, the target's management stands to lose the

most if a hostile merger succeeds: Their jobs, perks, and prestige lie on the line. If company insiders hold large blocks of stock, they have a good chance of fighting off unwanted merger bids.

However, when outsiders own large chunks of stock, their loyalty generally follows maximum profits.

4. What percentage of shares is owned by employees through their stock-ownership plans (ESOP's)? Employees will frequently oppose hostile takeovers—either because they distrust new management or because they have true company loyalty. Dallas-based LTV Corp., for example, ran into a major stumbling block when it made an unfriendly bid for Grumman. Through Grumman's employee investment plan, workers owned about one-third of the company's outstanding stock, and they didn't like LTV's raid one bit.

Reflecting the view of many Grumman employees, George Skurla, president of the Grumman Aerospace subsidiary, said: "I came here to work as a young man at the Grumman 'ironworks' [Grumman's nickname during World War II, when it built planes for the war in the Pacific]. I have no intention of retiring from the LTV 'steelworks.' Let the LTV guys go back to Texas and play with their subsidiaries."

LTV abandoned its pursuit of Grumman because Grumman employee-stockholders were so opposed to the merger. However, Grumman is in the courts on a related matter: Did its employee pension fund act prudently in acquiring so much Grumman stock and in voting against the merger?

Antitrust Considerations

Crying "foul" on antitrust grounds is one of the most frequent corporate defenses against unwanted takeovers. Lawsuits raising antitrust questions can destroy or fatally delay mergers. Once a company makes a hostile bid for another, investors should weigh the following factors:

1. How extensive are potential conflicts? Can the acquirer sell off a picayune division to resolve any problems—or does the conflict center on the very heart of both companies? Check the annual reports and 10-K's of both companies to see

- where antitrust snares may lie;
- what proportions of each company's revenues and profits the problem areas contribute.

2. How good are the PR campaigns and government relations of each combatant? It's the old "It's not what you know, but who you know" syndrome. To judge the relative mettle of each company's lobbying team, review the *Wall Street Journal* and *New York Times* indexes to see how the companies fared in previous government disputes. Did they win or lose?

3. How are the political winds blowing? In its antitrust enforcement, the Carter administration repeatedly took the position that "bigness is badness" and looked askance at any business combination between large companies. In contrast, Reagan's Justice Department has indicated that it will give the green light to vertical mergers (e.g., raw-material supplier/manufacturer), while still questioning horizontal mergers (companies competing in the same market segments). As you'll see in chapter 6, this differentiation became crucial in determining the outcome of the multibillion-dollar Conoco sweepstakes.

Warning Signals

Warning signals that a merger may be in trouble are detailed in chapter 10.

Merger Strategies

Factors influencing the chances of a merger's success were outlined earlier. Unfortunately, there's no hard-and-fast rule enabling anyone to say with certainty that *this* merger will go through, *that* one will fail. Investors will encounter constant tradeoffs. For example: How much weight does a potential antitrust hassle carry against the fact that the bidder's offer is for cash—at a substantial premium over current market value? Is a foreign company's juicy tender worth waiting up to two years for?

Not even professional risk arbitrageurs—the people who

"bet" on the success or failure of special-situation deals—have surefire answers.

Smith Barney arbitrageur Brian McVeigh says: "The first question I ask myself is, Is the deal logical? Does it make fundamental sense? If I were the CEO or investment banker, would I have done it this way?"

Another arbitrageur says: "You can't eliminate uncertainties, but you can reduce them."

"Good deals work, bad deals fall through," another shrugs.

Following the announcement of a merger offer, the target's stock price will rapidly approach the deal price—like water seeking its own level. For example, if a stock has been trading at $10 and a company makes a tender offer of $20, the target's price will soon rise to the $16–$19 level, depending on the perceived probability of the deal's success.

Therefore, if investors fear that a deal will collapse, they're best off with a take-the-money-and-run strategy—to sell the stock on the open market and forget the few extra points they could receive if the tender is successful. Nervous investors may also prefer this strategy.

Investors who feel confident that a merger will succeed should tender their shares to the bidding company, since this move will generally provide the highest payoff.

The market price of a stock will rise above the announced merger price in only one case: if Wall Street expects another bidder to emerge.

If More Than One Company Tenders . . .

. . . investors are sitting very prettily indeed. When a battle royal flares up between two or more corporate bridegrooms, rapid-fire offers and counteroffers bid up the price.

In 1978–79, Babcock & Wilcox stock was selling at around $28 per share. Then two prospective "bridegrooms" began to court the company. When the dust settled and Babcock was finally acquired by United Technologies, the final merger price worked out to around $64 per share—*more than double its premerger price.*

In the fall of 1980, Wheelabrator and McDermott locked

horns over Pullman. First McDermott made an unfriendly offer of $28 for Pullman, which had traded as low as $19.25 earlier in the year. After Wheelabrator entered the fray as Pullman's white knight, the offers quickly escalated, reaching the $50 range by mid-September. Wheelabrator ultimately won the battle with a $52.50 offer.

Rival tenders virtually assure investors that there will be a merger deal. The only question is *which* merger deal.

Using the same criteria outlined earlier, investors can analyze the probable success and time frame of rival merger offers. Two additional tip-offs help investors predict the merger's outcome:

Is There a "Lockup"? To combat unfriendly takeovers, companies under siege have gone beyond merely praying for white knights; they now actively recruit them by offering them a special advantage: the lockup. Not only can lockups aid friendly bids, they can cripple hostile offers.

A lockup involves stacking the deck in favor of the preferred contender. Wheelabrator's successful bid for Pullman used two popular lockup techniques:

• the stock option: Pullman gave Wheelabrator an option to buy 1.8 million new Pullman shares at the market price. If exercised, the option would have given Wheelabrator a healthy stake in Pullman.

• the asset option: Wheelabrator also received an option to buy Pullman's prized asset, its engineering and construction division, for $200 million. Without this division, Pullman was far less attractive to McDermott.

The battle for Crouse-Hinds included a different lockup strategy: To defend itself from InterNorth's unfriendly offer, Crouse-Hinds helped its white knight, Cooper Industries, obtain support pledges from several large Crouse-Hinds shareholders.

"Lockups can boost a friendly suitor's chances of success," says Oppenheimer vice-president Michael Metz.

Follow the Smart Money—that's the other tip-off. Little odd-lot traders, who buy and sell less than 100 shares of stock at a time, lack the expensive legal, accounting, and financial talent retained by the big arbitrageurs to spot a bidding war's probable winner. However, by following the smart-money's lead, other investors can cash in on Wall Street professionals' knowledge.

The stock market has a funny habit of being right about a deal's outcome. Investors should examine what Wall Street thinks will happen, as reflected in the stock price. If two rivals bid for a company, one offering $70 and the other offering $75, but the stock's price never gets above $68, this trading pattern indicates that the professionals seriously doubt the success of the $75 offer. Small investors should follow those professional suspicions.

Knowing Your P's and Queues

For shareholders leaning back to count their blessings during bidding wars, the moment of truth comes when they are confronted by final proration and withdrawal dates.

To review: When a company makes a tender offer for some —not all—of a target's outstanding stock, more shares may be tendered than were sought. In addition, if an acquirer offers both cash and stock in payment, investors may oversubscribe the cash portion. *Since all shares tendered by the proration date must be treated equally, the bidder must make proportional purchases from all eligible tenderers based on the total number of shares sought and received.*

If an acquirer has tendered for 51% of a company's shares and receives 60%, the bidder will purchase shares received by the proration date on a proportional basis. However, investors who miss the proration date will be left out in the cold. They have no assurance as to when, whether, and for how much the bidder will buy their shares. In payment, they may have to accept diluted stock (through the bidder's issue of new shares) instead of cold, hard cash. Meanwhile, after completion of a tender offer, the target's market price generally droops to its old trading level, so investors can't make much money there.

Similarly, investors who tender to the loser in a bidding war usually get shut out. In most cases, the loser withdraws its offer, which had depended on receiving a certain number of shares, and it may be too late to tender to the winner.

However, investors can "shop around" before proration dates, moving their shares from one bidder to another. Wall Street professionals call this "taking a free look," because shareholders can take back their shares anytime before the withdrawal date.

Shareholders should remember two interesting points about tender offers:

Eligibility for higher bids. Shareholders who tender to a company under its initial offer receive any subsequent increases in that bidder's price, so there's no need to constantly shift stock back and forth between bidders. Just watch out for the proration deadlines.

Preferential pools. All proration pools are not created equal. Let's say that Big Spender Company makes a tender offer for 51% of Targetrama, Inc., at $50 per share. You tender before the proration date. The offer draws only 30% of Targetrama's shares. Big Spender raises its offer to $75. By the new proration date, Big Spender receives 90% of Targetrama's shares. Since you tendered as part of the first "preferential pool," you will receive Big Spender's highest offer—$75—for *all* your shares, while Big Spender will purchase shares from later submissions on a pro-rata basis. As we'll see in chapter 6, du Pont used preferential pools to help draw early tenders and to win Conoco.

Because they benefit from preferential pools, investors should withdraw their shares from pools only for a good reason: e.g., a more favorable offer from another acquirer.

Incidentally, in cash-and-stock offers, there is no way of knowing—before the proration date—whether the cash portion of the offer is oversubscribed. You're flying completely blind because acquiring companies do not release counts on the number of target shares received until after the proration date.

GETTING IN AFTER THE ANNOUNCEMENT

Up until now, strategies have been structured for investors who buy potential targets before merger announcements. But what if an investor wants to get into the game *after* an acquirer makes a merger offer?

You can do it—but it's going to cost you more money to get into the game.

After a merger or tender offer is announced, the target's share price rises rapidly toward the "deal" price. Consequently, the investor who waits until a merger is announced will pay more for the target's stock than the investor who spotted the stock as a merger candidate months earlier. Table 7, from *Barron's,* shows the price behavior of 52 takeover targets during 1980. As you can see, investors who bought merger stocks early profited much more than those who bought the stocks after the news was out.

Since investors who jump on a merger bandwagon after the public announcement pay more for a stock, *they have greater risk that the shares will drop below what they paid for them if the deal goes "out the window."* As a rule of thumb, if a merger collapses, the target's stock price will drop to the general level at which it traded in the months before the announcement. Another way of estimating this *"sans* merger" price: Multiply the target's earnings by the going P/E multiple for other companies in the same industry.

Thus, if a merger offer comes in at $60 and the stock moves up to $55 after having lolled in the $20–$22 range, you're probably better off passing it up. Is a $5 profit really worth a potential $35 loss? As *Institutional Investor* pointed out in an August 1981 article: "The downside risk tends to be much greater than the upside potential. Near the conclusion of the Sohio-Kennecott deal, the ratio was about three to four points on the upside, versus 25 to 30 points on the downside."

Therefore, investors who consider dabbling in a little risk arbitrage of their own must examine an announced merger scrupulously to evaluate whether the deal will go through and how long it will take. Unfortunately, sometimes one dead deal can snuff out profits in three or four successes. As Jefferson Tarr, Oppenheimer's former arbitrageur who now heads his own company, puts it: "It's like tennis. Sometimes you win by winning. But most of the time you win by not losing."

TABLE 7

Before and After: Merger-Target Price Histories

DATE OF OFFER	TARGET-BIDDER	THE OFFER	PRICE 1 MO. BEFORE	PRICE 2 WKS. BEFORE	PRICE 1 WK. BEFORE	PRICE 1 DAY BEFORE	PRICE AFTER OFFER
7/25/80	American Distilling-Irwin Jacobs	Likely minimum $19 a share	17⅜	16	16½	16¾	20¼
2/6/80	American Investment Co.-Talcott National	$13 a share	9⅛	10⅜	10	10	11½
4/30/80	American Investment Co.-LLC Corp (formerly Liberty Loan Co.)	$8 plus two shs. LLC common (valued at $15.25 a share)	6¼	7½	7¾	10	10½
9/18/80	American Technical Ind.-Papercraft Corp.	$12.50 a share	7	7	7⅝	7⅝	12⅛
2/19/80	Ampex-Signal Cos.	.79 sh of Signal for each Ampex sh; can cancel if Signal trades above $51 or below $40	21	20¼	20¼	19½	27¾
10/10/80	Ampex-Signal Cos.	.85 sh of Signal for each Ampex sh	26¼	25⅜	26¼	33	33¼
7/23/80	Applied Digital Data Systems-Mitel	$11 a share for the common $25 a share for the preferred	6⅞	8⅛	8¾	9¾	12
8/25/80	Applied Digital Data Systems-NCR	$12 a share for the common $27 a share for the preferred	11¾	10	11	10¾	12
7/22/80	Belden Corp.-Ampco-Pittsburgh	To acquire a significant equity interest	18⅞	19⅞	24	24	25¼
9/9/80	Belden Corp.-Crouse-Hinds	1.24 shs Crouse for each Belden share	28¼	29½	34⅛	33	38½
9/5/80	Bob Evans Supermarket-Beatrice Foods	1.636 shs. Beatrice for each Bob Evans sh.	26¾ bid	24¾ bid	26 bid	27½ bid	31½ bid

TABLE 7 Continued

Before and After: Merger-Target Price Histories

DATE OF OFFER	TARGET-BIDDER	THE OFFER	PRICE 1 MO. BEFORE	PRICE 2 WKS. BEFORE	PRICE 1 WK. BEFORE	PRICE 1 DAY BEFORE	PRICE AFTER OFFER
8/20/80	Burns International-Pittston	Possible exchange of stk valued at $72 million, or about $24.80 a share	22⅛	21½	21¼	22⅝	24⅛
8/13/80	C&K Petroleum-Alaska Interstate	Principal holders offered $35 a sh; if accepted, offer to be made to other holders	25¼	23⅛	27	28¾	30¼
7/15/80	Cavitron-Cooper Laboratories	$20 a share	14⅞	14⅞	14½	16⅝	16½
10/23/80	Cavitron-Cooper Laboratories	$30 a share	20¾	20¼	21⅛	26¼	29⅞
5/20/80	City Investing-Temco Enterprises	an est. $30 a sh; subsequently raised to $32.50 a share	17½	18¾	20¼	22⅜	25¾
11/24/80	Coca-Cola Bottling of N.Y.-Coca-Cola	$10.375 a share	6¼	7¼	7⅜	7⅜	8⅞
12/22/80	CSE-La Guarantee Mutuelle des Fonctionnaires	$40 a share	32	36¼	35	35	35½
10/27/80	Cunningham Drug Stores-a private investor group	$18 a share	10½	10⅛	11½	12¼	15¼
9/2/80	Documentation Inc.-Storage Technology	.85 shs of Storage Technology	13⅛	14¾	16¼	17⅛	16⅜
9/5/80	Elixir-Industries-Ronald R. Sahm	$7.60 a sh; raised to $8.20 a sh (11/12/80)	3¾	4	4	4⅜	6
7/1/80	Fidelity Financial-H.F. Ahmanson	cash & stk valued at $21.20 a share	7⅜	8¼	12	11½	12¼

2/22/80	Fife Corp.-Clausing	$13.50 a sh. for up to 180,000 shs	11	11¼	12¼	13	14¼
1/24/80	Financial Federation-Gibraltar Financial	cash & stk valued at $45 a share; offer had a one-day limit	30⅝	28⅜	29⅛	34⅜	34⅜
6/2/80	Financial Federation-Great Western Financial	cash & stk valued at $52.65 a sh.	25⅝	27⅝	27	28½	38¼
2/26/80	Furr's Cafeterias-K mart	$28 a share	23½ bid	24⅜ bid	24¼ bid	26½ bid	27 bid
12/24/80	Franklin Mint-Warner Communications	$27 of Warner stk or package of $16 plus Warner warrants valued at $11 for each Franklin share	19	17⅝	19	19	25¼
3/26/80	Galveston-Houston-Smith Intl.	.7 sh of Smith Intl for each Galveston-Houston share	41	33	35⅛	35¾	37⅜
7/7/80	GK Technologies-Penn Central	$45 or .895 sh of a second series of Penn Central preference stock	26⅝	25	26½	29⅞	38⅝
10/6/80	Hardee's Food System-Imasco	$25 a sh.; subsequently raised to $28 a share	18½	19	16½	17¾	23¼
6/18/80	Hickory Farms Ohio-General Host	Had entered preliminary negotiations concerning possible merger, subsequently offered $20 a share	9⅛ bid	13 bid	12½ bid	13½ bid	15 bid
12/15/80	Hobart-Canadian Pacific Enterprises	$32.50 a sh for 52% of shs. out.	20	18¾	20¼	23¼	31⅜
12/9/80	Houston Oil & Minerals-Tenneco	Plans exch. of stk-.31 Tenneco sh for each Houston Oil sh. after distribution of Houston Royalty Trust	37¼	49⅜	50⅜	52⅝	51⅛
6/19/80	Huck Mfg.-Federal Mogul	$41 a share	32¼	33⅞	35	35¾	35⅜
7/30/80	Huyck Corp.-Wheelabrator-Frye	$22.125 a sh. for up to 35% of shares; each sh. not acquired convertible into .5 sh of Wheelabrator common	14¾	17⅜	17	20	21

TABLE 7 Continued

Before and After: Merger-Target Price Histories

DATE OF OFFER	TARGET-BIDDER	THE OFFER	PRICE 1 MO. BEFORE	PRICE 2 WKS. BEFORE	PRICE 1 WK. BEFORE	PRICE 1 DAY BEFORE	PRICE AFTER OFFER
8/1/80	Huyck Corp.-BTR Ltd.	$25.125 a share	14⅛	17⅞	17⅞	20⅞	24½
11/13/80	Integon-Ashland Oil	$40 a share for up to 45% of sh + exchange of 55% or more of remaining shs into Ashland convertible stock	25⅞	27⅛	26½	31	35
9/4/80	Intersil-General Electric	Discussions contemplate offer of $35 a share for all stockholders	26¾ bid	26¼ bid	25 bid	26⅜ bid	32⅞ bid
5/6/80	Ivey (J.B.)-Marshall Field	One share of new Marshall Field convertible pfd for each common share	18¼ bid	18¼ bid	18¼ bid	18¾ bid	23 bid
12/4/80	Kirsch Co.-Cooper Industries	$35.51 a share	22⅛	24	25¾	29½	32⅝
8/4/80	Koehring-Amca International	$37 a common share; redemption value or $30 a share for one series and $50 a share for two other series of preferred	20¼	22⅜	23¼	23¾	36⅜
4/14/80	Liggett Group-Grand Metropolitan Ltd.	Plans $50-a-share offer	38½	35½	33½	38	44¼
5/6/80	Liggett Group-Standard Brands	$65 a share for up to 45% of the shs.	33¾	40⅜	41¾	52⅜	58⅜
9/18/80	Manufacturing Data Systems-Schlumberger	.425 presplit shs of Schlumberger for each Manufacturing Data share	40 bid	46¼ bid	52¾ bid	58 bid	58¼ bid

8/25/80	McIntyre Mines-Brascan Ltd.	Offered to buy Superior Oil's 53% stake in McIntyre for $110 a sh; offer then to be extended to minority holders	72¼	74½	75¾	77½	84½
12/5/80	New England Nuclear-E.I. du Pont	1.3 shs of Du Pont for each share	35⅞	38½	39⅞	37⅞	43
6/24/80	NN Corp.-Engelhard Min. & Chem.	1.33 shs Engelhard for each NN share (to reconsider if value below $42.50 or above $50.50)	35½ bid	37½ bid	37¼ bid	39½ bid	40 bid
8/20/80	NN Corp.-Armco	1.5 shs Armco for each NN share but not less than $48	42 bid	45⅛ bid	46 bid	46⅝ bid	46¾ bid
8/18/80	Pacific Resources-Northwest Energy	$16.67 a share or Northwest preference stock	16¾ bid	16½ bid	15¾ bid	15 bid	14¾ bid
6/27/80	Pep Com Industries-Suntory Intl	$38 a share	29	30⅜	31¾	32¾	33⅛
8/28/80	Pneumo-LTV	$20 + 1.7 shs of $25 conv. pref. stk	38⅜	44½	46⅝	47¼	47
6/30/80	Pullman-McDermott	$28 a share for up to two-million shs; would raise stake to 23%	31½	28½	27⅞	27⅞	28¼
8/21/80	Pullman-Wheelabrator-Frye	$43 a share for two million shares and an exchange of stk for remainder	31	34	34⅞	36⅞	40⅛
8/7/80	Sav-On-Drugs-Jewel Cos.	$18 a share for up to 45% of out. shs; subsequently exchange of stk for remaining shs.	8⅞	9⅞	11	12⅜	17⅝
5/21/80	Scriptomatic-British General Electric	$16.25 a share	7½ bid	8 bid	8½ bid	10¾ bid	12¼ bid
10/8/80	Stange-McCormick & Co.	$13.25 a sh. for as many as 400,000 shs. & non-voting common for rest	10	10⅛	10	10½	11¼

TABLE 7 Continued
Before and After: Merger-Target Price Histories

DATE OF OFFER	TARGET-BIDDER	THE OFFER	PRICE 1 MO. BEFORE	PRICE 2 WKS. BEFORE	PRICE 1 WK. BEFORE	PRICE 1 DAY BEFORE	PRICE AFTER OFFER
10/15/80	Teleprompter Corp.-Westinghouse	$38 a share	24⅜	24	27¼		34½
8/21/80	Tesoro Petroleum-Diamond Shamrock		20⅞	20¾	26¼	27⅝	30⅛
9/22/80	Trans Union-Marmon Group	$55 a share	35	36¾	37	37¼	51½
12/10/80	United Refining-Coral Petroleum	$50 a share	23⅛	26⅛	26½	27	45
11/7/80	US Filter-Ashland Oil	$33 a share	24⅜	28	26⅜	26⅞	27¼
6/17/80	Valtec	Exchange of stock	20¾ bid	23⅜ bid	24½ bid	26½ bid	26¼ bid

Should You Always Tender?

Yes.

There's a high probability that the market will never reach the buyout price, so *always sell out on a merger. Do not hold on to your old stock or hold the new stock if the merger is for stock.* Investors who are bullish on the industry represented by the merger and want to maintain an investment in that industry will do better most of the time by buying the stock of a similar company.

As we'll see in chapter 6, the Conoco merger illustrates this rule eloquently. After du Pont's successful tender offer in early August 1981, Conoco's share price nose-dived over 30% by late September, when Conoco was last traded. Du Pont's stock dropped substantially, too, so that investors who took stock rather than cash saw the value of their investment shrink in less than two months.

What If You Don't Want to Sell?

Unfortunately, you don't have much choice. A buyer that acquires two-thirds of the target stock can force you out and make you accept the price that was offered. Your only alternative—if you're convinced you were rooked—is to exercise dissenter's rights by bringing a civil proceeding in a state chancery court and asking the court to determine the fair market value of your stock. If you're the only stockholder bringing the action, your chances are very slim; after all, your argument that the acquisition price was unreasonably low would be hard to maintain if 98% of your fellow stockholders accepted the offer. However, if you're part of a larger group —say, 20%–25% of the shareholders—you have a fair chance of receiving more for your stock. Weigh aggravation and court costs carefully.

What If the Deal Blows?

Chapter 11 offers a comprehensive discussion of warning signals that herald danger in any merger deal, and hedging techniques that can help you safeguard your investment.

Tax Considerations

To the stockholder of the acquired company, cash payments offer immediacy. Unfortunately, they also are immediately taxable at the capital-gains rate (either long- or short-term, depending on how long the target stock has been held).

However, if more than 50% of the total merger payment consists of the acquirer's stock—common, preferred, voting, or nonvoting—the IRS considers the deal a tax-free reorganization. Stockholders are then permitted to defer tax payments on the stock portion of the exchange until they sell the stock. Taxes on the cash portion, if any, fall due immediately.

To ensure that a deal will indeed qualify as a tax-free reorganization, the companies involved can submit a proposed transaction to the IRS national office for an advance ruling. Tax rulings normally take five months to secure, and are mandatory when the buyer is foreign.

Despite the long waiting period, many companies seek advance IRS tax rulings to prevent problems in the future. If a tax-treatment error occurs, the acquirer may have to assume the seller's tax liabilities. After ITT erroneously claimed that its acquisition of Hartford Fire Insurance would be tax-free, ITT had to assume Hartford shareholders' tax liabilities—to the tune of some $400 million.

If a deal must move swiftly, companies may decide not to seek advance rulings. Wheelabrator, for example, went ahead with its bid for Pullman without a ruling in order to beat out McDermott's hostile offer.

Investors should note that the IRS, with its 50%+ benchmark, has generally taken a more restrictive position than the courts on what constitutes a tax-free reorganization. Overruling the IRS, the Supreme Court, for example, has held that a transaction involving as little as 25% stock consideration constitutes continuity of ownership. When companies disagree with the IRS's ruling on a deal, they'll start litigation.

In most cases, a company making a tender offer will state the deal's tax status in its initial announcement.

If an investor receives the acquirer's stock in payment for his or her shares, the new shares take on all the characteristics of the old shares, for tax purposes. A so-called tack-on period applies: The holding period of the old shares becomes the holding period of their new shares. For example, if an investor has owned Oldco stock for five years and tenders the stock to Newco in exchange for Newco shares, the investor is immediately able to sell Newco shares and receive long-term-capital-gains treatment.

Investors should try to avoid receiving both cash and stock in payment for their shares. If investors receive both cash and stock, the cash portion will be treated as a *dividend* (taxed as high as 50%), rather than a long-term capital gain (taxed as high as 20%). An offeror's prospectus will state this possibility. If a deal's structure indicates that you might have to accept both cash and stock in payment, talk to an accountant as well as to your broker.

Another tax wrinkle should be noted: the treatment of the exchange of convertible securities. One of the most popular payments for merger transactions during the bull market of the 1960s, convertible securities are bonds or preferred stocks that can be exchanged for common stock at the option of the holder and under specified terms and conditions.

Convertibles offer two important tax advantages. First, the acquiring company's interest payments are tax-deductible. Second, the seller can defer capital gains until sale of the convertible. Because of the time value of money, this ability to defer payment on capital gains lowers the effective tax rate. In fact, thanks to the Economic Recovery Tax Act of 1981, investors who deferred realizing capital gains until after June 9, 1981, lowered their actual tax rate as well as their effective tax rate—from a maximum of 28% to a maximum of 20% on long-term capital gains.

Of course, purchase for stock or other securities has one major catch: The investor must figure out how the acquirer—and its stock—will perform in the future.

6

Mondo Conoco

There has never been anything comparable to what you are seeing before you
now.
—Mark Millard, Managing Director of
Shearson Loeb Rhoades, Inc.,
adviser to Seagram Company

"Baseball strike? What baseball strike?" quipped one Wall
Street arbitrageur. During the summer of 1981, Wall Streeters
hardly missed the action at Yankee Stadium.

Instead they concentrated on the curve balls, stolen bases,
and grand slams that added up to the largest merger game in
corporate history: the $7.6-billion takeover of Conoco by du
Pont.

In chapter 3, we analyzed the Conoco annual report and saw
that Conoco was vastly underpriced and was ripe for plucking.
In fact, a number of independent analysts had calculated
Conoco's breakup value at $115–$150 per share. Because of
these obvious charms, in 1981 Conoco attracted more beaux
than Scarlett O'Hara at the Tarletons' picnic.

A detailed analysis of the complex and varied Conoco case
will reveal to investors some of the options they face as a
merger unfolds, and how to deal with them. What follows is
a chronology of Conoco's famous courtship, along with suggested moves investors could have made as the drama un-
furled. (Note: The dates in the chronology generally refer to

when the newspaper headlines appeared; the events described will have occurred the *previous* day.)

October 29, 1980. "Trudeau Budget Sets Canadian Control of Oil and Gas Assets by End of Decade"—*Wall Street Journal* headline.

The handwriting was on the wall—and in the morning's newspapers. Canada's prime minister had announced a new national energy policy, aimed at returning ownership of the country's oil, gas, and coal reserves to Canada. At that time, about 70% of Canada's energy resources were owned by foreigners. By heavily taxing energy resources owned by non-Canadians, the new policy hoped to reduce foreign ownership to 50% by 1990.

In short, Canada was encouraging U.S. energy companies to get out of Canada. Consequently, investors, too, wanted out. They flocked to sell stocks of U.S. companies that owned Canadian resources. However, some careful analysis would have revealed that the Canadian move had bad news/good news implications for companies with Canadian investments.

The bad news: The downside was easily visible. The increased taxation would reduce profits of Canadian operations. Trudeau's policy immediately depressed the value of Canadian energy assets owned by non-Canadian companies. Conoco was one of those foreign companies; it owned 52.9% of Hudson's Bay Oil and Gas, which owned 265 million barrels of oil and 3.4 trillion cubic feet of natural gas. Within a week of Trudeau's announcement, Conoco sank from $61.625 to $51.625.

The good news: Not as apparent, but equally important, were the favorable implications for a special-situation play. Trudeau's program also included a number of investment tax credits and stipulations that favored Canadian-owned companies. In addition, Canadian banks eagerly agreed to lend Canadian companies huge amounts of money to finance oil and gas acquisitions. Soon numerous Canadian companies began compiling shopping lists of American companies with oil and gas operations or holdings in Canada. Dome Petroleum Ltd., a small but aggressive Calgary-based oil company, was one of the Canadian companies out window-shopping. It found Conoco.

Upon reading about Canada's new energy policy, investors should have considered how it would affect American companies with Canadian interests. If they had, they would have uncovered the special-situation potential of Conoco, which had traded between $41 and $73 in 1980.

January 2, 1981. Conoco sells for $65.375.

February 2. Conoco sells for $58.125.

March 2. Conoco sells for $59.125.

April 1. Conoco sells for $56.875.

May 1. Conoco sells for $49.875.

May 6. Dome Petroleum of Calgary offers $65 per share for 14 million shares of Conoco. Dome also reserves the right to purchase as many as 22 million shares. Following Dome's announcement, Conoco closes up 6⅝ points for the day, at 56½. (With benefit of 20/20 hindsight, we can say that investors should have held on to their shares. However, given the information at their disposal at this time, tendering to Dome looked like the best move, since the company was offering a 30% premium over Conoco's recent stock price.)

Dome's move was unusual and aggressive. Ironically enough, Dome did not seek a Conoco takeover. Instead, emboldened by Canada's new National Energy Program designed to end foreign domination of its oil and gas industry, the Calgary-based company wanted to force Conoco to sell off its 52.9% holdings in Hudson's Bay Oil and Gas.

Although Conoco's directors recommend rejection of the offer, *54.8 million* shares are tendered—about half Conoco's outstanding shares. This overwhelming response—coupled with the enormous undervaluation of Conoco's stock—alerts other hunters and investors that the company is ripe for plucking.

May 29. Playing the white knight, Seagram privately approaches Conoco and offers to buy 35% of the company. Seagram assures Conoco of its willingness to work a friendly compromise. Conoco shares close down 2 points for the day, at 51⅝. Of course, investors would know nothing about such behind-the-scenes moves.

June 1. Dome gets what it really wanted; the Conoco tender was merely a feint. To vanquish the specter of a takeover by Dome, Conoco agrees to sell Dome 52.9% of its Canadian holdings (Hudson's Bay Oil and Gas) in exchange for the 22 million shares of Conoco stock that Dome had acquired through its tender offer, plus $245 million in cash. Conoco shares rise to $53.

Next, Seagram's makes more behind-the-scenes moves.

June 4. Teams from Conoco and Seagram begin working out a deal allowing Seagram to buy 25% of Conoco for $2 billion. The formal offer includes Seagram chairman Edgar Bronfman's promise to leave Conoco's management alone for fifteen years.

June 17. Following the sale of Hudson's Bay Oil and Gas to Dome Petroleum, Conoco rejects two alternative offers from Seagram: to buy 28.6 million shares directly for $2 billion (or $70 per share); or to purchase 15.9 million shares at $75 per share and 9.6 million shares on the open market, for an estimated $1.7 billion.

June 18. Seagram begins open-market purchases of Conoco by buying 143,000 shares, for an estimated $7.7 million. Conoco closes at 54¼, up 1.

June 22. "Conoco Rejects a Foreign Offer, Mulls U.S. Union"—*Wall Street Journal* headline.

The article goes on to explain that Conoco has approached a major corporation in the United States about a possible merger. Conoco also discloses that it recently turned down a bid by a major foreign corporation to buy one-quarter of its stock. (The foreign corporation, of course, is Seagram.)

Here's a major clue for investors: If a company has been a merger target in the past, it becomes a likely target in the future. Moreover, Conoco clearly expresses interest in a friendly merger.

On June 19, the previous trading day, Conoco had closed at $56.25, fairly near its 12-month low of $47.50. Since any merger deal would probably come in at least as high as Dome's $65 bid, and even above the unnamed suitor's $70 offer, the risk-versus-reward consideration would suggest that investors buy Conoco if they didn't already own it.

June 24. "Seagram Tells of Bid for Conoco—Spurned Suitor May Buy Shares on Open Market"—*New York Times* headline.

In the article, Seagram discloses that it was Conoco's "mystery bidder," and that it notified the Justice Department and the Federal Trade Commission that it might buy at least 10% of Conoco's outstanding stock. Meanwhile, rumors circulated on Wall Street that Conoco was pursuing a merger with Cities Service.

For investors, Seagram's announcement confirms Conoco's status as a hot merger prospect. A look at Conoco's balance sheet should have convinced them even more: As we saw in chapter 3, Conoco's market value languished far beneath an adjusted book value of up to $150 per share.

In addition, Seagram matched the profile of a likely acquirer. It certainly had the money; in 1980 Seagram had sold its U.S. holdings in Texas Pacific to the Sun Company for $2.3 billion. "What are you going to do now? Buy Iran?" Charles Bronfman, deputy chairman, asked his brother Edgar, Seagram's chairman, following the sale. Seagram had also lined up a $3-billion-Eurodollar line of credit—a very nice shopping budget.

Seagram not only had the funds, it also had the desire. Seagram had clearly been looking for acquisitions. In March 1981 the company had made an unsuccessful tender offer for St. Joe Minerals.

June 24. Both Conoco and Cities Service ask the New York Stock Exchange to halt trading in their respective stocks. When trading halts, Conoco is at $62.

June 25. "Merger Bid by Conoco Is Expected—Cities Service Is Reported Target in Latest Talks"—*New York Times* headline.

The *Times* reports that Conoco and Cities Service verge on announcing a merger pact. A union of the two companies would create the nation's seventh-largest oil company.

Here's a potential danger. Conoco might *acquire* a company instead of *being acquired.* If Conoco acquired Cities Service for stock, the ensuing dilution would force its shares down, rather than up.

Investors should sit tight here, awaiting Seagram's response to Conoco's move.

Conoco does not trade today. For investors who don't yet own Conoco, now would be a particularly risky time to buy, given the situation's uncertainty.

June 26. "Seagram to Seek 41% Conoco Stake at $2.55 Billion; Cities Service Out—Surprise Offer of $73 a Share Expected to Start Today; Conoco Silent on Strategy"—*Wall Street Journal* headline.

Seagram makes an unfriendly tender of $73 per share for 41% of Conoco. In the text of the article, investors learn:

Seagram's proration date is July 17.

Seagram's withdrawal deadline is July 17.

Conditions: A minimum of 28 million Conoco shares—about a 32% stake—must be tendered and not withdrawn.

With the crucial proration and withdrawal dates weeks away, investors can tender to Seagram and still move their shares to another bidder if a better offer comes along.

Conoco closes at $65.25.

(Note: From this point on, developments will be discussed from the viewpoint of investors who *already own* Conoco stock. For investors who buy now, the potential risk has become nearly $20, the potential reward increasingly unpredictable. Although buying Conoco now could still be very profitable, explanations of how to play the game now become too complex for the scope of this book.)

July 1. "Conoco Votes to Oppose Seagram Takeover Bid" —*New York Times* headline.

Not only does Conoco's board unanimously vote to oppose Seagram's offer, the oil company also files a $1-billion lawsuit against the liquor company, charging that Seagram's violated Federal securities law as well as earlier alleged promises not to pursue a hostile bid. Investors can pretty much discount such suits; they're standard operating procedure in takeover battles.

If we take a look at how Seagram's offer measured up against our merger criteria on this date, we see that, all in all, Seagram's offer looks as though it stood a pretty fair chance of success (see table 8).

Conoco closes at $68.625.

July 7. "Du Pont Co. Agrees to Buy Conoco Inc. for Cash, Stock Totalling $6.82 Billion—Merger Would Be Largest in Corporate History, End Seagram Co. Hopes"—*Wall Street Journal* headline.

Du Pont announces that it has agreed to acquire 100% of Conoco's stock for $6.82 billion in du Pont common stock and cash. Under the terms of the merger agreement, du Pont would buy 40% of Conoco's 86 million outstanding shares for $87.50 cash each, and would exchange 1.6 shares of du Pont common stock for each remaining Conoco share. Based on du Pont's July 6 closing price of $46.375, the proposed agreement is worth $79.52 per Conoco share. The agreement also

TABLE 8
Comparison of Seagram Offer to Merger Criteria, July 1.

Merger Criteria	Seagram Offer	Outlook for Merger
Price	$73 (well above market)	Good
For what percentage of stock	41% (some shareholders will be left out)	Fair
Friendly vs. hostile	Hostile	Fair
Cash vs. stock	Cash	Good
Conditional?	Yes—minimum of 28 million shares (apx. 32%) must be tendered	Fair
Is target in a regulated industry?	No	Good
Foreign acquirer	Yes	Fair
Do Conoco management/directors own substantial percentage of shares?	No	Good—for hostile offer
Antitrust problems	None	Good

gives du Pont an option to buy 15.9 million Conoco treasury shares, also at $87.50 each.

Following the news, Conoco closes at $77, up 7⅜ from its close on July 2, the previous trading day.

At this point, the du Pont offer looks like a surefire winner (see table 9).

TABLE 9
Comparison of Seagram Offer to Merger Criteria, July 7.

Merger Criteria	Seagram Offer	Outlook for Merger
Price	$87.50 cash for 40% of Conoco; 1.6 du Pont shares for remaining 60% (estimated value of stock portion $74.20)— substantially above Seagram offer and recent stock price	Excellent
For what percentage of stock	100%	Excellent
Friendly vs. hostile	Friendly	Excellent
Cash vs. stock	Cash and stock. Some shareholders will get closed out of cash portion; institutional investors like stock for tax reasons. Deal will most likely qualify as tax-free reorganization	Good–Fair
Conditional?	Yes—du Pont must receive at least 51% of Conoco's shares	Fair
Is target in a regulated industry?	No	Good
Foreign acquirer	No	Good
Do Conoco management/directors own substantial percentage of shares?	No	Fair—substantial management ownership helps friendly offers
Antitrust problems	Minimal—vertical merger	Good

Astute investors would have noted that Conoco also granted du Pont the option to buy 15.9 million unissued Conoco shares (known as "treasury" stock) at $87.50 each. Such an accord is a popular "lockup" strategy, used to aid friendly bidders. This lockup becomes even more interesting when investors note that du Pont's investment banker is First Boston Corporation, the firm that used the same lockup edge to help Wheelabrator win Pullman.

Attractive and seemingly certain as the du Pont bid is, shareholders of Conoco do not need to make any moves yet: du Pont has merely announced an *intention* to make a tender offer —not the offer itself. Because of the speed with which events moved, du Pont's offer was still in registration. Shareholders could leave their shares with Seagram while awaiting the formal du Pont solicitation.

Conoco closes at $75.875.

July 13. "Seagram Decides to Battle Du Pont for Conoco, Inc., Increases, Widens Bid to $85 a Share for 51% Holding —Amended Offer Is Higher by an Average of $4.64 Than Rival's"—*Wall Street Journal* headline.

Seagram's new offer sets up a new schedule of proration and withdrawal dates. The withdrawal deadline is July 17; the proration date is July 22. (The withdrawal date moved automatically after du Pont raised its offer on July 6.) In its new offer announcement, Seagram waives the condition that its offer receive a certain minimum number of shares. Investors who tendered to Seagram under its previous $73 bid automatically become eligible for Seagram's higher offer.

Conoco shareholders now find themselves in the most advantageous merger situation of all: a bidding war. With Conoco's estimated book value of $110–$150 per share, the offers can soar far beyond their current $85 level.

At this point, the Seagram offer would appeal to investors who prefer cash, since investors who tender their Conoco shares to du Pont have no assurance as to whether they will receive cash or stock in payment. However, the du Pont offer will attract institutional shareholders, which prefer stock for tax reasons.

In addition, because Seagram tendered for only 51% of Conoco's shares, some investors feared that the offer would become oversubscribed. If that happened, Seagram would purchase up to 51% of Conoco stock on a pro-rata basis, leaving the fate of the remaining 49% of Conoco stock—and its owners—open. Because of this uncertainty, some large shareholders might prefer the du Pont bid for 100% of Conoco.

Conoco closes at $84.375.

July 14. "Mobil Signals Possible Conoco Bid, Seeks Loans with Citibank Group"—*Wall Street Journal* headline.

Enter Mobil. The nation's second-largest oil company signals its entrance into the Conoco fray by releasing a prepared statement saying that it is "arranging bank loans through a syndicate led by Citibank and [has] retained an investment banker in connection with recent developments relating to the acquisition of Conoco."

Prospects for Conoco shareholders will look even richer if a third bidder enters the game—particularly if that bidder is Mobil Oil, with over $14 billion in current assets alone.

Conoco closes at $86.125.

July 15. "Conoco Bid Increased by Du Pont; Oil Company Endorses Offer of $7.6 Billion"—*New York Times* headline.

Du Pont sweetens its offer, upping it to $95 per share for 40% of the company and 1.7 of its shares for each of Conoco's shares. Total value of the offer: about $7.6 billion. Conoco's board immediately endorses the offer.

Du Pont's new offer revises its proration and withdrawal dates:

Du Pont's proration date is July 24.

Du Pont's withdrawal deadline is August 4.

The offer remains conditional on du Pont's receiving 51% of the Conoco shares.

Meanwhile, Seagram takes a swipe at the tax status of du Pont's offer in today's *New York Times:* "We further believe that there is at the very least a very substantial possibility that the entire transaction proposed by du Pont is fully taxable." Obviously, Seagram is trying to dissuade investors from tendering their Conoco stock to du Pont.

Conoco closes at $87.875.

What should investors have done at this point? Nothing—crucial proration dates were still a week away. Ellen Greenspan, who heads the customer arbitrage department at Oppenheimer & Company, commented in *The New York Times* on July 16:

"In a situation like this, the best strategy for the stockholder is to sit back and enjoy it. What you have here is a bunch of big guys bidding for the company, and there is no reason to make a decision at this point.

"The momentum of the Conoco decision is such that the current offers may not be the final offers. Existing bids might be modified, or new bids from another company may surface. Du Pont and Seagram are playing hardball, and, in effect, have indicated their desire to stay in the game. And, presumably, there is Mobil standing in the wings."

July 17. "Mobil Joins Conoco Quest with $3.92 Billion Bid" —*New York Times* headline.

Mobil-ization: Mobil formally joins the Conoco war with a bid of $90 per share in cash for 51% of Conoco, and proposes to follow the tender offer (made July 16) with a merger, paying $90 per share in Mobil securities for Conoco's remaining shares.

Mobil's proration date is July 26.

Mobil's withdrawal deadline is August 6.

Conditions: Mobil must receive 51% of Conoco's shares.

Table 10 shows how Mobil's offer stacks up. In it we see the factors emerging that most strongly contributed to Mobil's loss:

Slow start. For reasons no one could clarify, Mobil waited until July 17 before announcing its bid for Conoco. This gave du Pont a critical lead time of 11 days in which to convince shareholders.

Antitrust mistrust—"The antitrust credibility discount factor," Joseph Perella of First Boston Corporation called it. In other words, "No one believed that Mobil would get antitrust

TABLE 10
Comparison of Mobil Offer to Merger Criteria, July 17

Merger Criteria	Mobil Offer	Outlook for Merger
Price	$90 cash for 51% of Conoco; offer very vague on payment for remaining shares	Fair— surprisingly, cash portion is lower than du Pont's
For what percentage of stock	51%	Fair
Friendly vs. hostile	Hostile	Fair
Cash vs. stock	Cash for 51% of company	Good
Conditional?	Yes—Mobil must receive 51% of Conoco shares	Fair
Is target in a regulated industry?	No	Good
Foreign acquirer	No	Good
Do Conoco management/directors own substantial percentage of shares?	No	Good—in hostile merger
Antitrust problems	Major	Fair–Poor

clearance." Investors, always anxious to take their profits fast, feared that major antitrust stumbling blocks would either delay or squelch a Conoco-Mobil merger. Said a Wall Street investment banker, "[Mobil] could have gone to $125 or even $130 and still lost. You just can't cross a credibility gap that wide with a bridge made of money."

And not enough money at that. As *The New York Times* commented on July 17, "The possible advantages to shareholders in tendering their shares at Mobil's $90 offering price were not immediately clear." Because many traders seriously questioned Mobil's ability to obtain antitrust clearance, Mobil needed to come in with a tempting offer to counteract this uncertainty. Mobil's $90 bid was *lower* than the cash portion of du Pont's offer, while having more conditions than Seagram's $85 bid. At $90, Mobil didn't look as tempting compared to the competition. "Far too low," said Stephen A. Royce, managing director of Bedford Partners, to *The New York Times* on July 23.

Conoco closes at $87.75.

July 21. "Conoco Vetoes Mobil's $90-a-Share Offer, Plans Trust Suit, Backs Du Pont Bid Anew"—*Wall Street Journal* headline.

Conoco immediately intensifies investor perceptions of Mobil's antitrust problems by planning an antitrust suit. In announcing the suit, Conoco chairman Ralph E. Bailey says: "It is clear that the Mobil offer raises major antitrust and other public-policy issues, which makes the successful completion of the Mobil offer highly problematical. If Mobil is permitted to acquire Conoco—which competes vigorously and broadly with Mobil in all phases of the petroleum business—a major restructuring of the U.S. energy industry is likely to result, with substantial energy enterprises like Conoco disappearing as vigorous competitors from the market."

Conoco closes at $84.50.

Now's when the fine art of juggling proration dates comes into play. Remember: After a bidder's proration date elapses, the company does not have any obligation to purchase tendered shares. As of today, the proration dates of Conoco's suitors are:

Seagram   July 22
Du Pont   July 24
Mobil   July 26

Because of the scheduling of the proration dates, investors should have tendered to Seagram at this point. The move did not commit them, since Seagram's withdrawal date was July 31. Instead, Wall Street professionals call this strategy "taking a free look." Investors had no need to decide whether to keep the shares with Seagram or move them to another bidder until July 24, du Pont's proration date.

July 24. "Conoco Bid Raised by Seagram—Increase to $92 a Share Could Conclude Fight"—*New York Times* headline.

In a well-timed move, Seagram raises its bid to $92 per share

—a total of $4.1 billion for a 51% interest. By its action, Seagram hopes to convince investors to keep their stock with Seagram, instead of moving it to du Pont when its proration deadline falls due at midnight tonight. Seagram also extends its withdrawal date to July 31.

At this point, decisions on strategy depended greatly on investor psychology. Investors who want cash on the barrelhead with reasonable assurance would have gone with Seagram. According to early counts reported in the papers, all stock tendered to Seagram by July 22 would receive full payment.

In addition, on this date Seagram announced that it would create a second proration pool for shares tendered after its original July 22 date but before August 1. By ensuring favorable treatment (i.e., no proration) for investors who tendered early, Seagram sought to discourage shareholder switches to other bidders.

In contrast, on July 24, investors who tendered to du Pont had *absolutely no assurance* as to whether they would receive cash or cash-and-stock for their Conoco shares. They were flying completely blind. As pointed out in chapter 5, tendering shares for both cash and stock poses serious tax penalties, since the cash portion will then be treated as a dividend, rather than a capital gain. Meanwhile, since du Pont's offer was contingent on its receiving at least 51% of Conoco's shares, investors had no assurance of getting *anything at all* from du Pont. Seagram's offer specified no minimum number of shares, although the company could still withdraw if another company raised its bid.

Unless you really wanted du Pont stock, you would have fared best by keeping your stock with Seagram while waiting for Mobil's next move.

Conoco closes at $86.75.

July 28. "Mobil Lifts Its Offer for Conoco—Per-Share Bid Is Raised to $105 in Cash"—*New York Times* headline.

Upward Mobil-ity: Mobil raises the cash portion of its offer to $105 a share for 51% of Conoco and simultaneously lowers the value of Mobil securities for the rest to $85. By revising its offer, Mobil hopes to encourage early tenders.

Meanwhile, du Pont also increases its offer, extending cash payments to 45% of the outstanding shares from 40%. Du Pont also announces that its tender offer drew 41% of Conoco's shares; 36% of those shares tendered requested cash.

As of today, the offers measure up as shown in table 11.

At this point, du Pont becomes undesirable for any investor who wants cash, since proration returns indicate that its cash portion is nearly completely subscribed. Investors tendering to du Pont now will have to accept stock.

According to many observers, Mobil made a fatal error by upping the cash portion of its offer while downgrading the securities portion. This was an attempt to encourage investors to tender early, in order to get the cash, but many Wall Street-ers feel that Mobil's strategy backfired. Already concerned about the vague descriptions of the Mobil securities, investors became even more nervous when Mobil reduced their value. A Wall Street takeover-stock trader asked, "How do you think

TABLE 11
Comparison of Offers as of July 28

	SEAGRAM	DU PONT	MOBIL
Total Value of Offer	$4.08 billion (51% of Conoco)	$7.43 billion (100% of Conoco)	$8.19 billion (100% of Conoco)
Per-share Value	$92.00	$85.41 (combined value of cash/stock offer based on duPont's closing price)	$95.00 (combined value of cash and Mobil securities)
Total Percentage of Conoco Shares Received	19.8%	41%	2%
Withdrawal Date	Friday, July 31	Tuesday, August 4	Thursday, August 6

somebody who previously tendered with the debentures in mind felt about that price cut?"

Meanwhile, in the financial press, speculation swirled about whether Mobil could pass antitrust scrutiny.

Week of July 27. It all depends on whose side you're on. Some quotes:

> Mobil believes that its acquisition of Conoco clearly does not violate antitrust laws. As we have said before, we believe that Mobil is free to acquire and operate all of Conoco's businesses. . . . Mobil strongly believes no Conoco shareholder should forgo the benefit of our offer because of exaggerated and uninformed antitrust concerns featured in the media, which may be inspired in part by Conoco and the other bidders.
>
> —Full-page Mobil ad in the
> *Wall Street Journal,* July 30, 1981

> [Regarding the Mobil offer] Who the hell wants debentures?
>
> —A. S. Tepper, St. Louis, who
> tendered his 200 Conoco shares
> to du Pont

> The du Pont transaction is the only one of the three offers which gives Conoco shareholders an opportunity to own a continuing participating equity interest in a strong combined high technology, chemical-energy enterprise.
>
> —Ralph Bailey
> Chairman of Conoco

July 29. "Seagram's New Tack on Conoco"—*New York Times* headline.

In an extremely interesting development, Seagram announces that on Saturday, August 1—only three days from now—it will start paying $92 for shares tendered to it. "Seagram is paying $92 in cash. Quickly," a Seagram advertisement directed at Conoco shareholders will say the following day. Investors wanting instant cash will grab the Seagram offer;

while others, taking a wait-and-see attitude, will hold out for higher bids from Mobil and du Pont as the Conoco battle intensifies.

One Wall Street speculator's point of view: "I can take Seagram's cash and run out and buy some other juicy takeover situations next week—or even have a second go at Conoco if it looks like the government will allow a bidding showdown between Mobil and Du Pont. I'll cry about getting only $92 all the way to the bank."

Conoco closes at $89.75.

July 30. "Du Pont Says Conoco Tender Offer Got 56% of Stock, with Cash Oversubscribed"—*Wall Street Journal* headline.

Du Pont's announcement confirms that any new tenders it receives will be for stock.

Conoco closes at $91.125.

August 3. "Du Pont Gains, Mobil Hits Snag in Conoco Chase —U.S. Seeks More Data from Mobil, Finds Only Single Flaw with Du Pont Bid"—*Wall Street Journal* headline.

A major move from Washington: On Friday, July 31, the Justice Department, which was reviewing both the du Pont and Mobil bids for antitrust implications, in effect gives du Pont a clean bill of health. The Justice Department finds only one possible conflict of interest between the chemical company and its oil and coal target: a petrochemical joint venture between Conoco and Monsanto. Du Pont feverishly begins negotiating with the Justice Department to eliminate the snag. If eliminated, du Pont can start purchasing Conoco shares within forty-eight hours—after its midnight, August 4, withdrawal deadline.

In contrast, the Justice Department asks Mobil to supply additional information. Automatically, this request extends by at least ten days the waiting period before Mobil can begin purchasing stock under its $105 bid.

This delay will prove crucial. Because of the uncertainty of Mobil's antitrust status and the delays it will entail, investors should have tendered to Mobil only if the company either made sudden progress on the antitrust front or substantially increased its bid.

Otherwise, investors should have tendered immediately to Seagram, which was buying Conoco shares for $92 on a first-come, first-served basis, up to 51% of the shares. So far, Seagram had received only about 20% of Conoco's shares.

Alternatively, investors could have sold their Conoco shares on the open market that day for $92–$96.

August 4. "Mobil Raises Bid for Conoco $10, to $115 a Share —Move, Tied to Effort to Defuse Antitrust Concern, Sparks Heavy Trading, Price Rise"—*Wall Street Journal* headline.

"Too little, too late," mutters one arbitrageur.

Mobil's move had pushed Conoco's stock to $96 the day before—$1 more than the cash portion of du Pont's offer. If prices held above this level, investors who tendered to du Pont would withdraw their shares and sell them on the open market.

However, later on August 4, du Pont raises the cash portion of its offer to $98. Conoco's price will never climb above the $98 level, although Mobil's bid is a hefty $115—indicating that the smart money doubts Mobil's ability to resolve its serious antitrust problems.

Mobil goes to federal district court seeking a temporary restraining order to prevent du Pont from purchasing Conoco shares after its midnight, August 4, withdrawal deadline. Otherwise, argues Mobil, "it will be all over but the shouting."

Events proved Mobil was right.

August 5. "Du Pont Apparently Wins the Fight for Conoco as Mobil Appeal Denied—Both Concerns Boost Offers; Mobil Fails to Get Delay on Du Pont's Deadline"—*Wall Street Journal* headline.

In hectic eleventh-hour maneuvering the day before, Mobil raised its bid to $120 per share.

But it's too late. Following the expiration of du Pont's midnight withdrawal date on August 4, the checks are in the mail. At 3:45 A.M. (EDT) on August 5, du Pont begins issuing checks for the 38.7 million Conoco shares attracted by its cash tender offer. An additional 9.4 million shares will be exchanged for du Pont stock. All in all, du Pont's tender offer has drawn 55% of the Conoco shares.

Final price tag for Conoco: $7.57 billion. The du Pont–Conoco merger will create the seventh-largest industrial company in the United States, with combined 1980 sales of $32 billion and net earnings of $1.3 billion.

Meanwhile, Seagram says that it will keep its $92-per-share tender offer open until Friday, August 7. Investors still holding Conoco shares thus have the choice of tendering to Seagram at $92 or selling their shares on the open market for $91.375–$92.00, Conoco's trading range today.

Should investors have kept their Conoco shares and waited for du Pont to swap each of them for 1.7 of its common shares? No way.

Conoco provides a tragic but classic example of the lost profits that can result from holding on to shares after a tender offer is completed. In early August 1981, Conoco shareholders could have sold their stock to Seagram for $92 or to du Pont for $98. By late September, Conoco had sunk to the $60–$65 range—a loss of over 30%.

Of course, it's possible that at some future time du Pont may want to clean up its balance sheet by making Conoco a wholly owned subsidiary and therefore buying the remaining Conoco shares outstanding. But that may be a remote possibility—certainly too weak to count on or to bank on. It's smarter to sell out for a guaranteed profit.

"Those who cannot remember the past are condemned to repeat it," wrote George Santayana.

Santayana's advice holds well for Wall Street. By analyzing the twists and turns of the enormous and expensive Conoco battle, investors can develop a better feel for what kinds of deals may succeed in the future. In particular, investors should be interested in "Big Rube."

"Big Rube" (for Rube Goldberg) is the affectionate name Bruce Wasserstein and Joseph R. Perella of First Boston Corporation, du Pont's financial adviser, give to the innovative and complex offer structure that helped du Pont win Conoco. Among "Big Rube's" components:

—*Tax-free transaction.* Institutional investors, who held some 62% of Conoco's outstanding stock, tend to prefer tax-free transactions. Du Pont's bid therefore proposed to acquire most of Conoco's shares for stock.

—*Stock options.* First Boston had successfully used a big stock option to help Wheelabrator-Frye win Pullman in 1980. Wasserstein and Perella adapted the strategy to the Conoco battle.

Du Pont persuaded the Conoco board to grant du Pont an option to buy 15.9 million Conoco treasury shares at $87.50 each. According to Wasserstein, the stock option offered du Pont some immediate advantages. "If we got in a struggle with somebody bigger and richer, as we feared we might, exercise of the option might let us quickly assume control, make it a lot more expensive for somebody else to get control, or prevent an opponent from assuming control by exercising and diluting their holdings after a successful offer to below a majority level." Furthermore, even if it looked as though du Pont would lose the fight for Conoco, "we could always exercise the option as a way of making money."

—*"Preferential" tender pools.* To attract institutional shareholders, du Pont had to structure the Conoco merger as a tax-free transaction. At the same time, du Pont did not want to risk losing other shareholders who might want cash.

To lure and hold these cash-hungry investors, First Boston applied another element of the strategy they had used for the Wheelabrator-Pullman deal: preferential tender pools. The strategy guaranteed early tenderers not only that they would receive cash, but also that they would stay eligible for the highest du Pont cash bid. Consequently, shareholders who tendered to du Pont would hesitate before moving their shares to either Seagram or Mobil, fearing to "lose their place in line."

In the same way that the du Pont deal used many of the elements of the successful Wheelabrator offer for Pullman, future deals will almost surely adapt some of the lessons and strategies of Conoco.

7

Taking Stock: Profiting from Repurchases

Offer to Purchase
1,700,000 Shares of Common Stock
of
The Standard Oil Company
(an Ohio Corporation)

For Cash at
$61.50 Net Per Share

The Offer Expires on Monday, August 6, 1979, at 5:00 P.M., New York City Time, Unless Extended

—The Wall Street Journal
Monday, July 30, 1979

Sounds like a typical tender offer, doesn't it?

There's one important difference, however. Standard Oil, the company that published the announcement, is tendering for its own stock.

Stock repurchases—also known as "buybacks" or "reacquired shares"—have become an increasingly prevalent special situation. In 1979 alone, observers estimate that companies repurchased over 100 million shares on the New York Stock Exchange.

As its name implies, a stock repurchase involves a company's buying back of outstanding common shares, in one of the following ways:

1. Privately negotiated purchases—i.e., buying large blocks from one or more major stockholders.

2. Open-market purchases—i.e., buying the shares on the New York Stock Exchange, American Stock Exchange, or over the counter at the prevailing trading price.

3. Tender offers—buying stock directly from shareholders, generally at a premium over market price.

Usually, a company's decision on whether to use open-market purchases or tender offers depends on the amount of stock it wants to reacquire, the stock's average trading volume, and the urgency of the buyback.

Let's say a stock has an average daily trading volume of 50,000 shares. If the company wants to reacquire 500,000 shares or less, it can generally accomplish the buyback in a couple of weeks (50,000 shares × 10 days). On the other hand, if it wants to repurchase 2 million shares, the program would take at least two months (50,000 shares × 40 days, with approximately 22 trading days in a month). Obviously, if a company was trying to foil a takeover attempt, it could not afford the extra time that open-market purchases take.

Since the first two buyback alternatives are not special situations (they can enhance long-term profits but don't offer an immediate payoff), we will limit our discussion to stock repurchase by tender offer.

Like mergers, stock repurchases via tender offer can provide shareholders with a nifty return on their investment. A study of all stock repurchases by tender offer on the New York Stock Exchange from 1963 through 1978 found that, on average, firms paid a premium of 23% for their shares. Table 12 provides some specific examples.

According to Michael Murphy, executive vice-president and chief financial officer of Consolidated Foods, "there is not a large company in the country today that's not assessing the stock buyback."

Stock repurchases weren't always so popular. In fact, people used to consider them disreputable, if not downright nefarious. According to Eric Dobkin, who conducts repurchase programs at Goldman, Sachs, "there used to be a stigma to a company's repurchasing its own shares, because it was said the management couldn't find any other investment opportunities it could tap."

Another observer stated it even more bluntly: "It used to be considered chicken to shrink your capital."

Originally, stock repurchases deserved their ill repute. Companies frequently used the practice to artificially boost their stock price. Some corporations even went as far as announcing repurchase programs that never materialized. Other

TABLE 12
Stock Repurchases Through Tender Offers

COMPANY	DATE TENDER ANNOUNCED	MARKET PRICE 1 MONTH BEFORE ANNOUNCE- MENT	PRICE ON DATE OF ANNCMT.	TENDER- OFFER PRICE	PREMIUM OVER MARKET PRICE 1 MONTH BEFORE ANNOUNCE- MENT
Ashland Oil	9/14/78	$35.625	$44.875	$47.00	32%
Weyerhaeuser	8/8/78	24.875	29.75	32.00	29%
Georgia-Pacific	1/29/79	24.25	28.25	31.00	28%
Standard Oil (Ohio)	7/26/79	52.50	53.375	61.50	17%
Levi Strauss	1/19/79	34.375	42.00	43.50	27%
Winn-Dixie	6/25/79	26.875	29.25	30.00	12%
Marriott	1/23/80	17.25	21.75	22.00	28%
Bendix	1/29/81	57.625	61.00	64.00	11%

seamy applications included using corporate funds to increase the control of individual owners and managers; after repurchases, these people owned a greater proportion of the outstanding shares.

Due to these questionable practices, "buying back your own stock was considered un-American," explained Howard Clark, manager of Blyth Eastman Paine Webber's industrial corporate finance department.

According to many Wall Street professionals, the turning point came when IBM spent $1 billion repurchasing 4 million shares in 1977. Spurred on by their own high cash reserves and low stock prices, other companies—including such household words as Sears, Levi Strauss, Quaker Oats, Norton Simon, and PepsiCo—quickly followed suit.

And after them, the deluge. States Bruce Nolop of Morgan Stanley's corporate finance department: "Now you're in good company if you repurchase; blue chip America is doing what many respectable companies might not have done in the past."

Today, concludes Robert Savage of Kehoe, White, Towey & Savage, shareholders consider buybacks as American as "motherhood and home-baked bread. The stockholders consider it a good use of money—better than paying all those high executive salaries."

Why do companies buy back their own stock? The following are some of the reasons.

Improved Earnings per Share

After stock repurchases, corporate profits are divided among fewer shares—meaning higher earnings per share, all other factors being equal.

Although the company hasn't actually grown, the earnings on the remaining shares, as well as return on equity, increases. These increases can have significant psychological importance. Financial analysts tend to favor stocks showing improved earnings and return on equity performance. A better corporate report card can mean an increased price/earnings multiple for the stock—and a higher share price on the market.

Teledyne provides the textbook example of a company that used reacquisition to enhance performance.

Henry Singleton, Teledyne's publicity-shy, brilliant, and inscrutable chairman, left the presidency of Litton Industries' electronic-equipment division in 1960 to form Teledyne. Starting from scratch, Teledyne grew to *Fortune* 500 proportions in six years. From its original product base in high-technology electronic systems, the company diversified rapidly through acquisitions, including Acoustic Research (stereo speakers), Ryan Aeronautical (pilotless aircraft), and Aqua Tec (shower massagers). The company passed the $1-billion mark in 1969, and led the *Fortune* 500 in both earnings and earnings per share for the ten-year period ending in 1971.

When the conglomerate bubble burst in the early 1970s, Teledyne fell out of favor. Its shares, which had traded as high as $143 in 1968, sank to a miserable $13 by 1970. That's when Teledyne started repurchasing shares.

All in all, Teledyne reduced the number of its outstanding shares from 81.8 million in 1971 to 21 million in 1981—a 75% reduction. Quite a turnabout for the conglomerate that had been one of the leading acquirers during the late 1960s, gobbling up 37 other companies in 1968 and 11 more in 1969. The massive repurchases spectacularly boosted Teledyne's earnings per share and return on equity.

To summarize Teledyne's performance from 1971 to 1980:

> REVENUES: + 165%
> NET PROFITS: + 516%
> EARNINGS PER SHARE: + 2,396%
> RETURN ON EQUITY: + 209%

Because of these stellar results, Wall Street has rewarded Teledyne's stock price handsomely. The shares, which traded as low as 7⅝ in 1974, sold for $148.75 at the beginning of October 1981.

Undervalued Shares

One of the most important factors encouraging stock repurchases is the severe undervaluation of issues on the stock market.

As we have seen in previous chapters, many companies are selling at historically low price/earnings multiples and at a considerable discount under book value. Moreover, as a recent article in *Institutional Investor* pointed out, many companies are doubly undervalued. Not only does their market price fall substantially below their book value, their book value itself carries assets at original cost—assets that would sell for far higher prices on the open market today.

Thus, paper companies such as Georgia-Pacific, Weyerhaeuser, and Boise-Cascade, which have all embarked on stock repurchases over the past few years, are "in effect buying back their own timberlands at a discount," as *Institutional Investor* put it.

Because, energy stocks plunged as much as 40% during the first half of 1980, many large oil companies—including Texaco and Gulf—also announced plans to buy their own stock.

Investment

Philip Roy, senior vice-president at Merck, which spends up to $50 million annually on stock repurchases, says, "We treat repurchasing just as we would treat any capital investment."

Merck, like most big companies, analyzes investments using the discounted-cash-flow method discussed in chapter 5: A company first calculates the expected cash flow from a project, and then discounts it to its present value. Using DCF, a company can compare the financial benefits of stock repurchases to alternative investments.

Stock repurchases can contribute directly to cash flow: The firm saves money by not having to pay dividends on the reacquired shares. Such dividend savings offer two big advantages:

—They are nontaxable (unlike interest earned on alternative investments).

—They are virtually risk-free.

Because of these features, stock repurchases can become attractive investments. In 1979, for example, Sears spent $180 million repurchasing 10 million shares. On these repurchases, Sears's vice-chairman Jack Kilcannon explained, "We made a 14% to 16% return, if you convert it to a pretax equivalent. It's not too easy to find returns equal to that these days."

Tax-Free Mergers

As previously discussed, the IRS considers a merger to be a tax-free reorganization if at least 50% of the purchase is for stock.

If a company's treasury lacks the shares needed "in house" to effect a merger, the company sometimes will turn to stock repurchases. To get the 1.7 million of its own shares it needed to acquire Webb Resources and Newco Exploration, for example, Standard Oil of Ohio made a $105-million tender offer in 1979. Similarly, in 1980, when Esmark announced that it would sell off its energy and fresh-meat businesses, the company said it would use the cash proceeds to buy back 50% of its outstanding shares, which it would then use to acquire other companies.

With the renewed popularity of stock in merger transactions, other companies will probably resort to similar stock repurchases in the future.

Avoidance of Takeovers

No contradiction here. The same factor that can make a company an active acquirer—cash surpluses—can also make it a takeover target.

Buying back shares offers a wary company several shelters from unwanted takeovers.

1. It uses up the cash surpluses that might attract hunters.
2. It makes the company too expensive to buy out. By boosting earnings per share and enhancing price/earnings ratios, buybacks can cure the undervaluing of shares that makes companies such vulnerable targets.
3. It eliminates disgruntled shareholders, unhappy over corporate performance, who might be the first to tender up their blocks of stock if an acquiring raider came along.

Balancing the Balance Sheet

According to investment bankers, companies are using stock repurchases to fine-tune their balance sheets. As Bruce Nolop of Morgan Stanley explains, "More and more companies are paying increasing attention to their capital structures and the appropriate relationship between debt and equity."

Just as some people believe in the "perfect mate," companies sometimes pursue an "ideal" debt/equity ratio—and use stock repurchases to bring their balance sheet into line.

Small Is Beautiful

Increasingly, companies have started questioning the old axiom that bigger is always better. Robert Salomon of Salomon Brothers observes: "There are so many companies that seek to be big—and do achieve bigness—but don't often achieve meaningful improvements in profitability. It's not clear that diversification is necessarily a good thing."

Salomon's point is well taken. Recent history has taught conglomerates some particularly brutal lessons. The 1970s witnessed several conglomerates faltering managerially with fingers in too many corporate pies, while other companies lost money propping up unprofitable subsidiaries. In fact, as Ralph Biggadike recounted in a recent *Harvard Business Review* article, conglomerates performed worse than their nondiversified counterparts.

Having observed the failings of so many conglomerates, many companies that might previously have become acquirers prefer to invest their money in a more risk-free proposition—their own stock.

Going Private

Some companies not only think that smaller is beautiful, they decide that private is prettier. For companies to go private, stock repurchase is the only alternative. Reasons for going private range from financial benefits to avoiding regulatory hassles.

General Maintenance

Sometimes corporate decisions to repurchase shares have less-exotic roots. Companies in need of shares for employee stock-option plans may prefer to buy back shares than to issue new stock, a procedure that dilutes equity. If the company reissues the stock, no changes in capitalization or shrinking of equity occurs. When Quaker Oats needed additional shares for its executive stock-option plan, it bought back 6% of its outstanding shares. Similarly, companies may require shares to meet obligations of their convertible securities. After raising the dividend on its common stock, U.S. Gypsum found itself flooded with shareholders of its convertible preferred stock who wanted to convert their preferred to Gypsum common stock. U.S. Gypsum bought the additional 1.6 million shares it needed in a tender offer and on the open market.

You Gotta Have Heart

At the very least, many experts think that stock buybacks indicate a corporate vote of confidence in its future—a way for a company to be its own best friend.

Myron Scholes, of the University of Chicago, comments: "The companies are putting their money where their mouth is, instead of just bellyaching."

STOCK REPURCHASES: SOME TIP-OFFS

In all probability, you won't be able to specifically identify a stock as a repurchase candidate, since repurchase tender offers look very much like merger tender offers. Similarly, repurchase candidates strongly resemble merger candidates.

Once again, we can paraphrase one of the fundamental laws of physics: Special situations cannot be either created or destroyed, but can change from one form to another. The same features that make a stock an attractive merger candidate—undervalued shares, cash surpluses—can also make a company a likely stock repurchaser. A company may either be bought out or take steps to avoid buyouts. It's the old law of the jungle: Kill or be killed; eat or be eaten.

The important point for stockholders to remember, however, is that *it doesn't matter.* Whether a company is acquired, or reacquires its own shares, stockholders will still realize tremendous profits.

Here's what to look for.

Undervalued stocks. Undervalued stocks have good repurchase potential for two reasons. First, their relatively low price makes them good investments. Second, with merger fever sweeping corporate America, repurchases can help forestall unwanted takeovers by improving stock price and earnings—making the company too expensive to buy out.

As with mergers, investors can identify undervalued stocks by comparing a stock's market value with

- its underlying adjusted book value;
- its value as indicated by the DCF method;
- various analysts' and brokerage house estimates of the stock's worth.

Companies that have repurchased in the past. A "try-it-you'll-like-it" philosophy seems to apply quite well to stock repurchases. A company that has undertaken repurchases once generally likes the results so well that it will use stock repurchases as a tool in the future. For example, to reduce its outstanding shares and to boost earnings, Teledyne used stock repurchases *on six occasions* between 1972 and 1979.

To find out which companies have repurchased their stock in the past, investors can check the *Wall Street Journal* index under "Reacquired Shares."

Cash cows. For companies that are net-cash generators—"cash cows"—buying back their own undervalued shares may be the best investment around.

Share repurchases have another advantage for companies with cash surpluses: Cash surpluses provide tempting bait for prospective acquirers; by repurchasing their own shares, companies can consume the excess cash before they themselves are consumed.

To help determine whether a cash-rich company might reacquire its own shares, Oppenheimer vice-president E. Michael Metz recommends that investors examine how the company currently uses its cash flow. This information appears in the annual report in the section titled "Statement of Changes in Financial Position," alternatively known as the "Sources and Uses of Funds" statement.

According to Metz, the most important clue will lie in a comparison of the capital expenditures with the depreciation figures. If depreciation is running higher than capital expenditures, the company is throwing off a lot of excess cash. This is a good sign for share reacquisitions.

Investors should also examine the company's "Ten-Year Review" to check whether its return on capital is increasing or decreasing. If a firm's return on capital is rising, it means not only that the company is generating excess cash, but also that it's an attractive industry to be in.

Low debt/equity ratio. Since equity is generally considered the most expensive form of capital, a comparatively low debt/equity ratio suggests that a company might not be managing its debt aggressively enough. Such companies may then resort to stock repurchases to bring their ratios into line.

Financial strength. Extensive stock repurchases can enhance corporate performance during good times—and put a company in the poorhouse during bad times. Therefore, only companies with generally strong balance sheets (as indicated by the financial ratios discussed in chapter 3) will usually have reacquisition potential.

The major risk of stock repurchases is the increased volatility in the price of the remaining shares because there are fewer outstanding shares to be traded. Teledyne, for example, sometimes trades up or down as much as 8 points in a day. Similarly, Monogram Industries, which repurchased about 60% of its shares between 1973 and 1981, can gain 4¾ in one day on a volume of less than 40,000 shares. In a down market, the shares would decline just as rapidly. If churning prices turn your stomach, volatile stocks don't belong in your portfolio. Or, if you must play the game, limit their presence in your portfolio to 5%–10%.

Furthermore, if a company's earnings nose-dive after a stock repurchase, the company might find itself with a precariously high debt/equity ratio. Although a too-low debt/equity ratio indicates that a company might not be maximizing profits, a too-high debt/equity ratio is even worse. It might lead to the ultimate disgrace for a company's chief financial officer: downgrading of the corporate bond rating. Said one executive with a shiver, "I can't think of anything worse for a CFO than to have your rating pulled. That sends cold sweat right down my back."

Less financially buoyant companies may also suffer if a recession follows upon the heels of a buyback. As business slows and receivables drag out from 30 to 60 to 90 days, smaller firms frequently discover that they could have used the excess cash as a safety net.

WHAT KINDS OF COMPANIES WILL NOT REACQUIRE?

Companies will generally not reacquire their shares if a possible unfriendly suitor owns a big block of stock. If the company repurchases shares but the potential acquirer does not tender, the acquirer's toehold in the target will increase proportionately, which strengthens its position in a takeover bid. Repurchases also reduce the absolute number of shares a buyer needs to gain control.

Nevertheless, this guideline shouldn't deter or discourage special-situation investors. After all, the company still has rich potential as a *merger* candidate.

However, investors should watch out if their reacquisition acquires another company itself. As previously discussed, a cash-rich company may either be a merger target, reacquire shares, or become an acquirer itself. Once a company buys another, its potential as a stock-repurchase candidate drops sharply because the acquisition generally uses up the cash previously available for share reacquisition. Although corporate managers intellectually understand the advantages of share repurchases, emotionally they long for growth. In 1979, for example, Transamerica canceled its plan to repurchase its shares to instead rescue Interway from an unwanted takeover. As Blair Pascoe, senior vice-president of Transamerica, comments, "The repurchase made sense numerically, but instead of shrinking the company, we were able to expand it, and that's always better."

Is there any way for an investor to predict which way a cash cow will jump: become a merger target, reacquire shares, or become an acquirer itself?

Not really, says E. Michael Metz of Oppenheimer. He recommends that you "try to determine as much as possible what management's interests are. Try to find a company where management interests parallel those of shareholders." This isn't usually true of family-run companies, or companies where management has fancy salaries and comfortable perks but owns very little stock in the company itself. Management's interests will probably mirror shareholders', Metz says, if corporate executives have themselves bought shares in the company on the open market. They'll be delighted to see the value of those shares go up.

Investors can get information about how much stock management owns from a company's proxy statement.

The length of time an investor should cling to a candidate while awaiting a buyback depends upon feel—"like a safecracker's fingers," one investor quipped. According to professionals, only practical experience in the Wall Street arena—the ability to say, "Hey, I've seen this repurchase pattern before" —can give some limited predictive ability. If you get tired of waiting for something to happen in a stock and you won't be losing money on it, you might as well sell and seek new investment opportunities.

Warning Signals

Additional information about warning signals that may foreshadow problems in reacquisitions, and about hedging techniques investors can use as safety nets, will be covered in chapter 11.

HOW REACQUISITIONS WORK

The SEC requires companies to file 13E-4 reports disclosing planned stock repurchases. The requirement also applies to a company's affiliates and corporate insiders. Companies planning to "go private" must submit 13E-3 filings. Investors can obtain information on 13E-3 and 13E-4 filings through the SEC.

In most cases, however, both shareholders and other investors generally first learn of a company's reacquisition plans through the daily financial press, which will carry articles and/or "tombstone" ads announcing the plans. Subsequently, shareholders are notified by mail.

The offeror must provide shareholders with stacks of information, including the reason for the buyback. On the last point, companies typically remain closemouthed: "General corporate purposes" is one popular explanation. For open-market purchases, a company must also disclose motives, if they are "material."

Tender offers for repurchases operate in much the same way as those for mergers. The offer has both a proration and withdrawal date and will usually specify a maximum number of shares to be repurchased. If the offer is oversubscribed, the company may accept shares received by the proration date on a pro-rata basis, although sometimes the company will decided to purchase all tendered shares even though it is not legally compelled to do so. Unless a stock repurchase is part of a plan to go private, you won't see the athletic bidding wars that characterize mergers. What you see is what you get: The initial offer is the price at which the company will buy back its shares, payment for which is usually made a week or two after the withdrawal date.

Because announced repurchases are virtually assured of going through, the stock's price rapidly rises to the level of the tender offer. Generally, the average investor won't find it profitable to buy a repurchase candidate after the announcement; the potential for profit is just too small.

Should Shareholders Always Tender?

Yes.

Stock prices typically fall off after a company completes its repurchases. If you still believe in a stock, you're usually best off tendering, getting your money, then waiting for the stock price to fall off, as it usually will. You can buy in again—more cheaply—and there's the possibility that the company will buy back more shares in the future, thus giving you additional potential profits.

One successful investor says: "There's a saying on Wall Street: 'Bulls make money, bears make money, but pigs don't make money.' Don't stick with a stock, hoping to wring every last cent of profit out of it. Take the money and run to a new stock, where you can make $20—instead of holding out for an additional $2 profit on one you already own."

TAX ADVANTAGES

People frequently compare stock repurchases to cash dividends, since both involve a cash flow from the company to common shareholders.

However, stock repurchases offer shareholders an important tax advantage: The proceeds from repurchases are generally taxed at the lower captial-gains rate—compared to dividends, which are taxed as ordinary income in their entirety. Buybacks thus help avoid the so-called double taxation of dividends, in which corporations pay taxes on their profits and then shareholders pay taxes on dividends received.

Teledyne's chairman Henry Singleton, for one, cites this double taxation as one reason behind his company's extensive stock repurchases. Despite the fact that Teledyne has been one of Wall Street's best performers, the company has never paid a cash dividend.

Investors should be aware that under Section 302 of the U.S. Tax Code, the IRS can treat stock repurchases as the equivalent of cash dividends. Robert Willens, a partner at Peat, Marwick, Mitchell, explains the three benchmarks that the IRS uses in determining whether a shareholder's repurchase profits qualify as capital gains.

1. If a shareholder sells back his or her entire holding in the repurchase, profits will be treated as capital gains.

2. If a shareholder "meaningfully" reduces (i.e., by at least 20%) his or her holdings, profits will be treated as capital gains.

3. For minor shareholders of major corporations, the IRS has ruled that any reduction in share ownership is meaningful. For example, if you own ten shares of IBM, which had 583,807,000 shares outstanding in April 1981, which you tender during a repurchase offer, and IBM takes even one of your shares, those profits will qualify as capital gains.

If a company says, "We are willing to buy ten percent of everyone's shares," Willens cautions shareholders against tendering only 5% of their holdings, since their proportional stake in the company would increase. "Surrender at least as much stock as everyone else," he advises.

If investors own shares of stock through their own corporation, they should remember that the tax laws treat a company's dividend income more favorably than its capital gains. (This benefit holds for professional corporations as well as general business corporations.) For corporations, the effective tax rate on capital gains is 28%, while the maximum effective tax rate for dividends is only 6.9%. Therefore, Willens recommends that corporations tendering shares during reacquisitions surrender a *disproportionately small* amount of stock, to ensure that their profits receive dividend treatment.

Willens also describes a very special type of reacquisition: the partial liquidation.

In a partial liquidation, a company first substantially reduces its activities through divestiture(s), and then distributes the proceeds to its shareholders by repurchasing their shares on a pro-rata basis. By a "substantial" reduction, the IRS means an average 15% reduction in a company's sales, assets, or number of employees.

The IRS has ruled that shareholder proceeds from partial

liquidations always qualify as capital gains, even if shareholders tender a disproportionately small percentage of their stock.

A company will state that a redemption is part of a partial liquidation at the time that it announces the deal, so stockholders will know how profits will be taxed before they tender their stock.

8

Going to Pieces: The Spinoff

If mergers illustrate synergy—the belief that 1 + 1 can add up to 3—then spinoffs demonstrate negative synergy. Through spinoffs, as a recent article in *Dun's Review* explained, 1 − 1 can also equal 3. When split apart, the sum of a company's various parts may be worth more than the whole.

A spinoff occurs when a parent company sets up one of its subsidiaries as a separate entity and distributes shares in it to the existing shareholders of the parent.

Spinoffs have increased in popularity in recent years. During the early 1970s, spinoffs crawled along at an average of two to three per year. By 1979, that figure had climbed to nearly a dozen. Observers expect that the number of spinoffs will continue to increase, with Oppenheimer & Company's executive vice-president Nathan Gantcher predicting, "The 1980s will be the 'deconglomerating' era."

Current spinoffs differ from those of the 1960s, when companies most often used them to get rid of small, money-losing operations. Today the "spin-ees" are frequently fast-growing subsidiaries in glamour industries that typically outperform their corporate parents.

Why do some companies spin off a rapidly growing subsidiary rather than keep it in-house? The reasons vary.

Increased Value

Even though a subsidiary may be highly profitable, Wall Street may not value the company and the subsidiary at "real" value. According to some observers, confusion about what highly diversified companies actually *do* may be the reason. Donald J. Mitchell, who heads a Cambridge, Massachusetts, management consulting firm, says, "When a firm is too diverse, investors have a hard time analyzing it." With conglomerates, analysts have a hard time answering such basic questions as "What industry is a firm in?" "Who are its chief competitors?" Because analyzing diversified companies is so complex, many investors prefer simply to stay away. Norman Weinger of Oppenheimer & Company states: "The thicker the annual report, the lower the price-earnings multiple."

Through spinoffs, a company clarifies its image—and frequently boosts its stock price as a result. According to Oppenheimer's Nathan Gantcher, "If you've got a piece of paper worth $20, you could have two pieces worth $40 [each] after a spinoff."

Spinoffs can enhance value for both the parent company and the subsidiary. Interestingly, although the former subsidiary is typically smaller than its parent, it generally outperforms the parent. A study by *Forbes* in 1968 and a follow-up in 1979 revealed that shares of the spun-off companies generally increase in value more rapidly than those of their parents. From 1969 to 1978, the price of the parents' shares rose by 99%, while their corporate children's shares grew by 133%.

Due in part to such excellent performance, one entrepreneur, Glenn W. Bailey, has gone into the spinoff business. Bailey, chairman and chief executive officer of Keene Corporation, a miniconglomerate producer of bearings, light fixtures, and insulation, formed a holding company called Bairnco, with Keene as its first—and, for a while, its only—subsidiary. According to Bailey's plans, Bairnco will eventually buy up other small growth companies, which it will spruce up and then spin off in whole or part to Bairnco's stockholders. Moving to implement its plans, Bairnco made tender offers for Ludlow Corporation (unsuccessful) and Lightolier (successful) in the summer of 1981.

Will Bairnco's spinoff plans fly? "You never know if you don't try," a recent *Forbes* article concluded.

Avoidance of Takeovers

Remember the old "Peanuts" cartoon of Linus sucking his thumb, clasping his security blanket, and sighing, "There's no heavier burden than a great potential"?

For many companies, unrealized potential—in the form of undervalued shares—has caused weighty takeover problems. As we've previously seen, undervalued companies are tantalizing prey for prowling acquirers. To defend itself against possible takeovers, a company may:

—Itself become an acquirer, to burn up excess cash or help boost its stock price.

—Divest, and then use the proceeds to reacquire its own shares, which can help improve a company's earnings-per-share and stock price.

—Spin off a subsidiary, to help close the gap between the company's "real" value and its market price.

"You don't realize what a sitting duck your corporation is," Coastal Corporation's chairman Oscar S. Wyatt, Jr., told employees at a closed-door meeting in May 1981. Wyatt was referring to rumors that Coastal, a refiner and marketer of oil and natural gas, was a prime takeover target. The speculation had caused Coastal's stock to soar from $29 in early April to $41 by the end of May.

To head off the takeover rumors, Coastal launched a study to determine whether it should spin off portions of its assets and operations to shareholders. As Coastal president Harry L. Blomquist, Jr., explained, the study will help decide if "Coastal should become three or four companies instead of one."

Coastal was no stranger to spinoffs. In January 1980, Coastal had spun off Valero Energy Corporation as part of a negotiated settlement with its customers, to resolve some $1.6 billion in lawsuits. According to various analysts' reports issued in the spring of 1980, a breakup of the rest of Coastal might yield a combined value of more than $90 a share—more than double the stock's price in June 1981.

Indeed, Coastal is not the only energy company whose undervalued shares have acquisition allure. Stock prices in June 1981, in the midst of the Conoco bidding frenzy, spotlighted the vulnerability of several oil issues.

Interestingly enough, the most undervalued oil companies were the fully integrated ones—those with extensive refining and marketing operations as well as exploration and production facilities. A study by Kurt Wulff, an oil analyst with Donaldson, Lufkin & Jenrette, found that recent stock prices for the ten largest integrated oil companies averaged *less than one-third* of their theoretical present value. In contrast, shares of companies that specialized in exploration-only traded at nearly four-fifths of their present value. "The more diversified the company," Wulff notes, "the bigger the discount."

Table 13, a chart compiled by Donaldson, Lufkin & Jenrette and reprinted from *Forbes,* shows the discounts from "real" value at which some oil and gas companies are selling.

Such "assets-in-distress" beckon to ravenous acquirers, and many Wall Street professionals expect that other oil companies will soon undergo "the Conoco syndrome." According to Kurt Wulff, "the best defense against moves like that is to get your stock price up on your own by restructuring. . . . If [companies] don't do it on their own, someone will do it for them."

Increased Price/Earnings Multiple

Due to wide price/earnings differences among industries, with "growth" or "glamour" sectors rating much higher P/E's than "mature" industries, a company might spin off a subsidiary in a glamour industry to allow it to take advantage of the higher price/earnings multiple it could command on its own. For example, Lanier Business Products, a manufacturer of business machines such as tiny portable dictating units, grew out of Oxford Industries, an apparel manufacturer. While the going price/earnings ratio for business machines is a healthy 12–14, apparel manufacturers merit a pedestrian 6–8.

By freeing up a powerful P/E multiple, a parent company does more than allow its child to reach a handsome stock price;

TABLE 13
Better off in pieces?

How much of a drag refining and marketing are on integrated companies' stocks is shown in the numbers below. The integrated oils are selling at much deeper discounts from the value of their oil and gas properties than nonintegrated companies. The judgment is confirmed in the higher premiums over understated book value for nonintegrated companies.

COMPANIES	RECENT STOCK PRICE	PRESENT VALUE*	STOCK PRICE AS % OF PRESENT VALUE	BOOK VALUE	STOCK PRICE AS % OF BOOK VALUE
Integrated					
Sun	33⅞	$130	26%	$34.38	99%
Getty	66½	250	27	50.44	132
Standard of Indiana	55¼	205	27	32.10	172
Standard of Ohio	48⅛	170	28	18.57	259
Atlantic Richfield	47	170	28	29.96	157
Phillips Petroleum	37¾	130	29	32.44	116
Marathon	60	210	29	31.97	188
Cities Service	47¼	130	36	30.96	153
Shell	44⅞	120	37	26.21	171
Conoco	65	147	44	42.45	153
Nonintegrated					
General American Oil	37¼	67	56	15.75	237
Natomas	26½	43	62	16.17	164
Southland Royalty	24⅝	40	62	2.30	1,070
Louisiana Land	36⅜	55	66	19.63	185
Superior Oil	184⅜	270	68	71.04	260
Williams Cos	28⅜	40	71	32.49	87
Mitchell Energy	28½	32	89	5.96	478
Helmerich & Payne	44	49	90	9.28	474
Mesa Petroleum	25¼	28	90	7.59	333
Texas Oil & Gas	35½	25	142	5.50	645

*Per-share value of oil and gas properties if sold separately.

SOURCE: *Donaldson, Lufkin & Jenrette*

in turn, the former subsidiary's higher stock price can enable it to embark on acquisitions beyond the parent company's means.

As Arthur Ainsberg of Oppenheimer & Company points

out, "If your [parent company's] stock is four times earnings and you get spun off as a division growing twenty-five percent a year and take a fifteen multiple in The Street, it's much easier to acquire for stock."

Harold Owen, president of Pengo Industries, which was spun off from Gearhart Industries in 1978, expressed a similar point of view: "We're doing better since the spinoff largely because of acquisitions, which is something we could do only as an independent."

The Thrill Is Gone

Mergers, like marriages, don't always work out. Companies, too, can "grow apart."

Take Engelhard Industries, which merged with Minerals and Chemicals Philipp, Inc., in 1967 to form Engelhard Minerals and Chemicals. The merger had seemed like a marriage made in heaven: Philipp, a leading world marketer of ores, metals, minerals, and other commodities, would help finance Engelhard, a producer of precious metals, chemicals, and mineral products. But after fourteen years together, Engelhard and Philipp Brothers called it quits in May 1981. "The synergy that brought us together is gone," said David Tendler, Engelhard's vice-chairman.

The mode of the divorce: a spinoff. Under the terms of the spinoff, shareholders received 100 shares of Philipp Brothers and 40 shares of Engelhard (a tax-free new issue) in exchange for every 100 shares of Engelhard.

Among the factors contributing to the Engelhard/Philipp Brothers breakup:

—Different growth rates. When Engelhard and Philipp Brothers merged in 1967, the two companies were roughly the same size. But the Philipp Brothers trading company soon began growing and rapidly outpaced Engelhard's industrial operations. Although labeled a division of Engelhard, Philipp Brothers contributed nearly 90% of Engelhard's total sales and profits in 1980. "We were the tail on the beast," said Irving Isko, chief executive of the spun-off Engelhard Corporation.

—Different business mentalities. Engelhard's operations demanded long-term planning and research and development, while Philipp Brothers could make or lose millions in minutes from a few cents' fluctuation in world commodity prices. Explains Engelhard's Isko, "If you're in the trading business, you don't have the mentality for spending ten years to develop a catalyst. You think you could make the same amount in three weeks of trading."

However, Philipp Brothers apparently believes that mergers may be lovelier the second time around. In the fall of 1981, the company bought Salomon Brothers, the nation's largest privately held investment banking firm.

Working Their Assets Harder

In the 1960s, conglomerates were the golden children of Wall Street, commanding price/earnings multiples of nearly 50 times earnings. By the early 1970s, the boom went bust: A pet conglomerate such as Litton Industries, which had sold for a high-flying $120.375 (43 times earnings) in 1967, shriveled to $2.875 (2 times earnings) in 1974.

Even today, many conglomerate has-beens still own doggy divisions acquired during the glory years. With today's high interest rates, these corporate losers have become increasingly expensive to subsidize. Therefore, more and more conglomerates are "unbundling"—selling or spinning off unprofitable divisions.

As Donald H. Ruttenberg, head of Studebaker-Worthington, explained: "Back in the late 1960s and early 1970s, you got paid—in the form of multiples—if you produced earnings. Now, unbundling those assets may, in certain cases, yield greater aggregate values for shareholders."

The $2-billion Philadelphia-based IU International Corporation was a typical conglomerate; its operations embraced everything from macadamia nuts to the nation's second-largest trucking fleet. The Gotaas-Larsen shipping operation had been one of the jewels of IU's empire, accounting for 75% of the parent's earnings in 1973. However, the collapse of the spot tanker market in 1975 swamped the shipping subsidiary in a sea of red ink. Soon the shipping operation was draining IU's resources to the tune of $100 million annually.

In late 1979, the conglomerate decided to spin off Gotaas-Larsen to its shareholders, giving 1 share of Gotaas-Larsen for every 3 shares of IU owned. Once freed of its capital-hungry problem child, IU could turn its attentions, and its cash, to strengthening its other lines of business—with profitable results.

At the time of the spinoff, IU sold for $13.75. Less than a year later, the combined value of IU and Gotaas-Larsen holdings was about $18.625—a 35% gain.

Backs to the Wall

Sometimes, companies spin off divisions because they have no other choice.

In 1979, for example, Coastal States Gas found itself up to its neck in hot water. During the 1960s, the company had entered into long-term, fixed-cost contracts to supply natural gas. When natural-gas prices doubled in 1973, Coastal tried to pass along the cost increases to its customers—and was immediately zapped with $1.6 billion in lawsuits. Faced with almost certain defeat in the courts and possible bankruptcy, Coastal was force to spin off a large chunk of its business to the angry customers and its shareholders. The spinoff—the largest in U.S. history—created Valero Energy Corporation, which instantly became the largest natural-gas pipeline company in Texas, with $1 billion in sales and $700 million in assets.

Former Coastal customers got 55% of the new Valero, while Coastal stockholders were given one Valero share for every Coastal share they owned. Coastal States Gas also changed its name to Coastal Corporation.

Much to Coastal's surprise, the spinoff benefited all concerned. Coastal stock, which had traded as low as $5 in 1978, rose to $25 within two months of the spinoff. Also within two months of the spinoff, the fledgling Valero Energy Corporation traded at $15—with keen investor interest in the issue frequently placing it on the most-active list. As Valero president and chief executive officer William Greehey explained, "The spinoff not only resolved the customers' problems, but gave shareholders a big value for their investment."

THE TIP-OFFS

In 1980, according to W. T. Grimm, a Chicago-based financial consulting firm, there were 1,889 mergers. In contrast, there were less than half a dozen rumored or actual spinoffs —among them M-G-M, Safeguard Industries/SBS, and General Tire/RKO.

As these numbers indicate, spinoffs, although they have become increasingly popular, are not exactly a dime a dozen. Because of the mere handful of spinoffs that occur each year, many investment advisers recommend that investors interested in pursuing this special situation use a different strategy from that of picking candidates for mergers or reacquisitions. *Instead of trying to select future spinoff candidates, wait until a company* announces *it is considering a spinoff.* Then, and *only* then, decide whether or not to speculate on the spinoff.

As Stanley Sanders, former president of Haas Securities, points out, "No professional investor tries to find a spinoff candidate in advance—because spinoffs happen so rarely. By trying to identify companies with spinoff potential, an investor will waste a lot of time and money trying to nail down something that seldom happens." Worse, Sanders goes on to say, the parent companies that might consider spinoffs tend to be in mature, regulated industries or have lackluster P/E ratios. In short, they're unattractive investments on their own. If a spinoff failed to materialize, investors would probably find themselves holding shares in a real dog.

Although an investor sacrifices some profits by waiting until a company announces spinoff plans, the loss isn't very great. Table 14 shows the prices of some parent companies one month before the spinoff announcement, on the date of the announcement, and on the day the spinoff was completed.

While trying to spot spinoff candidates in advance is risky, knowing what *kinds* of companies tend to spin off subsidiaries

TABLE 14
Effects of Spinoff on Price

PARENT COMPANY (Subsidiary)	DATE OF ANNCMT.	PARENT'S PRICE ONE MONTH BEFORE SPINOFF ANNOUNCEMENT	PARENT'S PRICE ON DATE OF SPINOFF ANNOUNCEMENT	PRICE OF PARENT AND SUBSIDIARY ON DATE SPINOFF COMPLETED	DATE OF COMPLETION
COASTAL CORP. (Valero Energy)	11/12/79	$24.75	$29.375	35.50 + 11.00 $46.50	12/31/79
SAFEGUARD IND. (Safeguard Bus. Systems)	6/18/79	$13.25	$16.625	28.75 + 23.75 $52.50	3/4/80
ENGELHARD MINERALS & CHEMS. (Engelhard Corp.)	3/25/81	41.75	53.00	42.25 + 28.75 $71.00	5/26/81

can help an investor decide whether an announced spinoff will actually go through. Here, then, are some guidelines for recognizing spinoff candidates:

Undervalued Companies

Undervaluing of shares—a stock selling at a market price significantly below its "real" or book value—is probably the single biggest tip-off to a stock with special-situation potential —either for mergers, share reacquisitions, liquidations, or spinoffs.

As previously explained, spinoffs can help a company realize the "true" value of its shares by enabling the parent to devote its time and capital to other, more profitable lines of business and helping the company to clarify its image.

Finally, there's the synergic twist that "the sum of the parts is greater than the whole." Following a spinoff, the market may value the separate stocks of a parent company and its former subsidiary more highly than it did the shares of the former parent alone.

By enabling a company to increase the value of its shares, spinoffs can help achieve two important corporate objectives: to increase the return to shareholders, and also, in doing so, to make the company less attractive as a merger candidate.

Regulated Industries

Companies may spin off subsidiaries to meet or beat out regulatory requirements.

The Bank Holding Company Act and the Public Utility Holding Company Act, both of 1935, brought banks and gas and electric utilities, respectively, under federal regulation. As a consequence, both acts spawned hundreds of spinoffs— which have since become an increasingly popular way for companies to escape regulatory requirements.

Recently, for example, General Tire and Rubber spun off its RKO General subsidiary in hopes that this would resolve its massive troubles with the FCC.

Through RKO, General Tire and Rubber owned four TV stations and twelve radio stations—franchises frequently described as "licenses to print money." In January 1980, however, the FCC stripped RKO of three of those licenses when it ruled that the company was unfit to run three of its television stations—in New York, Boston, and Los Angeles. The reason: transgressions by RKO's parent, General Tire—which allegedly included political payoffs, bribes, and antitrust violations. According to many observers, the FCC decision was one of the harshest ever delivered by that regulatory agency. It marked the first time the FCC denied licenses because of the *nonbroadcast* sins of a parent company.

With its remaining TV license (in Memphis) and twelve radio-station licenses in jeopardy, General Tire proposed spinning off the broadcast properties to its shareholders. Unfortunately, the dark clouds hovering over RKO have yet to yield any silver linings. In 1980 the FCC voted against the spinoff proposal. General Tire has stated it will try to rework the proposal and obtain FCC approval.

Another example. During the summer of 1981, two gas companies in the Midwest announced spinoffs that could shake up the structure of the industry. Both companies—Peoples Energy Corporation of Chicago and American Natural Resources Company of Detroit—plan to spin off their more profitable gas-production and transmission operations from their less lucrative and onerously regulated utility activities.

By spinning off the money-making gas-production and transmission activities, the companies would sidestep state regulatory commission requirements that earnings of nonutility subsidiaries be taken into consideration in determining utility rates. Once the utility operations are viewed on their own, according to the companies, they'll have an easier time persuading public rate commissions to grant increases.

Eugene A. Tracy, chairman-designate of Peoples Energy, commented: "The distinction makes it a lot clearer. The combined earnings of the companies distorted our condition, and state regulators confused the utilities with the nonregulated operations."

Although companies in regulated industries have spinoff potential, they may also have difficulty obtaining regulatory approval, as with the General Tire/RKO example. Similarly, because of the extensive public outcry against its proposals, the Peoples Energy plan was stalled, due to legal problems, as this book went to press.

Companies with Fast-growing Subsidiaries in Glamour Industries

A recent *Forbes* magazine article about spinoffs hypothesized that if Wall Street loves high-technology and energy stocks, it might become enamored of spinoffs in those industries, too.

Forbes identified nine diversified companies with subsidiaries in very fashionable industries—industries distinct from the parent company's main product line. Because very few of the parent companies would release operating data for the subsidiaries, sales and earnings figures are estimated in table 15.

Standing on its own, a high-growth subsidiary can generally command a higher price/earnings multiple than its parent. By spinning off its RKO broadcasting subsidiary, for example, General Tire not only hoped to cure its regulatory hassles with the FCC, but also hoped that an independent RKO would merit the flashier P/E multiple of 12, common in the pure broadcast industry, rather than the tired multiple of 6–7, for a tire manufacturer. Such a P/E play could double the price of the stock even without an increase in earnings.

Spinning off rapid-growth subsidiaries in industries with bright futures also has managerial importance. Frequently, the fledgling companies prosper better with entrepreneurial management than under the corporate wing. Large, diversified companies tend to have large, bureaucratic decision-making styles—unsuited to the fast-changing needs of growth industries.

High-Debt Parent Company/Capital-Intensive Subsidiary

Sometimes the decision to spin off is made to maximize borrowing power. If a parent has a high debt/equity ratio, it may find itself unable to quell the financial hunger pangs of a capital-intensive subsidiary. Freed from the burden of its for-

TABLE 15
Spinoff Possibilities?

If the stock market loves energy and high-technology stocks, then perhaps it will love spinoffs in those two industries, too. Here are nine companies with subsidiaries in these hot industries that are separate from the parent company's main product line. Sales and earnings figures for the subsidiaries are mostly estimates because only a few of the companies would release actual figures.

COMPANY POSSIBLE SPINOFF	PRINCIPAL BUSINESS	RECENT PRICE	PRICE/ EARNINGS RATIO	LATEST 12 MONTHS		
				SALES (MILLIONS)	EARNINGS (MILLIONS)	EARNINGS PER SHARE
Cabot Corp	chemicals, energy, engineered products	28⅞	5.9	$1,404	$153	$4.88
energy group	explor, dev and prod of oil and gas			399	52	1.64
Control Data	computer equipment and services	65	8.4	2,670	132	7.77
Service Bureau Corp	computer services			230	13	1.73
WR Grace	chems, natural resources, consumer prods	53¾	8.9	5,873	282	6.07
natural resources division	oil and gas			690	108	2.31
Mead Corp	paper products	25⅞	5.1	2,647	135	5.10
Mead Data Central	electronic information services			20	7	0.27
Mountain Fuel Supply	natural gas utility	44½	10.2	391	32	4.38
Wexpro	oil and gas explor and prod			50	11	1.46
Norlin	musical instruments, beer, electronics	14¼	NM	275	d2	d0.80
technology group	electronics			58	4	4.78
Quaker Oats	food processing	30⅝	6.8	2,473	95	4.48
Fisher-Price Toys	toys			380	34	1.68
Warner Communications	movies, records, television programs	37⅞	9.5	1,873	218	3.95
Atari, Inc	electronic games and microcomputers			400	48	0.87
Westburne Intl Industries	plumbing equipment, energy	22¼	5.1	918	34	4.40
Westburne Petroleum Serv	oil and gas drill and explor, oil field equip			183	12	1.75

d: deficit NM: not meaningful

mer parent's debt, the subsidiary can borrow to meet its own needs.

HOW A SPINOFF WORKS

Investors first learn about a company's spinoff intentions via a formal announcement. Generally, the spinoff announcement appears in the financial press, with company shareholders usually receiving notification by mail.

Because of the rarity of spinoffs, most investors will prefer to get involved after formal announcement. In deciding whether to speculate on a proposed spinoff, investors should check the formal announcement for several important pieces of information:

—Is the company planning a spinoff—or *only studying* the possibility of a spinoff? Obviously, an *actual* spinoff decision has more certainty of happening than a *considered* spinoff.

—What are the terms of the spinoff? How many shares of the subsidiary will investors receive for each share owned of the parent?

—Does the planned spinoff require shareholder approval? Most spinoffs do. If so, an investor should become an investigator and check whether a major stockholder might want to oppose the deal. Newspaper articles or a call to your broker should help provide the information.

—Is the spinoff tax-free? As we'll discuss later on, spinoffs are generally tax-free. Before announcing a spinoff, or spinoff intention, most companies get an advance ruling from the IRS concerning the deal's tax status. This information will usually appear in the spinoff announcement.

—Must the spinoff meet regulatory approval? If so, you may be in for a long wait before profits come dancing your way. General Tire has talked about spinning off RKO since 1976. Investors who bought General Tire back then at $25 are still standing at the altar. Slightly poorer, actually, in light of the dollar's decline since then: In late September 1981, General Tire still traded at around $24 to $25.

   Naturally, potential profits are among an investors most important considerations in determining whether or not to buy stock in a spinoff candidate.

   To determine potential profits, investors should first calculate the stock price of the subsidiary on its own. A company's 10-K (and sometimes its annual report as well) will break down its earnings and profits according to lines of business. To translate these figures into a stock price for the subsidiary, investors then use conventional security analysis. How do the subsidiary's *earnings, assets, growth rate,* and *market position* compare to the rest of the industry?

   Next, calculate how much the parent company might sell for after spinning off the subsidiary. Here's a quick way to arrive at a rough guesstimate:

   Let's say that Farblondget Industries makes baby food—worth a P/E of 7 because it's a declining industry. However, Farblondget's high-technology subsidiary manufactures biomedical devices of an incomprehensible nature. Using the market's rule of thumb—the higher the technology, the higher the multiple—Farblondget Biomedical should have a P/E of 30.

   The most recent annual report tells you that Farblondget Biomedical contributed $1 per share to the company's $5-per-share earnings. The company's stock is now selling at $40.

   Your calculations look like this:

	Earnings Per Share	Stock Price	P/E Multiple
Entire Company	$5	$40	?

And you find, when you divide the stock price by its earnings per share, that its P/E multiple is 8.

   Now you break out the company by its divisions:

Division	Earnings Contributed		Estimated P/E		Estimated Stock Value
Industries	$4	(×)	7	(=)	$28
Biomedical	$1	(×)	30	(=)	$30
					$58

You conclude that Biomedical's contribution to earnings is being ignored by the market. According to your calculations, the company's parts are worth $58, and it's selling at $40—a 31% discount from its estimated value. Even if you allow a discount of 8 points (15%) from the company's estimated market value if it were spun off into its component parts, the $40 price still seems like a good deal.

Combined, the projected stock prices of the parent and the subsidiary approximate your potential return after the spinoff. Now, you must compare this value with the present stock price of the company. Is the potential reward great enough to justify the risk (that the spinoff will fall through or stall endlessly; that the projected prices will fall short of expectations)?

To give you a better feel for spinoffs, let's work through a real-life example: the 1980 spinoff of Metro-Goldwyn-Mayer into M-G-M Film and M-G-M Grand Hotels.

October 1, 1979. M-G-M sold for $19.25.
November 1, 1979. M-G-M sold for $18.00.
November 15, 1979. Opening the *Wall Street Journal* this morning, an investor would have been greeted by the following headline: "M-G-M May Split Its Operations into Two Companies."

According to the article, M-G-M was "very seriously" considering restructuring the company into two separate, publicly traded companies: one to operate the hotel-casino activities, the other to handle movie and TV production.

An investor reading the article would note the following key points:

—M-G-M was studying the feasibility of the spinoff—not actually announcing it.

—The company announced that a shareholder would receive one share of the new film-company stock for each share owned of the old M-G-M.

—Any spinoff would require shareholder approval.

—Although the deal's tax-free status had not yet been verified with the IRS, the company thought that it would be tax-free.

—Any spinoff would require regulatory approval from the

state gambling commissions in Nevada and New Jersey, where M-G-M has or has planned operations.

The article also contained some interesting background on the proposed spinoff. Nearly point-for-point, M-G-M matched the profile of a company that might consider a spinoff:

—*A company with a fast-growing subsidiary in a glamour industry.* M-G-M's gambling operations had begun to overshadow the film activities that originally gave birth to the company. In 1979, hotel and gaming accounted for about 60% of M-G-M's $491 million in revenues. Following a spinoff, as Anthony M. Hoffman, an analyst at Bache Halsey Stuart Shields, Inc., pointed out, the pure gambling company was likely to "sell at a higher price-earnings multiple." Consequently, the gambling-only company could more easily "raise equity with less dilution to support M-G-M's new hotel-casino in Atlantic City, New Jersey, and for expansion of M-G-M hotel-casino operations in Reno and Las Vegas."

—*Undervalued shares.* Some analysts believed that the razzle-dazzle of M-G-M's hotel-casinos prevented the market from valuing the film operations at their intrinsic worth. Said one: "If you accept predictions about the coming video revolution, M-G-M's huge film library has a tremendous value and would get more attention from investors in a separate movie company."

—*Regulated industry.* Gambling is a regulated industry—and an intensely regulated one. Due to the stringent requirements of Nevada and New Jersey gambling authorities, M-G-M's film executives had to undergo the same personal scrutiny as the company's hotel-casino managers—even though the film people had little if any direct involvement on the gambling side. A spinoff would alleviate this problem.

Just from the morning paper, then, an investor can get a sense of the riskiness of the M-G-M spinoff's falling apart. Clearly, there was a moderate risk.

Next, an investor should calculate how much the M-G-M spinoff might be worth.

Using the same technique as in the Farblondget example, first we take M-G-M's 1979 earnings per share of $2.02 and divide them between the hotel/gaming operations, which accounted for about 60% of M-G-M's profits, and the film company, which accounted for about 40% of M-G-M's profits:

For Hotel/Gaming:
$2.02 × .60 = $1.21

For Film Company:
$2.02 × .40 = $0.81

Next, we multiply these per-share figures by the average P/E ratios for their respective industries. In 1979 the P/E ratios of hotel/gaming companies varied very widely. Resorts International had a P/E ratio of 7, while Caesar's World had an incredible P/E ratio of around 70. Because the spread of P/Es is so wide, we'll use a very conservative estimate of 20 for M-G-M's hotel/gaming operation:

$1.21 × 20 = $24.20

Average P/Es for film companies were clustered more closely; since Twentieth Century–Fox and Columbia Pictures had P/E ratios of 8, we'll just use 8 for this calculation:

$0.81 × 8 = $6.48

Thus we can estimate a combined value of slightly over $30 for the two M-G-Ms.

January 7, 1980. The plan looks like reality. At a stockholders' meeting, M-G-M president Frank E. Rosenfelt announces that the company will definitely propose spinning off its film division. No further details are announced.

With M-G-M closing at $21.00, the stock still looks like a good buy for aggressive investors.

On November 14, M-G-M closed at $19.625, up $1.875 following announcement of the spinoff study. Based on this current price of M-G-M stock, compared to the estimated value of an M-G-M spinoff and taking into account the moderate risk that the spinoff plan might collapse, most investors would probably take a chance on M-G-M.

March 11, 1980. M-G-M decides to go ahead. M-G-M announces it will hold a special shareholders meeting on May 30, 1980, to vote on the proposed spinoff of its film operations into the Metro-Goldwyn-Mayer Film Company, Inc.

The announcement also contains details on how the spinoff will work: Shareholders of record on May 30 will receive one new share of M-G-M Film for each share of M-G-M they hold. The old shares of M-G-M will now become M-G-M Grand Hotels, the hotel-casino operation.

M-G-M closes at $18.25. At this point, since M-G-M is trading slightly below its price about a month before the spinoff announcement, investors who don't yet own the stock might want to consider buying. As with mergers, the sooner you get involved with a spinoff candidate, the lower the price you'll generally pay for the shares.

May 6, 1980. Both *The New York Times* and the *Wall Street Journal* carry articles concerning M-G-M's proxy statement to shareholders about the spinoff. (Nonstockholders could have requested copies of the proxy statement from the company.) The proxy statement contains all sorts of interesting information about the spinoff:

—Kirk Kerkorian, the financier who owns 47% of the old M-G-M, has announced that he will increase his holdings in the two new companies by up to 5%. (Owning more than 50% of the stock, Kerkorian could then elect the entire boards of both companies. Obviously, with Kerkorian so strongly behind the spinoff, there's little chance of a shareholders' vote defeating the spinoff.)

—The proxy cautions that the spinoff might hurt M-G-M's financing plans for its Atlantic City hotel-casino, slated to cost nearly $200 million. It also states that the spinoff might adversely affect the ability of both the film and the hotel-casino divisions to raise additional financing, since neither could rely on the earnings, assets, or cash flow of the other.

Wall Street professionals usually discount such dire warnings in proxy statements, since they generally outline the "worst case" scenarios so that they are protected from potential SEC prosecution. Investors should have taken the proxy statement with a grain of salt.

How do these factors affect the spinoff investor? They will influence future stock prices of both the film and the hotel companies.

M-G-M closes at $20.75.

May 22, 1980. The *Wall Street Journal* carries a very small article noting that the Tracinda Investment Corporation, Kirk Kerkorian's wholly owned holding company, has requested that M-G-M consider amending the certificate of incorporation of M-G-M Film.

The proposed amendment would exempt tender offers for the film company's common stock from the requirements of Section 203 of the General Corporation Law of Delaware, M-G-M Film's state of incorporation. The Delaware statute requires that a company whose securities are the subject of a tender offer be notified of the terms of that offer 20 days in advance.

Tracinda requested the amendment to remove possible inconsistencies between the Delaware law and federal law, which requires that a tender offer begin within five days of the public announcement of the terms of the offer.

For astute investors, this rather dull article was the first tip-off that Kerkorian was planning some move on the film company—most likely, a tender offer. Such a move would help boost the new film company's stock price.

M-G-M closes at $21.50.

May 27, 1980. The Nevada Gaming Commission approves M-G-M's spinoff plans.

M-G-M closes at $22.00.

May 30, 1980. M-G-M shareholders overwhelmingly approve the spinoff.

In its last day of trading, the old M-G-M closes at $22.375.

June 2, 1980. On this first day of trading for the two M-G-M's, Kerkorian makes a $5-a-share tender offer for 1.45 million shares of the film company. These additional shares would give him 51% of the new company.

He had underestimated investors' enthusiasm, however, and Kerkorian withdraws the offer a few hours later, when the shares open at $9.25 on the NYSE. For the day, the film company closes at $8.25, down $1.25, while Grand Hotels closes at $21.25, down $1.25.

An investor who bought M-G-M stock on November 15, 1979—the day the M-G-M announcement appeared in the papers—and sold at today's closing prices would have realized a neat profit of $9.875 per original share ([$21.25 + $8.25] = $29.50 − $19.625)—just over 50% in less than seven months.

Should investors have sold their M-G-M stocks at this point? The question is difficult to answer. After completion of the spinoff, investors could have best evaluated prospects for both M-G-M Grand Hotels and M-G-M Film using conventional security analysis.

Forecasting is not an exact science, however. Perhaps nothing drove home that fact with such terrible reality as the fire that swept the M-G-M Grand in Las Vegas on November 18, 1980. Eighty-four people died in that fire and hundreds were injured. According to *Business Week,* damages against M-G-M Grand could amount to nearly $34 million—roughly equivalent to a year's earnings.

On December 31, 1980, M-G-M Film closed at $9.375. Due to Wall Street concern about pending lawsuits, M-G-M Grand closed at $8, far less than had been expected. (Just before the fire, the stock had been trading in the $13–$14 range.)

TAX SITUATION

All spinoffs are tax-free—but not all instances of a company setting up a subsidiary as an independent company qualify as spinoffs.

The IRS has established the following requirements for a transaction to qualify as a spinoff:

—The transaction must involve the pro-rata distribution of the stock of a controlled subsidiary. By "controlled," the IRS means at least 80%-owned by the parent. Therefore, if the parent company owns less than 80% of the subsidiary, the deal definitely is *not* a spinoff from the IRS's point of view.

—In addition, both the parent and the subsidiary must be involved in the active trade or conduct of a business.

—Both businesses must have been actively conducted for at least five years.

—The subsidiary concerned must have been owned by the current parent for at least five years.

These regulations should help investors screen companies with spinoff potential. If a company seems like a good bet for a spinoff—either because of undervalued shares, a subsidiary in a glamour industry, or whatever—but it owns less than 50% of the subsidiary or has owned the subsidiary for less than five years, you can erase the possibility of a tax-free spinoff. Similarly, investors weighing involvement with a company such as Bairnco will have to own the companies for at least five years to get full tax benefits.

If distribution of stock in a subsidiary is not a tax-free spinoff, then what is it? The IRS treats it as a dividend, taxable at the higher personal-income-tax rate. As Robert Willens, a tax partner with Peat, Marwick, Mitchell, points out, "With spinoffs, it's either feast or famine."

Once again, it's important to remember that the so-called tax-free spinoffs are really "tax-deferred": Investors defer paying taxes on the stock received in the subsidiary until they sell the stock; then the profits are taxed at the lower capital-gains rate. Remember that spinoffs treated as dividends can be taxed as high as 50%, payable the April 15 after the spinoff year. Spinoffs treated as capital gains would be taxed at a maximum of 20%, payable only when the stock is sold.

Willens explains how to calculate the capital gains on a spinoff. "Let's say you bought company A at $20. Company A then spins off Company B. The IRS takes the old cost—$20— and allocates the value over the two companies: $10 for Company A and $10 for Company B. Upon selling the stock in either company, the investor would have a capital gain—or loss—on the difference between the $10 and the selling price."

When can investors sell their stock to be eligible for capital-gains treatment? Like mergers, spinoffs are "tack-on" deals: The amount of time an investor has owned the parent company automatically applies to the stock of the former subsidiary. As long as the investor has owned stock in the parent for at least a year, the IRS will treat sale of stock in the subsidiary as a capital gain or loss.

During the summer of 1981, the IRS took an important stand for spinoff investors. For a deal to qualify as a spinoff, the IRS had a "continuity of interest" requirement: Shareholders in the old company had to receive a substantial equity interest in the new company. But is it enough that the parent-company shareholders *receive* the equity interest—must they *hold* it for any given period of time?

"No," argued the IRS on behalf of shareholders in *McDonald's of Zion.* As long as shareholders in the parent company have the right to sell the stock in the new company, they may do so, without affecting a deal's spinoff status.

In this chapter, we have discussed spinoffs as examples of "negative synergy," where a company is worth more in parts than as a whole. Next, we'll take a look at a more desperate scenario—the liquidation, where a company is worth more dead than alive.

9

Liquidations: Worth More Dead than Alive

Scene: The March 1979 shareholders' meeting of UV Industries. One investor stands up to thank UV's head, Martin Horwitz. "Most managers have their own interests at heart—they want to keep their jobs. But you are doing what is best for the shareholders, and I'm with you all the way."

Bringing on these good feelings was not record profits, fancy dividends, nor new stock price highs. Instead, it was Horwitz's decision to liquidate UV—enabling stockholders to obtain greater profits than if the company continued to function.

"Worth more dead than alive" is the phrase Wall Streeters frequently use to describe companies whose assets are far more valuable than their stock price. Sometimes a company can only realize its inherent worth by converting its plant, land, inventory, and equipment into cash. In the case of UV Industries, for example, the shareholders would receive an estimated $38–$40 per share after liquidation—a 100% premium over the $18 at which the company traded a month before the announcement.

There are three varieties of converting corporate assets into cash: bankruptcy, divestiture, and liquidation. Only one of these—the liquidation—is the kind of special situation from which investors can profit. Let's examine all three and define their differences.

BANKRUPTCY

As Eugene F. Brigham defines it in his popular financial text, *Financial Management: Theory and Practice:* "Bankruptcy is a legal procedure, carried out under special courts of law, for liquidating or reorganizing a business. It can either be *voluntary,* in which case the debtor petitions the court, or *involuntary* bankruptcy, in which case the creditors petition the court and prove the existence of one of the acts of bankruptcy as described in the bankruptcy statutes."

Although on occasion investors have made money buying stocks in bankrupt companies in hope of realizing profits after liquidation, the strategy is highly, highly risky. Owners of common stock have the very *lowest-*priority claims on the distribution of proceeds in a bankruptcy, while preferred shareholders have the second-lowest. In most cases, common shareholders are lucky if they ever see a few cents on the dollar after a company's bankruptcy.

Stay away from bankruptcy liquidation stocks.

DIVESTITURE

A divestiture occurs when a diversified company sells off part of its business. Although some people use "divestiture" synonymously with "partial liquidation," the two actions differ. As discussed in chapter 7, a partial liquidation occurs when a company first substantially reduces its activities (i.e., by selling off a division or subsidiary), then uses the proceeds to reacquire some of its shares. In contrast, after a company *divests* itself of an operation, it may distribute the money directly to shareholders or reacquire shares—*or* it might use the funds to acquire new companies. If the company acquires another, it might take a long time before investors see the acquisition's performance boost the parent's stock price. Sometimes the improvement never takes place.

Along with mergers, the pace of divestitures has picked up in recent years. According to W. T. Grimm, 35% of net merger-acquisition announcements in 1980 involved some kind of divestiture—either partial sales (involving 10% or more of a company's equity) or divisional sales (of a product line, subsidiary, or division). In addition, as table 16 shows, larger divestitures have increased in frequency—particularly in the $100-million–plus category.

Why the increase? As the chief reason, observers cite undervalued stock prices and high interest rates. In a recent article, "The Restructuring Game," *Institutional Investor* reported: "Tired of having investors undervalue their stocks, diversified companies have learned that by selling off profitable parts for huge profits, and by buying other going concerns with the proceeds, they can greatly enhance the appeal of their shares."

"Companies need to generate higher returns on their assets now, because of inflation," sums up Martin Siegel, merger and acquisition chief at Kidder, Peabody.

Although divestitures can help boost stock price by increasing return on equity or clarifying a company's identity for

TABLE 16
Value of Divestitures
1979–1980

| | PERCENT OF TRANSACTIONS | |
PRICE PAID VALUE	1979	1980
$ 5 million or less	35%	27%
$ 5.1–10.0 million	19%	21%
$10.1–15.0 million	9%	9%
$15.1–25.0 million	12%	9%
$25.1–50.0 million	13%	14%
$50.1–99.9 million	6%	8%
$100 million or more	6%	11%

SOURCE: *W. T. Grimm & Co.*

financial analysts, they are *not* special situations. Instead, divestitures provide a long-term strategy for increasing a company's intrinsic value.

LIQUIDATION

As the word is used in this chapter, a liquidation is a company's voluntary sale or spinoff of all its assets, followed by termination of corporate existence. This kind of going-out-of-business sale is indeed a special situation. As a recent *New York Times* article explained, "In a bankruptcy liquidation, the stockholders often end up with nothing, but in the dissolution of a going business, they can reap a windfall capital gain."

Nevertheless, companies generally consider liquidation only as a last resort because it can

—create confusion among suppliers and customers;
—result in loss of job and prestige for both employees and top management;
—involve mountains of paperwork about details;
—amount to an admission of "failure."

Finally, as a recent article in *Fortune* explained, top management tends to be "perpetually optimistic, ever-confident that the market will one day awaken to the values they so clearly perceive in their own companies."

Why do healthy companies choose to liquidate? The following are some of the reasons.

Undervalued Shares

Once again, the most important reason is the severe undervaluing by the stock market. Martin Lipton, a partner in the New York law firm of Wachtell, Lipton, Rosen & Katz, which specializes in acquisitions, states: "The market price of a stock is about half what you can sell the company for or get if you liquidate it. And as long as the market values a company so low, you'll see an increasing amount of this activity."

William E. Chatlos, a senior partner at Georgeson & Company, which specializes in handling proxy contests, expresses a similar view: "This new liquidation is about to explode. You are going to see more stockholder proposals thanking management for a good track record but asking for dissolution—not because they're unhappy with management but because the market is not reflecting their good job. It's been ten years since we've had a market that reasonably reflected value."

In the depressed stock market of the late 1970s and early 1980s, liquidation may be the only means for a company's shareholders (who frequently include top corporate management) to cash in on a company's true value.

"It's a sad commentary on the economy when it's necessary even to consider the possibility that the best strategy for a going concern may be to close up shop," concluded a recent *Wall Street Journal* editorial titled "Corporate Suicide?"

Rug Pulled Out from Under Them

For 19 years, Telecor had been the sole distributor of Panasonic electronic products in 12 western states—products supplied by Matsushita Electronic Industrial. Matsushita products accounted for 85% of Telecor sales. After Matsushita announced that it would distribute Panasonic products itself, Telecor decided to liquidate.

The Ultimate Takeover Defense

Like desperadoes facing that final shoot-out in a western movie, some companies swear they'll never be taken (over) alive. While fighting Seagram's unfriendly tender offer for St. Joe in early 1981, John C. Duncan, St. Joe's chief executive, vowed he would liquidate if he couldn't find a white knight willing to pay at least $60 a share for the company.

The Ultimate Tax Defense

If a company completely liquidates within 12 months of shareholder approval of the action, *it pays no taxes on the corporate level* on any gain from the sale of the assets. Profits from the sale go directly to stockholders, who are eligible for capital-gains treatment.

Consequently, a company that has sold off a major chunk of its business, at a considerable profit, may find itself facing a major tax bite. If the company sells the assets and remains in business, most of the profits are taxed at the capital-gains rate of 28%. If the cash is invested in securities, the IRS taxes interest on bonds up to 46%, while 15% of all stock dividends are subject to a maximum tax of 46%. To do better by its shareholders, the company may prefer to liquidate.

For example, in January 1979, Bates Manufacturing got an offer it couldn't refuse from American Natural Resources. Bates sold its largest property—Virginia Iron, Coal & Coke Company—to American Natural Resources for $104.5 million. Confronted by a huge tax liability of some $30 million, Bates instead decided to liquidate its whole operation within the 12-month, tax-free framework. Bates shareholders ended up receiving close to $70 a share—far higher than its stock-market price of $56.

LOOKING FOR LIQUIDATIONS

Like spinoffs, liquidations occur very rarely indeed. Therefore, Wall Street professionals recommend that investors seeking this special situation consider a company only *after* it announces definite liquidation plans.

In addition, investors should be as certain as possible that the liquidation will actually go through. Whereas, in selecting merger candidates, investors can look for stocks that have takeover potential *and* are good investments anyway, liquidation candidates are stocks with no foreseeable future in the market—otherwise, management wouldn't even consider dissolution.

In March 1980, for example, *Business Week* speculated, "Is Singer heading for self-liquidation?" Here's how one Singer executive described the company: "What Singer has is a group of high-cost factories, tooled up for a demand that existed perhaps twenty years ago, manned with union people who are not about to let the company off the hook. We're turning out machines there that cost exactly double what machines made in Taiwan cost, and we're serving a market that is dropping precipitously."

Not exactly the kind of company you'd want to invest in—without a special situation pending.

Other liquidation candidates share similarly bleak prognoses. Therefore, if a liquidation plan goes out the window, so may your investment.

Investors in the Chicago Milwaukee Corporation, parent company of the bankrupt Chicago, Milwaukee, St. Paul & Pacific Railroad, learned the hard way. After Chicago Milwaukee Corporation announced it was planning to liquidate the railroad's extensive timberlands, track, and equipment, speculators began bidding up the company's shares. From 13⅛ early in October 1980, the stock increased to 65½ by September 14, 1981. Randall D. Smith, a partner at Bear, Stearns & Company, estimated the railroad's liquidation value at $500 million—or "several hundred" dollars a common share. However, reports of the Milwaukee Road's death were greatly exaggerated. On September 15, the company's bankruptcy trustee released a plan for its reorganization as a smaller, hopefully profitable railroad. Unfortunately for speculators, the Milwaukee Road was worth less alive than dead—the stock price collapsed from 65½ on Monday to 47⅜ at Friday's close.

To avoid such pitfalls, special-situation investors should examine news about a possible liquidation for key information. As with other special situations, both shareholders and other investors most often learn of a company's liquidation plans through articles in the financial press. If a liquidation requires shareholder approval, as is generally the case, stockholders will receive proxy statements and ballots. Once a liquidation is in progress, a company's annual report will contain background information and updates.

In a company's initial liquidation announcement, shareholders should look for the following information:

How Specific Is the Announcement?

Is the company announcing a liquidation, or saying it is only *considering* liquidation? As the Milwaukee Road example illustrated, good intentions aren't enough. The more concrete the information about *how* a company's assets will be sold, *when* a company's assets will be sold, *to whom* a company's assets will be sold, the greater the probability of liquidation.

Barber Oil's liquidation announcement provides a model of straightforwardness. As reported by *The New York Times* on October 3, 1980:

"The Barber Oil Corp., a New York–based holding company with interests in oil and gas exploration, shipping and mining, said yesterday that its directors had adopted a plan for the company's complete liquidation. Distribution of proceeds from the sale of assets could be made within a year of shareholder approval, the company said." Barber also announced that it had reached a definitive agreement to sell its domestic oil and gas subsidiary to existing oil-income partnerships formed by the Petro-Lewis Corporation for $109.2 million, and that it had made a definitive agreement to sell its domestic shipping operations to Apex Shipping, Inc., for $25.5 million. The company scheduled a shareholders' meeting to vote on the proposal for late November or December.

Because of the definite information Barber's announcement contains—the fact that two of its major operations have found buyers, and the fact that there is a clear time framework—investors should have little doubt about the company's orderly liquidation within the 12 months required for tax advantages.

Who Is Proposing the Liquidation—Management or Dissident Shareholders?

Either corporate management or a company's shareholders, through a proxy fight, may propose liquidation. Although company managements seldom propose liquidation, the plan usually goes through when they do. Only rarely are liquidations accomplished through proxy fights; not only must the dissidents overcome shareholders' inertia and convince them to vote against management, but, even if the dissidents win, they must get the company to carry out the dissolution program.

In 1979, for example, a group headed by N. Norman Muller, chairman and chief executive officer of MacMuller Industries, launched a bitter fight to force SCM Corporation to liquidate. According to Bear, Stearns, the dissidents' investment banking firm, SCM, which traded for $18.375 in March 1979, could be worth from $36 to $47 a share. The SCM officials won, electing their board by a 69%–31% margin. However, the liquidation proposal lost by a smaller margin, 64%–36%.

Just about the only successful dissidents pushing for liquidation were those who in 1979 successfully elected their minority faction to the board of Vornado, Inc., the operator of the Two Guys chain. The dissidents had pledged to sell off 26 Vornado stores outside the New Jersey and Philadelphia markets and distribute the proceeds of the sales to shareholders.

Are the Assets Liquid?

Liquidity is an important component of a successful liquidation. How salable are a firm's assets?

Holly Sugar provides a good example of how *not* to invest in a liquidation.

On paper, at least, Holly Sugar looked like a dead doornail at the end of 1979. Its losses totaled about $12 million in fiscal 1978 and 1979, and forecasts indicated it might squeeze out a $6-million profit for fiscal 1980. Lurking beneath this mediocre financial performance, however, were some glistening assets. Holly's 10-K listed the replacement value of its sugar-beet refineries at more than $100 a share. With Holly selling for about $40 at the beginning of 1980, it looked like a good deal—buying $100 worth of assets for $40.

After Irwin Jacobs, the Minneapolis liquidation expert who owned about 10% of Holly's stock, announced in November 1979 that he wanted to force company management to consider liquidation, Wall Street arbitrageurs rolled into action. Big money moved in. According to *Forbes* magazine, the Goldman, Sachs arbitrage department picked up 6.7% of Holly at an average cost of $37, while the American General Enterprise Fund bought 9.9% at an average of $41. Morgan Stanley, meanwhile, purchased 5% of Holly at an average of $45 a share—a total outlay of $3.6 million.

One small problem, however. An asset is worth only what someone is willing to pay for it. Nobody wanted to buy any sugar-beet refineries—as a matter of fact, the United States has surplus capacity. Because of rising gas prices (sugar-beet refining is very energy-intensive) and depressed sugar prices, about a dozen sugar-beet plants had gone out of business in recent years and stood idle. Besides, anyone looking for a plant probably wouldn't have wanted one of Holly's; its most modern plant was 16 years old and not very energy-efficient.

In any case, no one wanted any sugar-beet refineries and, as Alan Greditor, a food analyst at Drexel Burnham Lambert, asked rhetorically, "What else can you use them for?"

The answer, of course, was nothing. Holly's assets were worth no more than the income they produced. Although Irwin Jacobs got out with over $3 million profit on his $4-million investment, a lot of the big guys on Wall Street got left holding a very expensive empty bag.

In contrast, Handy & Harman owns some very liquid assets: gold and silver.* In 1981 the company announced it was considering liquidation. After paying off current liabilities, according to Milton Berg, portfolio manager of the First Investors Natural Resources Fund, Handy & Harman's sale of its precious-metals stockpile plus other current assets would yield $21.10 per share—almost as much as the market value of the shares. In addition, the company has fixed assets, including property and a modern plant and equipment. Berg estimated that a Handy & Harman liquidation could fetch between $30 and $40 a share.

*In general—and subject to market conditions and interest rates—securities, gold and silver, and stockpiles of raw materials are assets that are relatively easy to liquidate. Real estate, whether developed or undeveloped, is less easy to liquidate and is extremely difficult to sell during periods of high interest rates and tight money supplies. Inventories and plant and equipment vary greatly in their ease of liquidation, depending on their nature, age, and other factors influencing their desirability and usefulness.

Investors can get information about the composition of a company's assets from its annual report and 10-K. In addition, the 10-K lists inflation-adjusted replacement costs for most of a company's fixed assets. These figures enable investors to see at a glance what the assets might fetch if the company liquidated them.

Liquidation goes easiest—and fastest—for small companies with a few highly salable assets, such as prime land and resources reserves, and for companies that operate in distinct, self-contained divisions that can be lopped off neatly and sold to various bidders. Liquidation moves more slowly for large companies with interconnected operations. For example, Kaiser's complexity, in part, caused its snail's pace toward liquidation. The company owned stakes in aluminum, steel, and cement companies, and operated broadcasting, aerospace, and engineering businesses. Kaiser Industries' liquidation ultimately took four years to complete.

Speed becomes important because of serious tax penalties if liquidation takes more than one year.

Beware of Regulated Industries

If regulatory agencies move slowly in approaching mergers or spinoffs, they often grind to a solid bureaucratic halt when considering liquidations. Investors considering investing in a company in a regulated industry, therefore, should factor the time element into their decisions.

Beware of Major Shareholders with Takeover Intentions

The jaws that snatch and the teeth that bite a liquidation plan to shreds may belong to a major shareholder who had planned an eventual takeover. Such potential raiders may not look kindly at corporate "Masadas" to avoid acquisition. For example, Victor Posner, the wily takeover angler whose Sharon Steel owned 22% of UV Industries, nearly undermined UV's liquidation plans.

For information about major shareholders, check a company's 10-K and proxy statement.

Of course, takeover intentions may not be all bad—the company may end up as a merger target rather than as a liquidation candidate. As discussed in chapter 5, investors can learn of takeover plans by following 13D filings.

HOW A LIQUIDATION WORKS

In action, a liquidation unfolds like a spinoff. First the company announces a liquidation or a liquidation study. Once again, investors usually learn of the plans through the financial press, while shareholders may also receive a news release. Since liquidation usually requires shareholder approval, company shareholders will receive a proxy statement outlining specific terms and ramifications of the liquidation and a ballot prior to the liquidation vote. The liquidation plan will either win or lose. If approved, the company has 12 months to entirely liquidate the company and pass along the proceeds tax-free at the corporate level. If the liquidation takes longer than 12 months, shareholders may be in for a nasty surprise, which will be discussed later on.

Following a company's liquidation announcement, special-situation investors will first want to estimate that company's worth. According to Stanley Sanders, former president of Haas Securities, investors should first look at book value as listed in the annual report or 10-K, and then adjust the figure up or down to reflect hidden assets or liabilities. In contrast to mergers, where predators frequently get swept up in the blood frenzy for the kill, liquidations usually involve rational decisions. Therefore, liquidation value generally stays near adjusted book value.

Also, when a company announces liquidation, the financial press usually includes an estimate from one or more analysts on the company's breakup value. Investors can use this figure as a benchmark—verifying for themselves, of course, the liquidity of the assets involved.

Let's return to UV Industries to observe the hows and whys of liquidations in the real world.

Background: In 1978, UV Industries, a diversified manufacturer of electrical equipment and producer of copper, gold, coal, and oil, had performed well. The company had ranked #357 on the *Fortune* 500 list. During its 15 years with Martin Horwitz at the helm, sales soared from $31 million to $600 million, and profits from $2.5 million to $40 million—thanks largely to acquisitions.

December 19, 1978. "Reliance Electric Set to Buy Unit of UV Industries"

                        —*Wall Street Journal* headline

UV agrees to sell its Federal Pacific subsidiary to Reliance Electric for $345 million. The *Journal* article went on to say that UV management "will study possible acquisitions with the sale proceeds and a possible plan of liquidation of UV industries." In addition, UV stated it would schedule a special shareholders' meeting before the end of March to vote on the Federal Pacific sale and consider management plans for UV.

At this point, outlook for a UV liquidation appears remote. UV had previously been an active acquirer; accordingly, most Wall Street professionals expected that the company would use the proceeds from the Federal Pacific sale for a new acquisition. Investors of a speculative bent might have taken a chance on UV, since the company closed at $22 on the NYSE —fairly near its trading level of recent months.

January 19, 1979. UV directors unanimouly vote that all the company's assets be sold or distributed to shareholders. The *Wall Street Journal* article mentions that the UV board has also unanimously approved the sale of UV's major asset, Federal Pacific, to Reliance Electric, and that the company has also begun preliminary discussions on the sale of its remaining assets—including a copper mine and U.S. Fuel, an oil, gas, and low-sulfur-coal producer.

Once again, the concreteness of UV's proposal, including the agreed-to sale of a major asset and the liquidity of its remaining assets, indicates a good possibility that the liquidation will go through.

Why did UV choose liquidation? Its reasons were common for companies opting for this route:

—*Undervalued shares.* Before UV announced its liquidation plans, its shares traded at $19. After the company's proposal, the stock zoomed to $30. When completed, according to one analyst, shareholders could realize over $33 a share. (An interesting note: Horwitz himself owned nearly 179,000 shares of UV. Consequently, liquidation would boost the value of his holdings by about $3.8 million.)

—*Tax bite.* In November 1978, UV announced plans to sell its Federal Pacific subsidiary to Reliance Electric for $345 million. Facing a capital-gains tax of about $42 million, UV decided that its shareholders would fare better under liquidation.

—*Merger avoidance.* UV's sale of Federal Pacific would give the company a lot of cash—making it more attractive than ever to a potential raider. Liquidation provided the last, best way out.

With regard to the last item, UV already had an ample takeover headache—with Victor Posner, the takeover artist. Since 1966 UV had performed an elaborate ballet to avoid the embrace of Posner, whose Sharon Steel owned 22% of UV.

Although Posner was not mentioned in the announcement article, Sharon's stake in UV was discussed in other recent news stories about UV. As for Posner's track record in corporate acquisitions, he was, as *Fortune* magazine commented in a February 2, 1979, article, "a man whose reputation precedes him." According to *Fortune,* "After taking over DWG, a Detroit cigar maker, in the mid-1960's, Posner launched a multitude of acquisitions, many of them hostile, which sent fear through executive suites and gave him control over corporations with sales exceeding $50 million."

Posner wanted to buy UV—not bury it; thus, wary investors should have weighed the likelihood of Posner's jeopardizing UV's liquidation. A Posner merger move might or might not have been advantageous to UV shareholders. If Posner tendered to obtain only a scant 50.01% majority of UV, he could force a merger in which the remaining 49.99% of the UV shareholders would have to accept stock or some kind of debentures—less appetizing than the cash payouts that liquidations generally deliver.

UV shareholders might have shivered a bit when they examined some of Posner's previous takeover techniques. In 1976 Posner went after Foremost-McKesson, a $3-billion company, by making a tender offer for 80% of Foremost-McKesson's shares, to be paid for with a new issue of Sharon Steel subordinated debentures. As the *Fortune* article concluded, "In other words, Posner was asking Foremost-McKesson's shareholders to lend him the money to take over their own company."

UV closes at $30.875. With UV's estimated liquidation value at $33+ per share, and the fact that the shares had previously traded in the $20–$22 range, the stock does not look like a good buy because of its current runup in price and the potential storm clouds.

February 1979. By a series of intricate legal moves and stock purchases, Posner attempts to gather enough votes to veto UV's liquidation plans. During the maneuvers, UV's stock price fluctuated in the $30 range. Therefore, investors who bought UV at $22 (when the company announced plans to sell Federal Pacific) could realize a nice profit from selling their shares on the open market. On the other hand, since UV is now selling at about a 50% premium to its pre-liquidation announcement price, buying UV now could prove quite risky.

Ultimately, Posner's tactics fail in the courts, clearing the way for UV's liquidation.

March 19, 1979. UV's shareholders approve the liquidation plans by a 71.7% to 14.4% vote (the rest were abstentions). At the same meeting, the shareholders also okay the sale of Federal Pacific to Reliance Electric.

Following shareholder approval, UV closes at $32.75, up $.125.

April 9, 1979. UV directors vote to pay stockholders an initial liquidating distribution of $18 a share. The payment was made on April 30.

July 23, 1979. Tenneco Oil agrees to buy UV's oil and gas properties for $135 million. (The purchase would be completed in October 1979.)

November 1979. Victor Posner's Sharon Steel beats out Reliance Electric to buy UV's remaining assets. For each share of UV, stockholders will receive $7 in cash and $27 in Sharon debentures. Total price for the remains of UV: $517 million.

Adding in the April liquidation distribution of $18 a share, this sale meant UV shareholders would receive a total of $52 a share for UV.

Up until this point, UV's liquidation plans ran like clockwork. Unfortunately for shareholders, the next stages became a textbook example of everything that can go wrong with a liquidation.

January 1980. The SEC announces that it's investigating Sharon Steel—delaying registration of the debentures needed to pay UV shareholders.

Also, Chase Manhattan Bank and the U.S. Trust Company, indenture trustees for two subordinated UV debt issues, sue Sharon and UV in federal court. The banks want to force UV to repay the debt for cash immediately, instead of allowing Sharon to assume the low interest (5⅜% to 9¼%) debt. The creditors would naturally prefer getting their cash out immediately and investing it at higher interest elsewhere. Other banks immediately jump on the litigation bandwagon.

As the going got tough, tough-minded investors should have gotten going—and sold their UV shares as fast as possible. On the open market, shareholders could still have sold UV for about $27 a share as these troubles unfolded. This $27, plus the $18 already received, could have given investors who bought UV in November 1978 a fine $23-a-share profit on their stock. Because of the lawsuits and SEC investigation of Sharon, investors might have a long wait before seeing any additional monies from UV. Once again, shareholders should "take the money and run"—and invest it in some new special situation.

Also, since UV was soon scheduled to stop trading as part of its liquidation, the open market escape hatch would soon slam shut entirely.

March 17, 1980. UV ceases trading on the NYSE as of today. Meanwhile, the SEC still has not cleared the Sharon debentures needed to pay for UV.

June 26, 1980. Big troubles: Reliance Electric sues UV's liquidating trustees and Sharon Steel in federal court, claiming it was "misled" regarding its purchase of Federal Pacific nearly a year and a half previously. The Consumer Product Safety Commission was investigating Federal Pacific circuit breakers (used in million of homes) for possible defects—and Reliance, Federal Pacific's new owner, could face extensive product recalls. Consequently, Reliance sued either to rescind the sale or collect damages of $345 million. Reliance also requested that all of UV's assets—including the anticipated payment from Sharon—be held in trust until its claims were satisfied.

September 29, 1980. Sharon Steel finally pays off the $518 million promissory note it had given UV, swapping $411.2 million in Sharon temporary debentures plus $106.6 million in liquid funds and $38 million in interest.

UV promises to distribute the cash portion as early as possible.

Final Outcome. UV shareholders are still waiting.

As of October 1981, UV shareholders have received additional aggregate cash payments of $10. They are still awaiting payment of the $27 in Sharon debentures. The Consumer Product Safety Commission is still reviewing whether or not to recall the Federal Pacific circuit breakers; the commission's decision will affect Reliance's lawsuit. Meanwhile, the courts have decided against Sharon in the bank cases; Sharon is appealing.

Although the final liquidation value of UV will reach $62 (compared to an original purchase price of $22), shareholders have had to wait since early 1979 to realize their payout. As pointed out, a better strategy in the case of UV would have involved selling the shares on the open market.

The UV example points out both the enormous profits— and perils—associated with liquidations. However, investors should be aware that some of the dangers will subside because of a little-noticed portion of the Economic Recovery Tax Act.

Under a provision of the "windfall profits" section of the act, companies that adopt a plan of complete liquidation before the end of 1981 and distribute all proceeds to shareholders within one year will not have to pay taxes on gains at the corporate level. Starting in 1982, companies using LIFO will have to recalculate their inventories on a FIFO basis, recapture the difference, and pay taxes on that difference. For companies with large, valuable inventories, these taxes can run into tens of millions of dollars.

Therefore, many companies have an additional important reason to speed their liquidation plans.

TAX IMPLICATIONS

As previously explained, if a company completely liquidates its assets within 12 months of shareholder approval of the plan, the company pays no capital-gains taxes on the profits. Instead, any proceeds flow directly to the shareholders, who are taxed on whatever capital gains they realize on their shares.

The problem, however, comes if a company fails to completely liquidate within the year. Then, any remaining assets generally go into a liquidating trust, on which shareholders must pay taxes—even if they haven't yet received any payments.

Robert Willens of Peat, Marwick, Mitchell explains how this tax trap works.

"Let's say you bought five shares in company XYZ for twenty dollars a share—a one-hundred-dollar investment. XYZ goes into liquidation. Within twelve months, they have not sold or spun off all their assets. At this time, XYZ distributes your share of the sold assets—let's say one thousand dollars—to you; your interest in the remaining unsold assets amounts to another thousand dollars and goes into a liquidating trust."

The IRS, Willens continues, treats that $1,000 interest in the liquidating trust as if it were actual money—already received by you. You would have to pay capital-gains taxes on

$1,900: the $1,000 in cash distributed and the $1,000 stake in the liquidating trust—less the original $100 for the stock. In other words, you have to pay taxes on $900 you haven't yet received.

Making matters worse, no "tack-on" period applies to assets in the liquidating trust. If assets in the liquidating trust are sold in less than a year from the time the company distributed them to the trust, a shareholder is not eligible for the long-term-capital-gains rate. Furthermore, if the shareholder's interest in the trust amounts to more than the original $1,000 after all assets are sold, he or she must pay tax on the difference.

Because of such pitfalls, Willens recommends checking—and double-checking—to be sure that a company can carry out its liquidation in a year or less.

How much longer can things drag out? Well, there's the Rocky Mountain Fuel Company. It's been in liquidation since 1946!

10

Buying Call Options: Speculation on a Budget

Many professional investors hold with the conventional Wall Street wisdom that smart investors don't buy options, they *sell* options on their own stocks, pocket the income, and enjoy more generous returns on their investments. This is true.

However, increased merger activity (and also, to a lesser extent, increased spinoff and liquidation activity) has changed some of the rules of the game. Now it seems reasonable to look at special-situation stocks in a new light and to increase return on investment by *buying* carefully chosen call options and benefiting from the leverage of controlling many times the number of shares than could be bought outright.

Special-situation investors needn't have thousands of dollars to get into the game. In fact, this investment technique is especially worthy of consideration for the small investor who may have a total portfolio of only $5,000 to $10,000 and wants to play the special-situation game with only a portion of his or her assets. Calls—option contracts to buy 100 shares of a stock at a set price (the "striking price") until a specified future date —give small investors a chance to make spectacular profits if they're right, at risk of losing only relatively small, limited sums of money if they're wrong on either price moves or timing. Here's where leverage seems to work mostly on the upside.

Using the Conoco merger as an example, the investors who made the largest profits on a percentage basis weren't the owners of Conoco stock, but the owners of certain Conoco calls who bought them at 1-16 ($6.25 per 100 shares) and sold their calls within a few weeks at 6 ($600 per 100 shares). That's a 9,600% profit! If they had been wrong, those call buyers would have lost a very small investment—much less than the cost of a movie and a hamburger nowadays.

In table 17 you can examine the calls that were available in early October 1981 for Eastman Kodak, whose stock closed at 66½ on October 2, 1981, and traded on the Chicago Board Options Exchange.

As you can see, an investor could pay $6,650 (plus commission) to buy 100 shares of Eastman Kodak outright, or could pay anywhere from $6.25 to $900 for the right to buy 100 shares of the stock at prices ranging from $60 per share to $90 per share at future expiration dates from the end of October 1981 to the end of April 1982.

In looking at the January calls, which in early October had

TABLE 17
Eastman Kodak Calls, October 1981

EXPIRATION	STRIKING PRICE	10/2/81 CLOSING PRICE
Oct.	60	7
Oct.	70	¾
Oct.	80	¹⁄₁₆
Oct.	90	¹⁄₁₆
Jan.	60	9
Jan.	65	6
Jan.	70	2⅞
Jan.	80	⁵⁄₁₆
Jan.	90	¹⁄₁₆
Apr.	60	2¾
Apr.	65	2¼
Apr.	70	4½
Apr.	80	⁵⁄₁₆

nearly four months to run before they expired, an investor could choose the following strategies:

January 60—cost $900 (plus commission): Starts profiting when the stock moves above 69 (60 + 9). Then, for every point above 69, makes $100 on $900 investment (11%).

January 65—cost $600 (plus commission): Starts profiting when the stock moves above 71 (65 + 6). Then, for every point above 71, makes $100 on $600 investment (17%).

January 70—cost $287.50 (plus commission): Starts profiting when the stock moves above 72⅞ (70 + 2⅞). Then, for every point above 72⅞, makes $100 on $287.50 investment (35%).

January 80—cost $31.25 (plus commission): Starts profiting when the stock moves above 80⅜ (80 + ⁵⁄₁₆ [=⅜]). Then, for every point above 80⅜, makes $100 on $31.25 investment (320%).

January 90—cost $6.25 (plus commission): Starts profiting when the stock moves above 90⅛ (90 + ¹⁄₁₆ [= ⅛]). Then, for every point above 90⅛, makes $100 on $6.25 investment (1,600%).

The longer the long shot, the less the probability of winning, but the greater the reward. Brokers at full-service brokerage houses should be able to get you professional advice from their options departments on the relative attractiveness of specific striking prices, expiration dates, and costs of calls on stocks. That's one advantage of a full-service brokerage house.

While it is not the province of this book to teach you "everything you always wanted to know about options, but were afraid to ask," here are some very basic rules of thumb.

For these Eastman Kodak options, those calls with a 60 or 65 striking price are referred to as "in-the-money" calls because the price of the underlying stock (66½) is higher than the striking price. The calls whose striking prices are higher than the prices of the underlying stocks are referred to as "out-of-the-money" calls. Obviously, if the stock should jump to 86, calls with striking prices of 70 or 80 would become in-the-money calls.

Professional investors feel that it's unwise to buy in-the-money calls; you're already paying for the stock's price, and if the price drops, so will the value of your call. They also feel that a call that's too far out of the money is a real crapshoot. In the case of Eastman Kodak, what is the probability that the stock will rise from 66½ to 90 by the end of January 1982, or even the end of April 1982? How often in the past has the stock risen 35% in a four-month or seven-month period?

But there are positive arguments for buying way-out-of-the-money calls, too. Eastman Kodak doesn't have to go to 90 for you to profit on your call. If it goes to 70 or 75, the price of the call will move up. And remember: A move from $\frac{1}{16}$ to just ¾ is a 1,200% profit! Cheap calls like these, too, are a good way for small investors to control larger blocks of stock than they could possibly buy. If a call is selling at ½, you can control 1,000 shares for $500.

Admittedly, this is a very speculative position to take. But there are some sophisticated ploys to soften that speculative edge.

First, let's say that your pet special-situation stock is selling at 50 and that you can buy nine-month calls with a striking price of 70 for $2. You could buy 100 shares of stock for $5,000. Or you could buy calls on 500 shares for $1,000—and put the remaining $4,000 in a money-market fund at approximately 18% (9% net in a 50% bracket) or a tax-free money-market fund at approximately 13%. Either way, the interest alone on the money-market fund will pay for over half the cost of the call if the stock drops so far that you lose your entire investment—a fairly unlikely scenario. Of course, you'd lose far more than your $1,000 investment if the 100 shares of stock that you owned outright took a 15-point drop. In addition, by buying calls, you've tied up only $1,000 (versus $5,000), and can control—and hopefully profit from—500 shares, rather than only 100 shares.

Another moderate strategy, which involves more money: Instead of buying 200 shares of your favorite special-situation stock, buy 100 shares outright and buy calls on as many additional shares as you like. As before, you can put any remaining funds into a money-market fund.

One final caveat: Stick to listed options (there are over 270 stocks whose options are traded regularly—see the list below), otherwise you'll find yourself paying too much for your options. On one stock, trading around 15 last spring, a six-month call cost $300—a premium of 20%. Investors would have a hard time making money buying options in which the stock had to rise 20% for them to just break even. Last warning, even at the risk of sounding repetitious: Stick to the listed options.

Put-and-call options

Stock	Exchange & Month	Stock	Exchange & Month
AMF	AF	American Tel. &	
ASA Ltd.	AF	Tel.	CBJ
Abbott Laboratories	PhF	AMP Inc.	CBF
Advanced		Anheuser-Busch	PhM
Micro-Devices	PaJ	Apache	CBM
Aetna Life &		Archer-Daniels-	
Casualty	AJ	Midland	PhM
Air Products &		ASARCO Inc.	AM
Chemicals	PhM	Ashland Oil	PhJ
Allis-Chalmers	PhJ	Atlantic Richfield	CBJ
AMAX	AM	Avco	PhM
Amdahl	CBF	Avnet	AF
Amerada Hess	PhF	Avon Products	CBJ
American		Baker International	PaM
Broadcasting Co.	PaF	Bally Mfg.	CBF, AF
American Cyanamid	AJ	BankAmerica	CBJ
American Electric		Bausch & Lomb	AJ
Power	CBF	Baxter Travenol	
American Express	CBJ, AJ	Labs	CBF
American Home		Beatrice Foods	AM
Products	AJ	Becton, Dickinson	PhM
American Hospital		Bethlehem Steel	CBJ
Supply	CBF	Black & Decker	CBF

Key:
A = American Stock Exchange
CB = Chicago Board Options
    Exchange
Pa = Pacific Stock Exchange

Ph = Philadelphia Stock Exchange
J = January, April, July, October
F = February, May, August, November
M = March, June, September, December

Stock	Exchange & Month	Stock	Exchange & Month
Blue Bell	PhJ	Datapoint	CBF
Boeing	CBF	Dean Witter	
Boise Cascade	CBF	Reynolds	PhF
Bristol-Myers	CBM	Deere & Co.	AM
Browning-Ferris		Delta Air Lines	CBJ
Industries	AM	Diamond Shamrock	PaJ
Brunswick	CBM	Digital Equipment	AJ
Bucyrus-Erie	AM	Disney	AJ
Burlington		Dr. Pepper	AF
Northern	CBJ	Dorchester Gas	PaF
Burroughs	AJ	Dow Chemical	CBM
Caesar's World	PhF	Dresser Industries	PhJ
Caterpillar Tractor	AF	Duke Power	PhJ
Cessna Aircraft	CBF	Du Pont	CBJ, AJ
Champion		Eastern Gas & Fuel	PhJ
International	CBM	Eastman Kodak	CBJ
Charter	PhM	EG&G	PhM
Chase Manhattan	AM	El Paso Co.	AF
Citicorp	CBJ	Engelhard	
Cities Service	PhM	Corporation	PhJ
City Investing	PhJ	Esmark	CBM
Coastal	AM	Evans Products	CBF,
Coca-Cola	CBF		CBM
Colgate-Palmolive	CBF	Exxon	CBJ
Combustion		Federal Express	CBJ
Engineering	PaM	Federal National	
Commonwealth		Mortgage	CBJ
Edison	CBF	First Charter	
Computer Sciences	CBM	Financial	AJ
Computervision	PhF	Fluor	CBJ
Comsat	PhJ	Ford Motor	CBM
Consolidated		Foster Wheeler	PaJ
Edison	AF	Freeport Minerals	CBF,
Continental			CBM
Telephone	AJ	Fuqua Industries	PhM
Control Data	CBF	GAF	PhJ
Corning Glass		General Dynamics	CBF
Works	CBF,	General Electric	CBM
	CBM	General Foods	CBF
Data General	PaM	General Instrument	PhM

Stock	Exchange & Month	Stock	Exchange & Month
General Motors	CBM	International Paper	CBJ
General Telephone		International Tel. &	
& Elec.	AM	Tel.	CBM
Georgia Pacific	PhJ	Johns-Manville	CBF
Getty Oil	PhM	Johnson & Johnson	CBJ
Gillette	AM	Joy Mfg.	PhF
Global Marine	AM	Kaneb Services	AM
Goodyear Tire &		Kerr-McGee	CBJ
Rubber	AJ	K mart	CBM
Grace (W.R.)	AF	LTV	AM
Great Western		Lear Siegler	PhM
Financial	CBJ	Levi Strauss	PaJ
Greyhound	AJ	Lilly (Eli)	AJ
Gulf & Western	CBM	Litton Industries	CBM
Gulf Oil	AJ	Lockheed	PaM
Halliburton	CBJ	Louisiana Land &	
Harris	CBF	Expl.	PhF
Hercules	AM	Louisiana Pacific	AF
Heublein	PaF	MACOM	AF
Hewlett-Packard	CBF	MGIC	AF
Hilton Hotels	PaF	MGM Grand Hotels	PaM
Holiday Inns	CBF	MAPCO	PaJ
Homestake Mining	CBJ	Marathon Oil	AM
Honeywell	CBF	Marriott	PhJ
Hospital Corp. of		Martin Marietta	PhM
America	PaJ	McDermott	PhF
Household Finance	AJ	McDonald's	CBM
Houston Natural		McDonnell Douglas	PaF
Gas	PaJ	Merck & Co.	CBJ
Hughes Tool	CBM	Merrill Lynch	AJ
Hutton (E.F.)		Mesa Petroleum	AJ
Group	AJ	Middle South	
INA	CBJ	Utilities	CBM
Inexco Oil	PhF	Minnesota Mining	
International Bus.		& Mfg.	CBJ
Mach.	CBJ	Mobil Oil	CBF
International Flav.		Mohawk Data	
& Fr.	CBF	Sciences	PaM
International		Monsanto	CBJ
Harvester	CBJ	Motorola	AJ

Stock	Exchange & Month	Stock	Exchange & Month
NCR	CBM	Resorts	
NL Industries	PhF	International A	PaJ
NLT	AM	Revlon	CBM
National Distillers &		Reynolds Industries	CBF
Chem.	AF	Reynolds Metals	PaF
National Medical		Rockwell	
Enterprises	AF	International	CBF,
National			CBM
Semiconductor	CBF, AF	Ryder System	PaF
Natomas	AM	Safeway Stores	CBF,
Newmont Mining	PhM		CBM
Northwest Airlines	CBJ	St. Joe Minerals	PhM
Northwest		Santa Fe Industries	AM
Industries	CBM	Santa Fe	
Norton Simon	AF	International	PaJ
Occidental		Schering-Plough	PaF
Petroleum	CBF	Schlumberger Ltd.	CBF
Owens-Corning	PhM	Scott Paper	PhJ
Owens-Illinois	CBM	Searle (G.D.)	AF
PPG Industries	PhF	Sears, Roebuck	CBM
Penney (J.C.)	AF	Signal Companies	PaF
Pennzoil	CBJ	Skyline	CBF
PepsiCo	CBJ	SmithKline	
Perkin-Elmer	PaM	Industries	PaM
Pfizer	AM	Southern Company	CBF
Phelps Dodge	AJ	Sperry	CBJ
Phibro	PhJ	Squibb	CBJ
Philip Morris	AM	Standard Oil—	
Phillips Petroleum	AF	California	AM
Pitney-Bowes	AJ	Standard Oil—	
Pittston	PhF	Indiana	CBF
Pogo Producing	PaJ	Standard Oil—Ohio	AM
Polaroid	CBJ, PaJ	Sterling Drug	AF
Prime Computer	AM	Storage Technology	CBJ
Procter & Gamble	AJ	Sun Company	PhF
RCA	CBM	Superior Oil	CBM
Ralston Purina	CBM	Syntex	CBM
Raytheon	CBF	TRW	AJ
Reading & Bates	PaF	Tandy	AJ
		Tektronix	CBM

Stock	Exchange & Month	Stock	Exchange & Month
Teledyne	CBJ, PaJ	USAir	PaM
Tenneco	AF	Valero Energy	AM
Texaco	AJ	Virginia Electric &	
Texas Instruments	CBJ	Power	PhJ
Texas International	AF	Jim Walter	CBF
Texas Oil & Gas	PhM	Wang Labs Class B	PaJ
Tiger International	AF	Warner	
Time	PhM	Communications	CBF
Tosco Petroleum	AF	Warner-Lambert	AJ
Transamerica	PhF	Waste Management	PhF
Trans World	PaM	Wendy's	
Travelers Corp.	PaF	International	PaM
UAL	CBF	Western Union	PhJ
UNC Resources	CBF	Westinghouse	
Union Carbide	AJ	Electric	AJ
Union Oil—		Weyerhaeuser	CBJ
California	PaJ	Whittaker	AM
Union Pacific	PhF	Williams Companies	CBF
U.S. Home	AM	Woolworth (F.W.)	PhF
U.S. Steel	AJ	Xerox	CBJ, PaJ
United		Zapata	PaM
Technologies	CBF	Zenith Radio	AF
Upjohn	CBJ		

11

Warning Signals

According to Dr. Douglas V. Austin, a frequent contributor to
Mergers & Acquisitions and a man who has been researching
takeovers for 24 years, over 95% of all uncontested (friendly)
takeovers go through, and over 75% of all contested (unfriendly) takeovers are successful. Contested takeovers go
through at higher prices than originally offered, so investors
make even more money from successful contested takeovers
than from successful uncontested takeovers.

However, there will inevitably be some situations in which
the deal falls through. It is vital for every investor to be able
to recognize the signs of possible failure, and to know how to
protect his or her investment. In this chapter we will look at
key warning signals and discuss methods for minimizing your
risk.

Mirror Images

Remember all those tip-offs in chapter 2 that indicated that
a special situation might be brewing? Be wary if their "mirror
images" or opposites develop, most notably:

- sudden price drops;
- sudden volume drops;
- both together—as usually happens—a much stronger signal.

These reversals mean that the professionals—primarily the arbitrageurs—have had a change of heart about the imminence of a special situation.

Since risk arbitrageurs make their living betting on the outcomes of special situations, they have developed elaborate, expensive, and often exotic means of gauging the success or failure of a deal. For example, after one arbitrageur learned—by calling a New York hotel—that the chief executive of a company to be acquired in a friendly deal had suddenly canceled his room reservation, he immediately unloaded his position in the merger candidate. The next day, the deal was called off.

Arbitrageurs not only have a working relationship with top-level company executives and investment bankers, they also can afford squadrons of lawyers, accountants, and investigators to constantly monitor a deal's health.

Obtaining information through legwork is strictly legal. Quoted in the August 1981 issue of the *Institutional Investor,* Joseph Perella of First Boston Corporation explained: "[The arbitrageurs] are just using the same sources as other investors can use. The information is there if you go looking for it. Everybody can hire a lawyer in Kansas City, but not everybody does. Only a few people have enough at stake to pay for one."

If price and volume figures start indicating that the smart money may be pulling out of a stock, it may mean that their retinues of high-priced legal and financial talent see trouble ahead. Therefore, you should prepare to protect your investment by using one of the techniques described at the end of this chapter.

External Events

Sometimes deals fail because of events entirely outside a company's control. Record-high interest rates and credit restraints in the fall of 1979, the spring of 1980, and on and off in 1981 squelched many corporate plans for mergers and other deals. Fortunately for special-situation investors, the probusiness "anti-antitrust" attitude of the Reagan administration has nevertheless facilitated many megabuck mergers and acquisitions.

Merger Warning Signals

Most warning signals have to do with mergers because mergers involve two companies. Repurchases, spinoffs, and liquidations don't. Since over 95% of friendly merger offers are consummated, they will not be discussed here. However, when merger offers are hostile (by definition, contested), the deal may fail. Warning signals can help investors avoid folding with the deal.

BEFORE THE MERGER ANNOUNCEMENT

Perhaps you've bought a stock that you think is merger bait. Change your mind and use the defensive ploys at the end of this chapter if one of the following scenarios unfolds:

The Company Buys Shares from Only One or a Few Shareholders

This is absolutely the worst scenario, so it's being presented first. One company or individual buys a toehold stake in another company, reported dutifully in a 13D filing. The purchaser has the reputation of being a lean and hungry acquirer; the target has all the signs of a fat, juicy, cash-rich or under-valued victim.

The arbitrageurs heat up the action. You, the investor, scanning balance sheets and price-and-volume charts, decide to take the plunge.

Then—the target company buys back the toehold stake from the presumed acquirer, often at a tremendous premium. And how does the company finance its repurchase? By using the surplus cash or increasing its debt. The pseudoacquirer laughs all the way to the bank. Meanwhile, now that what had all the earmarks of a merger is off, the ex-target's shares plummet. The small investor gets stuck holding shares in a company that has gobbled up its cash and eroded its debt/equity ratio—i.e., a company that is no longer desirable as a merger target.

When a company pays a premium to buy back its stock from a potential raider, only one stockholder—the raider—gains. All other shareholders lose money if they don't bail out in time.

Unfortunately, there's little an investor can do beforehand to avoid this tiger trap. The best advice professional traders can offer: If a company or individual buys a toehold stake in a corporation, try to know the buyer's modus operandi. What has been its pattern in the past—accepting the buyback or pushing for the merger? Gulf & Western Industries, for example, has been amenable to buybacks. In September 1980 the company purchased a 7.4% interest in Oxford Industries and a 10.4% interest in Robertshaw Controls. Two months later, both companies bought back their shares—for a total of $2.1 million more than Gulf & Western had paid for them.

Carl Icahn, an arbitrageur, has shown himself equally cooperative—for a profit. He sold his interest in Saxon Industries back to the company for $10.50 per share—a $2.37-per-share premium over the stock's market price—for a 29% profit.

Investors can get a handle on a potential acquirer's track record by reading through the entries on the acquirer in the *Wall Street Journal Index* or *Business Periodicals Index.* However, past performance is not an ironclad guarantee of future behavior; many acquirers have played the game both ways.

If a company announces a stock buyback from one shareholder or a small group, start looking for one of the storm shelters described at the end of this chapter.

The Company Revises Its Charter and/or Bylaws

One of a company's best defenses involves amending the terms of its charter or bylaws to make it harder or take longer for a hostile bid to go through. Such revisions may or may not require shareholder approval. If shareholders must approve the resolutions, information will appear in the proxy statement, which shareholders receive automatically and which nonshareholders can request from the company or business services (see Appendix). Among the specific changes, watch out for those that involve the following:

Increasing the proportion of shareholders required to approve a merger or acquisition. Often this provision will require a "super-majority" of 80% of the shareholders to approve the plan—virtually precluding the possibility of a hostile takeover.

Raising the quorum requirements for meetings of shareholders. This provision makes it harder for dissident stockholders who favor a merger against management's wishes to call a meeting.

Limiting the right of shareholders to call special meetings. This provision also makes it harder for dissident stockholders who favor a merger against management's wishes to call a meeting.

Restricting stock transfers to foreigners. If an industry has become especially attractive to foreign buyers, a company that wants to avoid becoming a target might limit the amount of stock a foreign company can own.

Setting up special classes of voting preferred stock. During the conglomerate heydays of the late 1960s and early 1970s, companies frequently used this maneuver to enhance their flexibility in carrying out acquisitions. Today this technique has become a popular strategy in avoiding acquisition. If approached by an unfriendly suitor, the target can issue the preferred stock to a friendly party, who could then vote against the merger.

Staggering the terms of board members. By staggering the number of directors elected each year, rather than having all directors elected in one year, incumbent management can keep control of the board out of unfriendly hands for several years.

The Company Acquires Another Company Itself

As we saw in earlier chapters, "cash cows"—those companies with millions of dollars of loose change jingling in their pockets—are popular merger targets. To defend themselves against takeovers, the companies may embark upon acquisitions themselves.

If they acquire a company for cash, it reduces their cash surplus and makes them less attractive targets.

If they acquire a company by using debt, the borrowing increases their debt/equity ratio and reduces their future borrowing power, and thus their attractiveness to suitors.

If they acquire a company for stock, the acquisition and new stock issue dilute the holdings of other shareholders. Most important, this process reduces the power of a potential acquirer with an existing toehold stake in the company.

Of course, the acquisition can be a good move, signaling new aggressiveness on the part of company management to improve return on equity for shareholders. However, the stock then becomes a good long-term investment—not a rapid-profit special situation.

The Company Acquires a Company in a Regulated Industry

As previously seen, if a merger requires approval of a regulatory agency, it can add years to the time needed to close a deal. Many targets take advantage of this slow bureaucratic pace by buying a company in a regulated industry to reduce their attractiveness as targets. For example, B. F. Goodrich, fearful of a takeover, acquired a trucking company. Trucking is regulated by the ICC—one of the slowest agencies of all, whose statutory waiting period is 30 months. Now Goodrich probably has nothing to worry about.

The Company Buys a Company in an Industry that Cannot Be Owned by Foreigners

If a company fears that its prospective suitor may be foreign, it can purchase a company in an industry that prohibits foreign ownership—e.g., trucking, communications, or defense contracting.

The Company Puts Large Blocks of Shares in Its Employees' Hands Through Employee Stock Ownership Plans (ESOP's)

Since employees generally feel threatened if their company changes hands, they would be reluctant to tender their stock in a hostile offer. In fighting a takeover attempt by Texas

International Airlines, Continental Airlines sought to double the number of its shares outstanding and to set up an employee trust to control 51% of the airline, thus diluting Texas International's stake from 48.5% to under 25%. The plan would have made Continental the nation's largest employee-controlled firm—but, because of various problems, most notably difficulties in raising financing, Continental's proposal never got off the ground. Texas International finally won President Reagan's approval of the takeover in October 1981.

The Company Reincorporates in a State with Strong Antitakeover Laws

This perennial ploy may soon fall by the wayside, depending on a Supreme Court ruling in the Court's 1981–82 session.

Certain states, such as Idaho, have elaborate antitakeover laws that protect companies incorporated in their states. These laws require complicated filings of offers, long waiting periods, higher-than-majority shareholder votes, all of which can stall a hostile tender offer into oblivion. Many fearful targets reincorporate in these states as a defensive measure.

However, these state laws conflict with federal law, which treats hostile bids more favorably. And federal law generally supersedes state law. The entire issue will come before the U.S. Supreme Court, which, in the fall of 1981, agreed to hear an appeal by Illinois officials who defend that state's 1978 antitakeover law. A federal appeals court struck down that law, citing discrepancies with federal law, and commenting that the Illinois law interfered with interstate commerce by favoring in-state targets over out-of-state acquirers.

The Supreme Court decision will affect the corporate takeover laws of more than 30 states.

AFTER A FRIENDLY MERGER OR HOSTILE TENDER IS ANNOUNCED

The potential merger may be in trouble if the target resorts to any of the strategies previously mentioned. Here are some other problems that might arise:

The Target Says No

When a target says no, its rejection can come in various degrees of hostility, with attendant ramifications for shareholders.

Playing hard-to-get. By initially spurning a suitor's offer, a company can often elicit a higher bid—either from the original bidder or from a white knight. To detect whether a company might be willing to say yes if the price is right, examine the language the target's management uses in rejecting the offer. If it calls the offer "inadequate" or even "grossly inadequate," that's a good sign. Think of the elegant, stylized language of diplomacy and you'll get the idea. Even more obvious semantically is the more demure reply: "The offer does not fully reflect the value of the company."

Responses in this vein mean that the company is willing to talk merger—for a price. The target's initial rejection may elicit a higher price from the first hunter—or bring in a white knight.

Playing hard-to-get pays off very handsomely if a white knight gallops in. Despite gnashing of teeth by the shareholders when management rejects a merger bid at a substantial premium over market price, sometimes management is right; an offer may indeed be too low. By holding out, management may find another suitor that values the company more highly.

"If somebody covets what you've got, there may be somebody else out there who covets it even more," *Forbes* Magazine said in a March 17, 1980, article about "reluctant brides." Table 18, reprinted from that *Forbes* article, retraces the fortunes of ten companies that rejected their first suitors—and clinched more profitable deals later on. More recent and highly profitable examples are white-knight Wheelabrator-Frye's acquisition of Pullman against a hostile offer from McDermott, Inc., and white-knight du Pont's acquisition of Conoco against a hostile offer from Seagram.

Limited war. The target prefers to remain independent and will defend itself vigorously. But management is unwilling to burn any bridges should a takeover become inevitable. If the

TABLE 18

Ten companies that said no . . .

the first time around, and had no subsequent cause for regret.

TARGET—SUITOR	ANNOUNCEMENT DATE	TARGET'S PRICE PRIOR TO ANNOUNCEMENT	FINAL OFFER	PREMIUM	SUBSEQUENT BUYER	ANNOUNCEMENT DATE	TARGET'S PRICE PRIOR TO ANNOUNCEMENT	FINAL OFFER	PREMIUM	INCREASE OVER PREVIOUS BID
Dictaphone—Northern Electric	9/24/74	8¾	$12.00	37%	Pitney Bowes	12/15/78	18⅞	$28.50	51%	138%
Anaconda—Crane	8/7/75	15⅛	20.00	32	Atlantic Richfield	3/16/76	22	33.25	51	66
Southern Industries—Marquette	3/23/76	9¼	12.50	35	Dravo	12/15/78	11¼	15.97	42	28
Unitek—Airco	5/7/76	23⅛	30.00	30	Bristol-Myers	11/29/77	38¾	52.21	35	74
Gabriel Inds—Papercraft	4/27/77	10¾	15.40	43	CBS	5/5/78	16⅛	17.90	11	16
Falcon Seaboard—Raytheon	6/9/77	24⅛	29.75	23	Diamond Shamrock	11/2/78	32	33.41	4	12
Pemcor—Maremont	7/22/77	13	16.75	29	Esmark	6/23/78	29⅜	29.01	−1	73
Medusa—Moore McCormack	10/10/77	27	38.50	43	Crane	8/21/78	44	50.00	14	30
Microdata—AM International	11/8/78	13¾	20.50	49	McDonnell Douglas	7/10/79	29⅞	32.00	7	56
Hess's—Marshall Field	11/23/78	12¼	17.38	42	CrownAmerica	9/13/79	14⅜	25.70	76	48

FORBES, MARCH 17, 1980

target is confronted by a determined acquirer offering a fair price, the "blushing bride" will probably submit.

In cases of limited warfare, the target will generally resort to complex-but-clean legal maneuvering. The preferred tactics include:

  • claiming that the acquirer violated provisions of the Williams Act, which require a warning to the target of takeover intentions, filing of information concerning the takeover, and disclosing sources of financing
  • claiming that the acquirer violated Federal Reserve margin rules
  • citing state antitakeover laws (as mentioned earlier, this defense has become shakier because of federal challenges to the state laws)
  • citing conflicts of interest on the part of the acquirer's bank's or lender's board of directors
  • alleging misleading, untruthful, or fraudulent statements by the acquirer
  • claiming that the proposed takeover would violate antitrust law

This last point requires further discussion. Antitrust difficulties can range from the minor to the catastrophic. Investors should examine how much foundation the antitrust questions raised have. Where the conflict arises, how much money is involved? What proportion of each company's business is involved?

What is the government's attitude on antitrust issues? During President Reagan's first year in office, several officials of the administration went on record with the position that corporate bigness is not necessarily bad. William Baxter, the assistant attorney general for antitrust, said: "I have no hostility against large mergers, as such. . . . Former administrations were concerned with fairness to smaller competitors. Even in situations where the companies were less efficient, heroic efforts were made to keep them in business. There was also concern with large size. If corporations obtained large size by a merger, that alone was sufficient to taint the merger. But my view is that is not so."

If an antitrust conflict centers on a small operation that contributes very small profits to a company's bottom line, chances are fairly good that the acquirer can solve the problem by selling off the conflicting enterprise. If, however, the antitrust issue centers on operations that are the very lifeblood of both companies, the merger can founder right there.

The scorched-earth policy. Finally, some managements will fight takeovers to the bitter end, even if they destroy their companies in the process. "I've heard it called the 'scorched-earth defense,' " one securities analyst said.

According to some analysts, Wetterau Foods adopted a scorched-earth strategy to repel a takeover by Empire Inc., which had acquired a stake in the company. Wetterau, an attractive candidate because of its surplus cash, went on a buying spree, acquiring other companies and "paying too much money," one analyst said. Wetterau acquired these companies with newly issued stock, which diluted the holdings of Empire, along with all Wetterau's other shareholders. Finally, Wetterau used its cash to buy back its shares from Empire at a premium, which left all its other shareholders high and dry. In the analyst's opinion, "Wetterau is now worth much less money than ever before." Wetterau shares, which had sold as high as $49.50 in early 1981, fell to $10.625 in November 1981.

Companies adopting the scorched-earth defense will go for the jugular in attacking their opponents. Instead of legal quibbling, lawsuits and charges escalate into the "felony punishable by five years in jail" variety. Joseph R. Perella, a merger specialist and managing director of First Boston Corporation, comments: "You don't create the other guy's vulnerability. But if it's there, you really attack it."

In takeovers that use stock, the traditional strategy involves disparaging the quality of the acquirer's securities. In cash offers, since the target can't attack the quality of the acquirer's money, the target will question the integrity of the bidder and its management instead. If an acquirer has anything even slightly embarrassing in its past, it might prefer to withdraw from the merger arena while all its skeletons remain safely tucked away in their respective closets. During the Conoco wars, according to a *Wall Street Journal* article of July 23, 1981, sources hinted that Conoco would expose Mobil's close ties with Saudi Arabia to pressure the oil company into dropping out of the contest. "There are going to be some embarrassing discovery requests made of Mobil," one insider reportedly warned.

Although stockholders have increasingly taken action when a company's directors decline an offer or embark on a scorched-earth campaign, lawsuits and proxy fights are complicated, expensive, and generally unsuccessful. As long as corporate directors make a good-faith determination that an offer "is not in the best interests of the stockholders," the courts will usually uphold their position. Therefore, investors are better off using one of the hedging techniques described at the end of this chapter.

The Acquirer's Shareholders Say No

In today's litigious society, investors have a new worry: Shareholders of the acquirer have started suing to block mergers, claiming that their company is shelling out too much money for the target. Shareholders of the Penn Central Corporation—including the Hunt brothers and two former executives of a Penn Central subsidiary—brought suit in October 1981 to block Penn Central's proposed $1.4-billion purchase of Colt Industries. As this book went to press, the suit was still pending. Although at this time it is uncertain whether lawsuits against acquisitions will be any more successful than suits to force a company to be acquired, investors should consider this new stumbling block as part of the risk in mergers.

Once again, however, readers should note that, although much space has been devoted to possible problems in merger deals, problems do not crop up often, and most of them are merely strategies to bid up the acquisition price. Discussing all these problems so thoroughly is the author's contribution to full disclosure in investment planning.

BEFORE OR AFTER THE REPURCHASE
ANNOUNCEMENT ON REACQUIRED SHARES

As we have seen, a company may become a merger target because of excess cash or undervalued shares. Similarly, a company may strive to avoid acquisition by buying back its own shares—hoping to reduce cash surpluses and increase earnings per share on its remaining shares.

Since mergers and reacquisitions stem from similar underlying factors, it follows that the two special situations share similar danger signals. Potential stock repurchases may fall through if—

—the company repurchases shares from only one or a few shareholders.

When a company buys back shares from only one or a few stockholders, these sellers are the only ones who gain. Since the limited buyback consumes surplus cash and/or credit, the remaining investors are left holding shares with vastly reduced special-situation potential.

—the company becomes an acquirer itself.

Reacquiring shares costs money—obtained from the company's cash surpluses or by borrowing. If a reacquisition candidate uses its cash or credit to buy another company, it will lack the funds to buy back stock from its shareholders.

—the company adopts any other large-scale alternate use for its cash—such as greatly increasing capital expenditures.

Once again, this cash drain precludes repurchase of shareholders' stock.

—the company starts losing money.

If business slumps or a huge lawsuit threatens, the company may prefer to keep a healthy cash cushion, rather than disbursing it and then having to borrow money.

—a possibly unfriendly suitor buys a big block of stock.

When the company sets about reacquiring its shares, the suitor could choose not to tender. The suitor's stake in the target would thus increase proportionately, and eventual takeover would be facilitated.

If any of these scenarios develop, use the hedging techniques discussed in the last section of this chapter.

AFTER THE SPINOFF ANNOUNCEMENT

If you follow the guidelines in chapter 8 for analyzing spinoff announcements, you should experience no problems with your spinoff investments. Remember: Spinoffs are rare. Don't buy a stock because it has spinoff "potential." Many stocks have had spinoff "potential" for the past ten years, and may see this potential unrealized for another ten years. Investigate spinoff stocks only after *definite announcements* have been made, and investigate the tax treatment of the subsidiary that will be spun off, as discussed in chapter 8.

AFTER THE LIQUIDATION ANNOUNCEMENT

Like spinoffs, liquidations rarely occur. Moreover, a company will liquidate only if it is undervalued by the market. Therefore, investors should speculate only in special-situation liquidations, as discussed in chapter 9, and only after a company announces *specific* plans for its liquidation.

Well-planned liquidations go through and make money for their investors. However, a liquidation may be in trouble if—

—*an agreement to sell a major division falls through.*

One of the points stressed in chapter 9 is that investors should make sure that a company that announces its liquidation has lined up purchasers for all its major divisions. Even so, a sale may collapse, and the entire liquidation may be jeopardized. The company may no longer need to close up shop to avoid paying taxes on the huge capital gain generated by the sale. Furthermore, unless the company can rapidly find another buyer, the liquidation process may well take longer than a year. This unfortunate scenario creates the tax penalties for shareholders that are discussed fully in chapter 9.

HEDGING YOUR BETS

Even with all these pages of dire scenarios, all is not bleak, and all is not lost. There are three major strategies investors can use to protect their profits or limit their losses.

Before discussing them, however, let's quickly go over the whole concept of risk. An investor's risk on a special-situation stock is the difference between what he or she paid for the stock and the price at which the shares would trade if a deal fell through.

Example: Merger Marvel, Inc., has been trading in the $20 range for a few months. You become interested in the stock when Acquirer, Inc., buys a 7% stake, reported in a 13D filing. Meanwhile, Merger Marvel shares rise from $20 to $25 in a week on high volume. Following a careful analysis of the company, you buy shares at $25. Your risk would be $5: the difference between the $25 you paid for the shares and the $20 level they would probably return to if the merger failed to materialize.

It's important for investors to realize that "risk" and "missed opportunities" refer to two different concepts. If you buy Merger Marvel at $25 and the shares soar to $50—then drop to $30—you haven't *lost* $20; you've still gained $5—although you'll probably feel crummy about the additional gain you missed out on.

If investors spot any of the warning signals previously described and think that a special-situation deal will soon go down the drain, they can protect their financial stake by using one of the following techniques:

Sell the Stock

If the stock is still trading above or slightly below what you paid for it—sell. Don't waste your time and energy figuring out hedging techniques; instead, start prowling around for a new special-situation candidate who can earn you big returns. Also, don't worry if you've owned the stock for less than a year. Never hold on to a stock that turns sour just to qualify for long-term-capital-gains treatment. Sell stock because of investment decisions, not tax considerations.

Buy Put Options

Put options are exactly the opposite of calls. They enable a buyer to sell a certain stock at a set price—the striking price —within a certain time period. For the purpose of this book, only buying puts on stocks you already own—a hedging strategy—will be discussed.

With puts, you can protect your investment if a stock's price goes down—as generally happens if a special-situation deal collapses. As Mark Rubenstein, an associate professor of finance at the University of California at Berkeley, explains, "If you buy a stock and buy a put against it, it's like insurance." According to him, such a hedging strategy guarantees a loss no larger than the put price.

As with calls, investors should limit themselves to puts listed on the major exchanges; other puts are generally too expensive. Although 270 different calls are listed, only about two-thirds of those stocks also have puts, so check the situation for stocks you own.

Here's how a put can help you hedge. Let's say that Good Buy, Inc., stock has a 1981 low of $10. You purchase it at $15. Following rumors of a possible takeover, Good Buy jumps to $20. To protect your investment, you can buy a put on Good Buy at $15. To lock in your current profit, you can purchase a Good Buy put at $20. The $20 put would cost you more since it is "in the money"—i.e., in the stock's current trading range.

By purchasing either put, you would limit your downside risk to the cost of the option plus transactions costs. You've successfully protected your stock investment—even if the underlying shares fall back to $10.

Buying puts also appeals to investors who foresee a near-term slump—but a later gain—in the prices of stocks they already own. They can hold on to their shares for long-term gains, while buying puts to weather short-term losses.

Investors should note, however, that buying a put interrupts a stockholder's holding period on a stock for the purpose of creating long-term capital gains. Because the IRS holds that owning a put makes stock ownership relatively risk-free, the put may affect your chances of favorable treatment for long-term capital gains when the stock is sold. For further information, investors can consult a booklet concerning the tax implications of options, published by the Chicago Board Options Exchange and available through brokers.

Selling Short

Selling short on stock you don't own is a highly complicated and risky proposition and falls outside the scope of this book.

If you *own* a stock . . . if gathering warning signals indicate its price will soon plummet beneath the level you paid for it . . . *and* if puts on the stock are not listed, you might want to consult your broker about "selling short against the box." ("Against the box" comes from jargon meaning "against stock already in your safe-deposit box.") By selling short, you limit both your losses and your potential profit.

Let's return to our previous example where you bought shares in Good Buy at $15. The stock is now trading at $22. If you sell short at $22, your profit is the difference between $22 and the price to which the stock falls—e.g., a 7-point profit if the stock drops back to $15. However, if the stock price rises to $30, you're out of luck—you no longer own the shares. In comparison, if you owned a put at $22, you could just let the option expire and sell your stock at $30.

These hedging techniques will help you protect your profits and limit your losses.

12

Going for Broker

In order to buy or sell stock, you're going to need a broker. Your first step will be to decide what kind of broker you'll feel most comfortable dealing with: full-service or discount.

DISCOUNT BROKERS

For do-it-yourself investors, discount brokers are probably the best choice. They are the "no-frills" segment of the market: no elaborate analyst recommendations, no intellectual research department; the discounters specialize in "transactions only." You call up, get an anonymous clerk on the phone, place your order—that's it.

Although some firms began offering brokerage services at fees below prevailing commissions in the early 1970s, discount brokerage firms really took off in 1975, when the SEC prohibited fixed brokerage commissions. They have a growing share of the brokerage market, presently accounting for about 10% of all retail brokerage transactions and 5% of retail brokerage commissions.

In general, discounters charge about 50% less than full-service houses for stock transactions, but the savings can amount to as much as 75% because discount brokers compete on the basis of price. Rummage through the financial pages and you'll find a bundle of ads from rival brokers: "Far lower

than Merrill Lynch, even lower than Quick & Reilly Schwab."
Typically, the ads contain neat tables showing how a given
discount broker undersells all the others on various trades.

There's the catch. The prices quoted refer to trades of a
certain number of shares at a certain price. For example, one
broker uses 100 shares at $40; 200 shares at $25; 400 shares
at $15; 700 shares at $40; and 1,000 shares at $10, and comes
out lower than his competitors. Another broker uses 100
shares at $60; 500 shares at $50; and 1,000 at $15. That firm
also throws in a 25% volume discount—but doesn't explain it
in the ad. A discounter's fees will vary more than those of a
full-service house. Also, some discounters have "hidden"
charges, so investors should scrutinize their rate sheets carefully. Although a discounter may be dirt-cheap for a small
trade, prices for a bigger trade can offer less of a saving.

To paraphrase Abraham Lincoln, a discounter can undersell
some of the competition all of the time, and all of the competition some of the time—but can't be cheaper than all of the
competition all of the time.

Some Pointers on Discount Brokers

They're safe. Both full-service and discount houses have to
comply with the same regulations. In addition, there's the
Securities Investor Protection Corporation. A kind of FDIC
for the securities industry, the SIPC insures an investor's account up to $500,000.

Try the phone test. Some discounters shave overhead by
keeping staff to a minimum. That's admirable—until you fran-
tically try to phone your discounter to buy some just-
announced spinoff candidate, only to get a busy signal for a
solid two hours. Meanwhile, other eager investors have bid up
your special-situation darling by 25%. A good test to diagnose
such snafus: Call up the discounter on a day the market is
active, to see if you can get through.

You'll pay about the same price for the stock itself—whether
you use a full-service house or a discounter.

Some discounters won't handle certain transactions. Discounters are fine as long as you're buying listed stocks or bonds for

investment. However, on more-exotic trades, especially for options, discount brokers may lack maneuverability. Although discount brokers cost less than full-service houses for options trades, they don't offer special services, such as evaluating options, which involves a complex mathematical procedure. Consequently, even with the commission savings, many options traders prefer having a full-service broker watching the market, where a small gain can become a big loss in just a few hours.

Interestingly, some discounters are adding back the frills. For example, Source can provide investors with an account executive who offers personalized advice just like a traditional broker. (Investors pay higher commission fees for this service than for "no-frills" transactions.) Source has also diversified into commodities trading and has added a bond specialist.

Other discounters have lured investors with premiums, such as low-cost subscriptions to various stock-market newsletters and other financial publications. According to the companies involved, the newsletters help investors who want ideas but don't want to pay full-service brokerage commissions.

FULL-SERVICE BROKERS

Discounters are great if you just want someone to execute orders. However, if you want *help,* you need a good full-service broker.

What's a good broker? "Part financial wizard and part psychiatrist," answered one anonymous investor.

Finding a good broker is rather like finding a good doctor. Start by taking an informal poll of some of your friends. Then, perhaps, talk to your banker. If the same name appears on two or three lists, you may be on to someone. If the broker in question has "CFA" after his or her name, so much the better. CFA stands for "Chartered Financial Analyst." Like CPAs, CFAs have to pass rigorous qualifying exams.

If dealing with a large house, check out the quality of its research department. Get copies of their newsletters and research reports from a year or so ago, and then see how recommended stocks actually performed.

Finally, meet your prospective broker. Chemistry is an important part of any broker/investor relationship. Is the broker receptive to clients' ideas? Will he or she call you with stock opportunities, or wait for you to call? And which style do you prefer? Some clients love to phone and be phoned; some prefer to do the phoning. Similarly, some brokers like to call their clients; some may feel that frequent phoning can look like account-churning for commissions—Wall Street's own "Dialing for Dollars." Therefore, when you first meet, discuss ground rules about how frequently you should call. Many brokers get justifiably annoyed when clients with time on their hands call in the middle of a heavy trading day to find out how a pet stock is doing. And brokers have a habit of calling annoying clients last when they have a good research idea.

If you don't want to wait until the next day to find your favorite stock's closing price, find out whether the broker's secretary can give you the information. Most of them can, and do.

Each broker has particular likes and dislikes. Some avoid "junk" stocks just as they avoid junk food. Others don't feel comfortable with special-situation issues. How does a broker's investment style match your investment goals?

A *Business Week* article of June 15, 1981, urges readers, for their own protection, never to deal with a broker who blind-calls you, claims that a mutual friend suggested the call, and touts a certain "surefire deal." In many cases, the "good deal" may be a stock that the broker is trying to unload after his house took a position in the issue.

If you're investigating a large brokerage house, try to stay away from "the broker of the day." The "broker of the day" title isn't an award marking a job well done; it merely designates the broker who gets stuck handling nuisance phone calls and strangers on a given day. Their reward: any new accounts that develop that day. Although most brokerage houses generally rotate this awful assignment, some of the top brokers on staff frequently can avoid it. "It's comparable to KP in the army," says one broker.

Another Wall Street professional thinks that investors should have visible proof of a broker's track record. "If a broker says that he or she is an expert at picking special-situation stocks, ask which stocks he or she specifically recommended to clients. Then ask him or her to show you the account records (covering up the clients' names, of course) so that you can see for yourself. Most brokers will do this."

Generally, a broker will want to meet with you, too—or at least have a lengthy phone discussion. Some brokers won't accept accounts below a certain amount; others don't want clients who will hold on to a stock for ten years (they'll never earn any commissions).

Once you decide on a broker, you can judge performance firsthand. Does the broker return your calls? How quickly? Does the broker have good ideas? How good is the back office —the behind-the-scenes department that handles all paper work? Do confirmation slips arrive promptly? Research reports? What about your checks?

And then the acid test for any broker: "He or she should make money for you over any given three-year period," says one investor, who's had the same broker since 1969, through some of the most erratic and depressing markets since the Depression.

Finally, there's the question of where to go when you need help against your helpers. If it's a relatively minor complaint, like receiving checks late—or even a somewhat more serious one, like your feeling that your broker's churning your account —you can write or phone the New York Stock Exchange's Department of Member Firms for help. For more serious problems, it's the Securities Investor Protection Corporation.

Although the Securities Investor Protection Corporation resembles the FDIC, it is *not* a government agency. Completely funded by the securities industry, the SIPC helps protect the customers of securities firms that go out of business. In such cases, the SIPC becomes a party to the liquidation process.

During the summer of 1981, for example, the SIPC sought and oversaw the liquidation of John Muir & Company after that firm failed to meet the New York Stock Exchange's minimum capital requirements for member firms. Muir was the first NYSE member firm to be ordered liquidated since the SIPC was established in 1970.

When a firm is ordered liquidated, the SIPC first sends customers securities that are in their own names or are being registered. Next the SIPC returns, on a pro-rata basis, all other cash and securities held by the firm but belonging to customers. Finally, the SIPC's giant insurance pool (created through assessments on the securities industry) reimburses customers for any remaining claims. In October 1980, the SIPC raised its maximum coverage to $500,000 per claim. The SIPC covers claims for cash, securities, stock options, commercial paper, CD's, and even oil and gas ventures registered as securities with the SEC. It does not, however, insure commodity claims.

Fortunately, Muir had sufficient capital to pay off all creditors' claims without additional funds from the SIPC.

The Securities Investor Protection Corporation is headquartered in Washington, D.C.

Appendix

Information and Where to Get It

According to Martin J. Whitman, coauthor of *The Aggressive Conservative Investor*, corporate disclosures, as demanded by law, are generally adequate. The people who prepare the documents generally do so honestly and comprehensively. If they don't, the law provides stiff penalties for intentionally misleading the public or omitting material facts.

The trick for the special-situation investor, then, involves finding out what documents to look at—and where to get them. A brief description of SEC corporate filings as of March 1981 follows. Generally, these and the company's annual report will be the only documents you'll need. Information concerning the filings comes from a Disclosure Incorporated brochure, "A Guide to SEC Corporate Filings." Under contract with the Securities and Exchange Commission, Disclosure converts to microfiche the more than 110,000 documents filed each year by the 11,000 publicly owned companies whose securities are traded on the New York Stock Exchange, the American Stock Exchange, and over the counter.

DISCLOSURE STATUTE

A basic purpose of the Federal securities laws is to provide disclosure of material financial and other information on companies seeking to raise capital through the public offering of their securities, as well as companies whose securities are already publicly held. This aims at enabling investors to evaluate the securities of these companies on an informed and realistic basis.

The Securities Act of 1933 is a *disclosure* statute. It generally requires that, before securities may be offered to the public, a registration statement must be filed with the Commission, disclosing prescribed categories of information. Before the sale of securities can begin, the registration statement must become "effective," and investors must be furnished a prospectus containing the most significant information in the registration statement.

The Securities Exchange Act of 1934 deals in large part with securities already outstanding and requires the registration of securities listed on a national securities exchange, as well as over-the-counter securities in which there is a substantial public interest. Issuers of registered securities must file annual and other periodic reports designed to provide a public file of current material information. The Exchange Act also requires disclosure of material information to holders of registered securities in solicitations of proxies for the election of directors or approval of corporate action at a stockholder's meeting, or in attempts to acquire control of a company through a tender offer or other planned stock acquisition. It provides that insiders of companies whose equity securities are registered must report their holdings and transactions in all equity securities of their companies.

SECTION I: GENERAL DOCUMENTS TO HELP INVESTORS IDENTIFY SPECIAL SITUATIONS

Form 10-K

The 10-K is an annual report that goes into much greater detail than the company's glossy annual report. Special-situation investors can find such important information as the value of patents, licenses, and franchises (often carried at negligible cost on the balance sheet), the identity of majority stockholders, and the company's real-estate and other investments. This information is useful for *all* special situations.

Effective December 15, 1980, the Securities and Exchange Commission adopted and proposed major changes in its disclosure systems under the Securities Act of 1933 and the Securities Exchange Act of 1934. These changes were intended to reinforce the concept of an integrated disclosure system.

The changes that were adopted include amendments to Form 10-K, amendments to the Proxy rules, expansion of end amendments to Regulation S-K (which governs non-financial statement disclosure rules), uniform financial statement instructions, a general revision of Regulation S-X (which governs the form, content and requirements of financial statements), as well as a new simplified optional form for the registration of securities issued in certain business combinations.

The integrated disclosure system is based on the belief that investors expect to be furnished the same basic information package, both to support current information requirements of an active trading market and to provide information in connection with the sale of newly issued securities under the Securities Act.

The program is intended to:

☐ Improve disclosure to investors and other users of financial information

☐ Achieve a single disclosure system at reduced cost

☐ Reduce current impediments to combining shareholder communications with official SEC filings.

Part I

1. *Business.* Identifies principal products and services of the company, principal markets and methods of distribution and, if "material," competitive factors, backlog and expectation of fulfillment, availability of raw materials,

importance of patents, licenses, and franchises, estimated cost of research, number of employees, and effects of compliance with ecological laws. If there is more than one line of business, for each of the last three fiscal years, a statement of total sales and net income for each line which, during either of the last two fiscal years, accounted for 10 percent or more of total sales or pretax income.

2. *Properties.* Location and character of principal plants, mines, and other important properties and if held in fee or leased.

3. *Legal Proceedings.* Brief description of material legal proceedings pending; when civil rights or ecological statutes are involved, proceedings must be disclosed.

4. *Principal Security Holders and Security Holdings of Management.* Identification of owners of 10 percent or more of any class of securities and of securities held by directors and officers according to amount and percent of each class.

Part II

5. *Market for the Registrants' Common Stock and Related Security Holder Matters.* Includes principal market in which voting securities are traded with high and low sales prices (in the absence thereof, the range of bid and asked quotations for each quarterly period during the past two years) and the dividends paid during the past two years. In addition to the frequency and amount of dividends paid, this item contains a discussion concerning future dividends.

6. *Selected Financial Data.* These are five-year selected data including net sales and operating revenue; income or loss from continuing operations, both total and per common share; total assets; long-term obligations including redeemable preferred stock; cash dividends declared per common share. Also, additional items that could enhance understanding and trends in financial condition and results of operations. Further, the effects of inflation and changing prices should be reflected in the five-year summary.

7. *Management's Discussion and Analysis of Financial Condition and Results of Operations.* Under broad guidelines, this includes: liquidity, capital resources and results of operations; trends that are favorable or unfavorable as well as significant events or uncertainties; causes of any material changes in the financial statements as a whole; limited data concerning subsidiaries; discussion of effects of inflation and changing prices. Projections or other forward-looking information may or may not be included.

8. *Financial Statements and Supplementary Data.* Two-year audited balance sheets as well as three-year audited statements of income and changes in financial condition.

Part III

9. *Directors and Executive Officers of the Registrant.* Name, office, term of office and specific background data on each.

10. *Remuneration of Directors and Officers.* List of each director and 3 highest paid officers with aggregate annual remuneration exceeding $40,000 and total paid all officers and directors.

Part IV

11. *Exhibits, Financial Statement Schedules and Reports on Form 8-K.* Complete, audited annual financial information and a list of exhibits filed. Also, any unscheduled material events or corporate changes filed in an 8-K during the year.

Schedules

I. Marketable securities. Other security investments

II. Amounts due from directors, officers, and principal holders of equity securities other than affiliates

III. Investments in securities of affiliates

IV. Indebtedness of affiliates (not current)

V. Property, plant, and equipment

VI. Indebtedness of affiliates (not current)

VII. Reserves for depreciation, depletion, and amortization of property, plant, and equipment

VIII. Intangible assets

IX. Reserves for depreciation and amortization of intangible assets

X. Bonds, mortgages, and similar debt.

XI. Indebtedness to affiliates (not current)

XII. Guarantees of securities of other issuers

XIII. Reserves

XIV. Capital shares

XV. Warrants or rights

XVI. Other securities

XVII. Supplementary profit and loss information

XVIII. Income from dividends (equity in net profit and loss of affiliates)

Form 10-Q

The 10-Q is similar to the 10-K, but is filed quarterly. Thus its information is more current and more useful.

This is the quarterly financial report filed by most companies, which, although unaudited, provides a continuing view of a company's financial position during the year. It must be filed within 45 days of the close of a fiscal quarter.

Part I

1. Income Statement

2. Balance Sheet

3. Statement of source and application of funds

4. A narrative analysis of material changes in the amount of revenue and expense items in relation to previous quarters, including the effect of any changes in accounting principals.

Part II

1. Legal Proceedings. Brief description of material legal proceedings pending; when civil rights or ecological statutes are involved, proceedings must be disclosed.

2. Changes in Securities. Material changes in the rights of holders of any class of registered security.

3. Changes in Security for Registered Securities. Material withdrawal or substitution of assets securing any class of registered securities of the registrant.

4. Defaults upon Senior Securities. Material defaults in the payment if principal, interest, sinking fund or purchase fund installment, dividend, or other material default not cured within 30 days.

5. Increase in Amount Outstanding of Securities or Indebtedness. Amounts of new issues, continuing issues or reissues of any class of security or indebtedness with a reasonable statement of the purposes for which the proceeds will be used.

6. Decreases in Amount Outstanding of Securities of Indebtedness. Amounts of decreases, through one or more transactions, in any class of outstanding securities or indebtedness.

7. Submission of Matters to a Vote of Security Holders. Information relating to the convening of a meeting of shareholders, whether annual or special, and the matters voted upon, with particular emphasis on the election of directors.

8. Other Materially Important Events. Information on any other item of interest to shareholders not already provided for in this form.

Form 8-K

Form 8-K is useful for special-situation investors because it details *material changes* that were considered by the SEC to be so important that they couldn't wait for the next 10-Q.

This is a report of unscheduled material events or corporate changes deemed of importance to the shareholders or to the SEC.
1. Changes in Control of Registrant.
2. Acquisition or Disposition of Assets.
3. Bankruptcy or Receivership.

4. Changes in Registrant's Certifying Accountant.
5. Other Materially Important Events.
6. Resignations of Registrant's Directors.
7. Financial Statements and Exhibits.

Form 13-F

Form 13-F is the equivalent of form 10-Q for financial companies. The portfolio breakouts, which usually don't appear in annual reports, can be quite useful.

A quarterly report of equity holdings is required of all institutions with equity assets of $100 million or more. This includes banks, insurance companies, investment companies, investment advisers, and large internally managed endowments, foundations, and pension funds.

Proxy Statement

Proxy statements signal something so important that stockholders—rather than the board of directors—must vote on it. Shareholders receive proxy statements automatically; other investors can request them from the company or find them in business libraries.

A proxy statement provides official notification to designated classes of stockholders of matters to be brought to a vote at a shareholders' meeting. Proxy votes may be solicited for changing the company name, transferring large blocks of stock, electing new officers, or many other matters. Disclosures normally made via a proxy statement may in some cases be made using Form 10-K (Part III).

Annual Report to Shareholders

The Annual Report is the principal document used by most major companies to communicate directly with shareholders. Since it is not a required, official SEC filing, companies have considerable discretion in deter-

Quick Reference Chart to Contents of SEC Filings

Legend: A—always included —included—if occured or significant F—frequently included ▮ special circumstances only

REPORT CONTENTS	10-K	19-K / 20-F	10-Q	8-K	10-C	6-K	Proxy Statement	Prospectus	F-10 8-A 8-B (34 Act)	"S" Type (33 Act)	ARS	Listing Application	N-1R	N-1Q
Auditor														
☐ Name	A	A	▮					A	A	A	A		A	
☐ Opinion	A	A	▮						A		A		A	
☐ Changes				A				▮						
Compensation Plans														
☐ Equity	▮		▮				F	F	A	F		▮		
☐ Monetary							F	A	F			▮		
Company Information														
☐ Nature of Business	A	A				F		A	A	A	▮			
☐ History	F	A						A	A		▮			
☐ Organization and Change	F	F		A	▮	F		▮	F	A		▮		
Debt Structure	A					F		A	A	A	A		A	
Depreciation & Other Schedules	A	A				F		A	A	A				
Dilution Factors	A	A	F			F		A	A	A	A			
Directors, Officers, Insiders														
☐ Identification	F	A				F	A	A	A	A	F			
☐ Background	▮	A				F	F	A	▮	A				
☐ Holdings		A		▮			A	A	A	A				
☐ Compensation		A					A	A	A	A				
Earnings Per Share	A	A	A			F		A			A		A	
Financial Information														
☐ Annual Audited	A	A							A		A		A	
☐ Interim Audited		A						▮		▮				
☐ Interim Unaudited	▮		A	▮		F		F		F				
Foreign Operations	A							▮	A	A	▮	F		
Labor Contracts		▮		▮				▮	F	F				
Legal Agreements	F							▮	F	F				
Legal Counsel								A	A	▮				
Loan Agreements	F		F					▮	F	F		▮		
Plants and Properties	A	F					F	A	F					
Portfolio Operations														
☐ Content (Listing of Securities)														A
☐ Management													A	
Product-Line Breakout	A							A		A	▮			
Securities Structure	A	A			▮			A	A	A				
Subsidiaries	A	A						A	A	A				
Underwriting								A	A	A				
Unregistered Securities	▮			▮				F		F				
Block Movements				F				A				▮		

Legend   **A**—always included —included—if occured or significant

F—frequently included   ▮ special circumstances only

TENDER OFFER/ACQUISITION REPORTS	13D	13G	14D-1	14D-9	13E-3	13E-4
Name of Issuer (Subject Company)	A	A	A	A	A	A
Filing Person (or Company)	A	A	A	A	A	A
Amount of Shares Owned	A	A				
Percent of Class Outstanding	A	A				
Financial Statements of Bidders			F		F	F
Purpose of Tender Offer			A	A	A	A
Source and Amount of Funds	A		A		A	
Identity and Background Information			A	A	A	
Persons Retained Employed or to be Compensated			A	A	A	A
Exhibits	F		F	F	F	F

mining what types of information this report will contain and how it is to be presented.

Recent changes (effective December 15, 1980) required by the SEC were made to standardize the presentation of disclosure items in annual reports to make them consistent with similar requirements in SEC filings. For example, selected financial data relating to a registrant's financial condition and results of continuing operations will be presented in the Annual Report in the same manner as in the 10-K.

SECTION II: DOCUMENTS TO HELP INVESTORS AFTER STOCK ACQUISITIONS AND TENDER OFFERS HAVE BEEN MADE

When special-situation investors read in the *Wall Street Journal* or other daily newspaper that these documents have been filed with the SEC, they should read them to determine whether a deal is good or bad, and whether it looks as though it will be consummated.

Form 13G

An annual report (short form of 13D) which must be filed by all reporting persons (primarily institutions) meeting the 5% equity ownership rule within 45 days after the end of each calendar year.

1. Name of issuer
2. Name of person filing
3. 13D-1 or 13D-2 applicability
4. Amount of shares beneficially owned
☐ Percent of class outstanding
☐ Sole or shared power to vote
☐ Sole or shared power to dispose
5. Ownership of 5% or less of a class of stock
6. Ownership of more than 5% on behalf of another person
7. Identification of subsidiary which acquired the security

being reported on by the parent holding company (if applicable)

8. Identification and classification of members of the group (if applicable)

9. Notice of dissolution of the group (if applicable)

Form 13D

Similar information of 5% equity ownership in connection with a tender offer filed within ten days of the acquisition date.
1. Security and issuer
2. Identity and background of person filing the statement
3. Source and amount of funds or other consideration
4. Purpose of the transaction
5. Interest in securities of the issuer
6. Contracts, arrangements or relationships with respect to securities of the issuer
7. Material to be filed as exhibits which may include but are not limited to:
   a. Letter agreements between the parties
   b. Form formal offer to purchase

Form 14D-1

Tender offer filing made with SEC at time offer is made to holders of equity securities of target company, if acceptance of offer would give the offeror over 5% ownership of the subject securities.
1. Security and subject company
2. Identity and background information
3. Past contacts, transactions or negotiations with subject company
4. Source and amount of funds or other consideration
5. Purpose of the tender offer and plans or proposals of the bidder
6. Interest in securities of the subject company
7. Contracts, arrangements or relationships with respect to the subject company's securities
8. Persons retained, employed or to be compensated

9. Financial statements of certain bidders

10. Additional information

11. Material to be filed as exhibits which may include but are not limited to:

a. The actual offer to purchase

b. The letter to shareholders

c. The letter of transmittal with notice of guaranteed delivery

d. The press release

e. The summary publication in business newspapers or magazines

f. The summary advertisement to appear in business newspapers or magazines

Form 14D-9

A solicitation/recommendation statement that must be submitted to equity holders and filed at the SEC by the management of a firm subject to a tender offer within ten days of the making of the tender offer.

1. Security and subject company

2. Tender offer of the bidder

3. Identity and background

4. The solicitation or recommendation

5. Persons retained, employed or to be compensated

6. Recent transactions and intent with respect to securities

7. Certain negotiations and transactions by the subject company

8. Additional information

9. Material to be filed as exhibits

Form 13E-4

Issuer tender offer statement pursuant to the Securities Exchange Act of 1934.

1. Security and issuer

2. Source and amount of funds

3. Purpose of the tender offer and plans or proposals of the issuer or affiliates

4. Interest in securities of the issuer

5. Contracts, arrangements or relationships with respect to the issuer's securities

6. Persons retained, employed or to be compensated

7. Financial information

8. Additional information

9. Material to be filed as exhibits which may include but are not limited to:

The offer to purchase which is being sent to the shareholders to whom the tender offer is being made.

Most of these reports are available upon request to a company's Office of the Secretary. Also, the principal filings are available for inspection at SEC regional and branch offices:

CALIFORNIA

*10960 Wilshire Boulevard, Suite 1710
Los Angeles, California 90024
(213) 473-4511

450 Golden Gate Avenue, Box 36042
San Francisco, California 94102
(415) 556-5264

COLORADO

410 Seventeenth Street, Suite 700
Denver, Colorado 80202
(303) 837-2071

FLORIDA

Dupont Plaza Center
300 Biscayne Boulevard Way, Suite 1114
Miami, Florida 33131
(305) 350-5765

GEORGIA

1375 Peachtree Street, N.E., Suite 788
Atlanta, Georgia 30367
(404) 881-4768

*Public Reference Room

ILLINOIS

*Everett McKinley Dirksen Building
219 South Dearborn Street, Room 1204
Chicago, Illinois 60604
(312) 353-7390

MASSACHUSETTS

150 Causeway Street
Boston, Massachusetts 02114
(617) 223-2721

MICHIGAN

1044 Federal Building
Detroit, Michigan 48226
(313) 226-6070

NEW YORK

*26 Federal Plaza, Room 1102
New York, New York 10278
(212) 264-1636

PENNSYLVANIA

600 Arch Street, Room 2204
Philadelphia, Pennsylvania 19106
(215) 597-2278

TEXAS

411 West Seventh Street
Fort Worth, Texas 76102
(817) 334-3821

Federal Office and Courts Building
515 Rusk Avenue, Room 5615
Houston, Texas 77002
(713) 226-4986

*Public Reference Room

UTAH

Boston Building
9 Exchange Place
Salt Lake City, Utah 84111
(801) 524-5796

VIRGINIA

Ballston Center Tower 3
4015 Wilson Boulevard
Arlington, Virginia 22203
(703) 557-8201

WASHINGTON

3040 Federal Building
915 Second Avenue
Seattle, Washington 98174
(206) 442-7990

Disclosure itself has organized all corporate filings dating from 1966 to the present to allow corporate executives, bankers, attorneys, investors, and others to have access to facts about public companies. For further information and costs, contact:

Disclosure Incorporated

5161 River Road
Washington, D.C. 20016
(301) 951-1300

SECTION III: OTHER SOURCES OF INFORMATION AND SERVICES

Newspapers

The Wall Street Journal. Published Monday through Friday by Dow Jones & Company, the *Wall Street Journal* is internationally recognized as the most complete source of daily information about both individual companies and the securities market in general. The *Journal* reports daily price and volume data for the New York Stock Exchange, American Stock Exchange, the NASDAQ-OTC market, bond market, options market, and commodity exchanges. For a change of pace, the *Journal*'s front page also features colorful articles on everything from the sex life of bullfrogs to the self-proclaimed "Garlic Capital of the World." (It's Gilroy, California, and it produces around 90,000 tons annually.)

The Wall Street Journal

22 Cortlandt Street
New York, New York 10007
(212) 285-5000

The New York Times. In addition to serving up "All the news that's fit to print," the *Times* has an extensive daily business section that recaps major market data, as well as covering and analyzing financial news about companies, the economy, and international implications.

The New York Times

229 West Forty-third Street
New York, New York 10036
(212) 556-1234

Barron's. Published weekly by Dow Jones & Company, *Barron's* provides weekly listings of prices and quotes for all financial markets as well as information on individual stocks, including updates on earnings and dividends. *Barron's* also includes an in-depth statistical section, which recapitulates the previous week's stock-market activity.

Barron's

22 Cortlandt Street
New York, New York 10007
(212) 285-5243

Business and Financial Magazines

The following publications are oriented towards a general business audience, providing both relevant news stories and in-depth looks at individual companies and the business environment.

Business Week (weekly)

1221 Avenue of the Americas
New York, New York 10020
(212) 997-2511
(800) 257-5112 (subscribers' service)

Forbes (biweekly)

60 Fifth Avenue
New York, New York 10011
(212) 620-2200

Fortune (biweekly)

1271 Avenue of the Americas
New York, New York 10020
(212) 586-1212

Investment-Information Services

Investment information itself has become big business—in fact, Americans shell out millions annually for investment advice.

The following are the key investment-information sources publishing daily, weekly, monthly and/or annual reports. Subscriptions to these services are tax-deductible. Also, major public libraries and business-school libraries generally have several of them for reference.

Standard & Poor's

STANDARD & POOR'S CORPORATION RECORDS. These massive volumes contain basic information on individual corporations, arranged alphabetically. Topics include capitalization and long-term debt; corporate background (such as subsidiaries, affiliates, principal properties, officers and directors, etc.); bond descriptions; stock data; earnings and finances. A separate volume summarizes recent news stories about all corporations listed. Since the volumes come in binders, S & P can update information continually during the year.

STANDARD & POOR'S STOCK REPORTS. At least three to four times a year, Standard & Poor's releases comprehensive two-page reports on the major stocks traded on the NYSE, ASE, and OTC. Reports are organized by exchange. Information includes near- and long-term sales and earnings prospects, recent news developments, pertinent income and balance-sheet figures for the past ten years, dividend data, and a graph of stock price and volume movements.

STANDARD & POOR'S STOCK GUIDE. For quick, easy reference, S & P publishes the monthly *Stock Guide* containing pertinent information about the 5,100 most actively traded common and preferred stocks. A separate section covers performance of over 400 mutual funds. The *Stock Guide* includes historic and recent price ranges, volume, yield, P/E ratios, dividends, earnings, financial position, and institutional holdings.

THE OUTLOOK. Each week, Standard & Poor's *Outlook* surveys general market conditions, with indexes for various industry categories. *The Outlook* also features in-depth looks at specific groups of stocks or industries, such as growth stocks, stocks likely to increase their dividends, convertible securities, and the like. S & P also publishes a special annual edition of *The Outlook* which forecasts market performance for the coming year. Topics include rapid-growth stocks for long-term profit, best low-priced stocks, and other timely investment areas.

Standard & Poor's

25 Broadway
New York, New York 10004
(212) 248-2525

Moody's Manuals

Published once a year in bound volumes, Moody's manuals contain key information on thousands of firms. They examine capital structure, income accounts, financial and operating data, capital stock and management. Moody's organizes its volumes as follows:

INDUSTRIAL MANUAL. Covers industrial companies listed on the NYSE, ASE, and regional exchanges, and also includes a special section on international industrial firms. Moody's also publishes supplementary news reports to update information.

OTC INDUSTRIAL MANUAL. As the name suggests, this volume is similar to the regular *Industrial Manual,* but instead covers firms traded over the counter. Moody's also updates this manual with supplementary reports.

PUBLIC UTILITY MANUAL. Deals with electric, gas, gas-transmission, telephone, and water companies. Moody's also publishes supplementary news reports to update information.

TRANSPORTATION MANUAL. Includes railroads; airlines; steamship, bus, and trucking companies; as well as oil-pipeline and bridge companies; and automobile and truck leasing firms. Moody's also publishes supplementary news reports to update information.

BANK AND FINANCE MANUAL. Covers banks, savings and loan associations, U.S. government credit agencies, the insurance industry, investment companies, real-estate firms, real-estate investment trusts, and other financial enterprises.

MUNICIPAL AND GOVERNMENT MANUAL. Contains information on federal, state, and municipal organizations and agencies, as well as listings for foreign government and international organizations.

Moody's

99 Church Street
New York, New York 10007
(212) 553-0300

Value Line Investment Survey

Value Line is published in several parts. The 2,000-page *Investors' Reference Service* presents basic historic information on more than 1,700 widely traded stocks, as well as analytic measures of earnings stability, growth rates, etc. For the 1,700 firms covered, there are also detailed short- and long-term forecasts of performance. *Value Line's Ratings and Reports* provides a new, full-page report for each stock every 13 weeks.

Each week *Value Line* publishes a summary and index with weekly updates on key data and ratings for each stock. Perhaps most important for investors, this section also identifies stocks selling at a discount from liquidating value, stocks selling at the widest discount from book value, the biggest "free-flow" cash generators—all tip-offs to possible special-situation action.

Meanwhile, *Value Line*'s weekly *Selection and Opinion* section forecasts the economy and the stock market, and also provides investment advice, in-depth analyses of specially recommended stocks, market averages, and other features.

Value Line

711 Third Avenue
New York, New York 10017
(212) 687-3965

Brokerage Firms

Nearly all the major brokerage firms prepare publications, newsletters, and reviews analyzing both the stock market and individual companies. In general, the firms provide the materials free, as a goodwill gesture to attract customers.

Recommended Reading

Badger, Ralph D.; Torgerson, Harold W.; and Guthmann, Harry
G. *Investment Principles and Practices.* 6th ed. Englewood Cliffs,
N.J.: Prentice Hall, 1969.

Brigham, Eugene F. *Financial Management: Theory and Practice.* 2nd
ed. Hinsdale, Ill.: Dryden Press, 1979.

Edwards, Robert D. and Magee, John. *Technical Analysis of Stock
Trends.* 5th ed. Springfield, Mass.: John Magee, 1966.

Graham, Benjamin, Dodd, David L., et. al. *Security Analysis:
Principles and Technique.* 4th ed. New York: McGraw-Hill, 1962.

Graham, Benjamin and McGolrick, Charles. *The Interpretation of
Financial Statements.* 3rd rev. ed. New York: Harper & Row,
1975.

Pring, Martin J. *Technical Analysis Explained.* New York:
McGraw-Hill, 1980.

Roth, Harrison. "Trading Put Options" (booklet). New York:
Drexel Burnham Lambert, 1981.

Whitman, Martin and Shubik, Martin. *The Aggressive Conservative
Investor.* New York: Random House, 1979.

Index